THREE AMERICAN COMPOSERS

Edith Borroff

State University of New York at Binghamton

UNIVERSITY
PRESS OF
AMERICA

LANHAM • NEW YORK • LONDON

Copyright © 1986 by

University Press of America,® Inc.

4720 Boston Way
Lanham, MD 20706

3 Henrietta Street
London WC2E 8LU England

Library of Congress Cataloging in Publication Data

Borroff, Edith, 1925-
    Three American composers.

    Bibliography: p.
    1. Fischer, Irwin, 1903-1977.   2. Finney, Ross Lee,
1906-   3. Crumb, George.   4. Composers—United
States—Biography.   5. Music—United States—20th
century—History and criticism.   I. Title.   II. Title: 3
American composers.
ML390.B76   1986   780'.92'2   [B] 86-9090
ISBN 0-8191-5371-0 (alk. paper)
ISBN 0-8191-5372-9 (pbk. : alk. paper)

All University Press of America books are produced on acid-free
paper which exceeds the minimum standards set by the National
Historical Publications and Records Commission.

to

American Music

and

The Three Composers

whose work

has

enlarged me

TABLE OF CONTENTS

TABLE OF MUSICAL EXAMPLES

vii

Chapter 4: George Crumb
Examples from the works of George Crumb have been made
available through the courtesy of C. F. Peters Corporation, with the exception of Night Music I, which has
been made available through the courtesy of Belwyn-
Mills, Inc.

PLATES

PREFACE

I have enjoyed the warm support of the three composers central to this study. All three of them have welcomed me to their homes and, over a number of interviews, afforded me a deeper knowledge of their working methods and philosophies. All statements attributed to them in the text derive from these interviews; they are dated in endnotes wherever the date is relevant. All three of them have manifested genuine interest in and remarkable patience with the issues I have raised and with the many questions I have asked. My gratitude to them for their welcome, their lively encouragement, and their generosity to me is beyond my ability to repay.

The Research Foundation of the State University of New York awarded to me in 1975 the moneys to fund several trips to interview the composers and to attend performances; the award was repeated (and the moneys doubled) in 1976, permitting me to attend premieres of works commissioned for the Bicentennial. Without the help of the Research Foundation I would not have been able to travel to these performances nor to benefit from the attendant interviews. I am grateful to the Research Foundation for their support.

Portions of Chapter One appeared in a short article, "American Music: Checks and Balances," in the November 1977 Newsletter of the Sonneck Society, and in the monograph, Liberal Arts, History and Hope (State University of New York Press, 1979); portions of Chapter Two are included in the article, "The Music of Irwin Fischer," in the June 1978 (final) issue of Music and Man. I would like to thank the editors of these publications for permission to use these materials in the present study.

I would like to thank the American Composers Alliance for permission to use examples of the music of Irwin Fischer. Rosalie Calabrese, Executive Director, has been not only a tremendous help but has also provided moral support which I have valued greatly.

I would like to thank C. F. Peters Corporation, and in particular Don Gillespie, for valuable help. Through their courtesy I have been able to reproduce most of the musical examples of this volume. For the chapter on the music of Ross Lee Finney they have provided examples from the 32 Piano Games, the Sixth String Quartet, the Concerto for Percussion and Orchestra, Symphony No. 1 (Communiqué 1943), Variations for Orchestra, Summer in Valley City, Spherical Madrigals, Edge of Shadow, and Still Are New Worlds. For the chapter on the music of George Crumb they have provided examples from the Sonata for Solo Violoncello, Makrokosmos, Volume I, Songs, Drones, and Refrains of Death, Ancient Voices of Children, Eleven Echoes of Autumn, and Black Angels.

I would like to thank Belwin-Mills, Inc., for permission to use the examples from George Crumb's Night Music I. Linda Santiago, in New York, and Carol Cuellar, in Hialeah, both cut through difficulties to help me, and I am grateful to them.

I would like to give warm thanks to Professor Paul Jordan, whose support and encouragement in this work have meant a great deal. In addition, he read proof on the entire manuscript, lending the finished product an accuracy of text which I could not have achieved without his help.

Finally, I would like to thank the many people who have given their blessing to my work: the Administration of the State University of New York at Binghamton; the colleagues who have responded to my enthusiasm with sustained--and sustaining--interest; and those friends and family members who have seen me through a long project with exemplary kindness and loving support.

Binghamton, New York
March 24, 1986

Three
American
Composers

Chapter 1
A HALF-CENTURY IN THE UNITED STATES

Musical life in the United States in the twentieth century has provided a lively and challenging array of types and styles. Music for the concert hall, for the theatre, and for the church has been rich indeed. And popular music, from ragtime, jazz, and blues to a commercial country and rock, has been increasingly independent in style.

That independence is new. For two centuries and more, popular and concert music had shared musical theory and technique: the harmonic system of a Dittersdorf divertimento was the same as that of a Mozart symphony; the melodic entities of a Strauss waltz were based in the same tonal theory as those of a Brahms intermezzo; the rhythmic notation of Dvorak's "Songs My Mother Taught Me" was the same as that of a Wolf Lied. So was the technique of the singers. The general styles were in fact very much the same: both the Dittersdorf and the Mozart are considered "classical," both the Dvorak and the Wolf are considered "romantic." Even the songs of von Tilzer and the theatre music of Sousa and Herbert shared in romantic ideals and techniques.

The gap between popular and concert music at the end of the nineteenth century was one of context and complexity; by the middle of the twentieth century, the differences between popular and concert music were so great that the two types were considered two separate musical arts. The gap between an album of hard rock and a piano recital at Carnegie Hall begins with the very nature of music's basic constituents.

Even within concert life itself, with which this book is concerned, the music scope was extraordinary. In Europe, Schoenberg and Respighi, Lutoslawski and Walton were composing at the same time,--and using different harmonic systems, different rhythmic notations, and calling for widely ranging styles of performance. And they professed widely divergent aesthetic commitments as well.

In the United States the scope of concert music was dramatic: Cowell and Chasins, Cage and Beach, Babbitt and Still were displaying a variety of the

musical art that strained the capacity of professional
or layman to absorb it all. That composers with such a
vast range of style could all have existed in one place
in the span of a few years and offer so rich an art is
an amazing cultural phenomenon deserving of attention.
If this richness is to be savored to the fullest, it
must be understood.

A Time of Change

The fifty-year period that bracketed the middle of
this century was a time of musical upheaval, a change
of basic assumptions not experienced since the change
from polyphony to monody in the seventeenth century.
This new change was potent in Europe, but it was
perhaps even more potent in the United States, where
the European art had been transplanted but had been
variably influenced by native elements.

In the years immediately following the first World
War, American concert music was still following the
established tradition of European domination. The
Columbia lectures of Edward MacDowell were lively
memories; books by Baker, Coerne, and Mason were
educational staples; the popular musical summaries of
Elbert Hubbard (in support of the Chautauqua movement)
were going into several printings; European performers
(and managers) monopolized the important stages and
podiums; the modernists were the Paris-centered post-
Debussy French and Russo-French composers of chamber
music, song, and ballet, along with the Germanic post-
Wagner composers of orchestral and operatic scores;
the avant-garde combined the fringes of what seemed a
musical madness stemming from Dada and Surrealist
promulgations on the one hand and expanding mathematical theory on the other. American hopefuls still took
the mandatory study in Europe for granted, knowing that
their chief hope of success lay in re-entry to the
United States after a considerable orbit in European
circles.

By the end of the 1970s a remarkable turnabout had
been effected; the Columbia lectures of Edward MacDowell were not only forgotten but were turned inside
out; the entire basis operandi of Coerne, Hubbard, et
al, was moribund; American performers were given
preference--and deference--on European and Oriental
stages; Americans studied abroad not as humble
hopefuls asking to be allowed into the secrets of a

European art, but as Government or Foundation-funded young artists enjoying a broadening vista in a general sense, to cap an American education with international experience; and the three categories of music defined earlier by the traditionalists who had been securely in control of the musical establishment--traditional, modernist, and avant-garde--had shrunk to two, defined now by the avant-garde--the new and the old.

The story of the turnabout, accomplished so swiftly in the long terms of history, is a fascinating one. It is, of course, complex. To the extent to which America has been a musical subcontinent, discussion of developments in the music of the United States is to be illuminated by seeing it vis-à-vis the European patterns of music history in which they are based. Yet that subcontinent by definition is an entity in itself, within which native elements interact with those imported for its formation, and within which the European patterns become less and less useful as the native elements strengthen.

Discussions of American music as a whole have often focused upon those native elements that have proved so much stronger than a self-satisfied European musical elite in the early years of this century would have believed: the song schools of the early republic and their descendants (such as shape-note, revival, and gospel singing), the roof-raisings and hoe-downs whose very names ring with the memory of community celebration after community labor in pioneer days, the folksongs of the mountain men and women of the east and the lonesome cowboys of the west, the banjo picking of the plantations, the rag dancing and the cakewalk prizes of the slaves, and above all the music of the urban blacks that developed the arts of ragtime, jazz, and the blues. Composers have been seeking their musical roots as Americans and entering into noble experiments, hoping to define an American style.

But the Coming of Age of American concert music, however much it lay in the examination and incorporation into concert works of a mosaic of types and styles, took place in American schools, particularly in higher education and in the training of composers. And in the story of American schooling lies a key to the turnabout that explains not only its force but also its particular nature, not only its character but its details and resonances. For in the half-century from 1925 to 1975, the center of power in American musical professional education shifted from the conservatories to the universities, and that shift is fascinating and rich in ramification.[1]

At the end of the first World War the conservatory was still the accepted training-ground for professional musicians, and composers were still considered as general practitioners who seldom managed to become financially independent through composition alone. For hundreds--no, thousands--of years, the interactions of a musician's performing and composing activities were essential: Bach's music was heard because he played it himself; the same was true of Beethoven, Chopin, Schumann, and virtually all other instrumental composers. They all established themselves as performer/composers before they could branch out into the music of other mediums or into orchestral work--and by then they had orchestral connections. The forums in which composers could be heard (not only the places but also the systems that supported them) were called venues.

Conservatories had been founded to institutionalize the apprenticeship system through which all composers were taught until the nineteenth century. Many elements of apprenticeship were maintained in the conservatory curricula, not least of which were the connections to performance venues that enabled good students to find opportunities to be heard by the public.

Conservatories today are basically college-level facilities, and we think of study there as following high-school graduation or being relegated to a "preparatory" department. But earlier in the century this distinction was much less powerful. In most cases training began much earlier, a gifted child taken under the wing (and often actually into the home) of an acknowledged master. Daily lessons might begin as early as the age of three and continue in the conservatory with which the master was affiliated as soon as the child was sufficiently advanced.

Training in this system would be much the same as it had been for two hundred years: daily ear training and sight-singing, keyboard practice (including technical studies, harmony, sight-reading, transposition, and improvisation), a sufficient competence in strings to play in string quartets if the student were a pianist, nine hours a week of chamber music class, and composition (including the traditional arts of variation and transcription of both concert and popular repertoire). The amount of literature covered would stagger a piano major today: a representative trainee early in the century would play all the Beethoven sonatas, all the standard works of German, Polish, Russian, French, and Nordic schools, plus an ever-expanding component of American works from both concert and popular traditions. Popular works were always subjected to the imagination of the performer, transformed by the imagination in transcription and arrangement, standard practice in that time--in a dual concept of both literal and fanciful performance. The training aimed at both versatility and virtuosity.

But conservatories trained more than professionals; just as few English majors become professional writers, so did few music students become professional musicians. And the large number of non-professional music students assured an audience that was knowledgeable and in the best sense appreciative.

It also gave strength to patronage. Musical patrons had often had a certain amount of early training with private teachers, in many cases strong professional training that they did not complete--or, as women, completed, briefly practiced, and put aside at marriage. Some of these women became powerful figures in American patronage, shaping the music (and other arts) in their cities.

Historically, and to a large degree in the first half of the twentieth century, apprenticeship meant the total immersion into musical experiences, of many kinds, from early childhood, in the home of a master and (from the nineteenth century) in an institution devoted to musical professionalism. As a teacher affiliated with an institution, a master was always willing to audition, to find time for a young person who applied for a hearing. Sponsorship of young talent was a salient aspect of the work of a maestro. This intensive, protracted, and consummately musical training produced practitioners whose careers included performance and therefore provided ready entree to performance venues: the church organist or choir director, orchestral musician (or conductor), civic band leader, all of these could function easily as composers because they held control of performing groups. Such musicians used their own music and also opened the network to their students and to young performer/composers recommended by other masters. Concert bureaus maintained a wider (national and international) communication between masters. The system as a whole assured the health of two very important factors in professional life: first, it provided means for the recognition and sponsorship of young talent and a place from which to launch public careers; and second, it saw to the training of a host of amateurs in the same work and maintained a creative interaction with the public, who would take interest in maturing local apprentices. Discussion of emerging musical personalities could take on the lively aspects of sports fans comparing the new crop of college football players. The inclusion of the public dimension was a vital aspect of this system; this social interpenetration may be related to the fact that conservatories accepted women as composition students without fuss or feathers--the apprenticeship tradition had included women from ancient days.

The University System

A new training system for composers was beginning to expand. A few eastern universities (in the beginning only Yale and Harvard) began to hire conservatory masters to teach the theory of music and offer composition lessons. Men like Horatio Parker, at Yale from 1894, regarded their university duties as part-time, secondary work, and continued to function as music masters in the public arena and to maintain their career venues (for the benefit of their students as well as themselves).

The universities had a thousand-year tradition of theoretical studies that included music (with arithmetic, geometry, and astronomy) as part of the Quadrivium of the Liberal Arts, a discipline which gave its name to American college education long after its early history was forgotten. (Harvard, for example, used Boethius as a text well into the nineteenth century.) In this tradition, theory was more cosmic than practical, its students were called "philosophers," and the subject differed diametrically from the study of practical music, which was the province of apprenticeship. Early twentieth-century conservatory studies in harmony, counterpoint, and form analysis were based on apprenticeship, where every subject had the ramifying and deepening of participating musicianship as its only goal.[2]

It was doubtless to bridge the gap between musical philosophy and living music that the universities brought in practitioners to teach theory courses. These instructors could not provide a complete system, however; performance was not part of university work, and would not be until after the second World War.

So the new composers coming out of the university system were a very different breed from their conservatory counterparts. As the traditionally trained composers developed through performance, the university group developed through theory courses. Generally, a choir was the only performing group in a college or university, but that was not a sufficient force to maintain a composer or career (except perhaps for the choirmaster himself). To the extent that theory and composition instruction in a university were offered by a master active in public musical life, young composers in this system had a connection to musical performing groups. But because the young composers were not practicing musicians they could not replace their teachers. In 1925, when this study begins, universities were at a low point relative to performance; during the half-century to follow they would build the performing groups that served to make the university itself a performing venue;[3] university composers were supported chiefly in university jobs. Such men as Walter Piston were professors rather than practitioners; their acceptance in the public arena was shaky and not always friendly.

As the decades went on, university composers were further deepening their hold on exciting theoretical innovations but weakening their connections with performers. Whereas the conservatory composers saw performers as their colleagues, as fulfilling their works by bringing them to life, university composers saw performers increasingly as their servants, duty-bound to perform works whether they understood them or not, whether they liked them or not. The relationship at its worst was antagonistic, but as performance began to enter university curricula, a number of fine musicians started to specialize in the performance of avant-garde music by university composers. This led in turn to segregation of new and old music in separate concerts within the universities.

The great disadvantage suffered by university composers was the separation from a public audience. The colleges and universities in the United States

7

trained audiences in a new way: by teaching courses in "Music Appreciation" to non-music students. This potential audience was not given training parallel to that of composers, as in the conservatories, but were subjected to an indoctrination parallel to that in literature: as Shakespeare and Milton and perhaps Browning or Emerson were taught as authors one should read and revere if one were to be considered literate, so were Bach and Beethoven and perhaps Brahms taught as composers one must listen to and revere if one were to be considered cultured. The public, thus programmed, became increasingly obedient and conservative; even the new conservatory composers, whose goal was to join the tradition in order to move it forward, were too modern for this audience--the university composers seemed to inhabit another planet.

The great compensating advantage enjoyed by university composers was the university control of publishing, criticism, and foundation grants. Theory and appreciation texts for university consumption, supporting works for the general public (such as Roger Sessions's The Musical Experience) and newspaper reviewing became the province of university-trained writers,[4] And foundation grants, whether government or private, were awarded according to adjudication by university faculty and kept for themselves. This enabled virtually an entire generation of university composers to work abroad after the second World War. The group of university composers was a small one at the beginning of the century, and although the group expanded in number, it continued (in the long tradition of the university) to be exclusively male. Only after 1975 would women make significant entry as composers into American university music.

Two Camps

The conservatory and university composers squared off not just as two groups differently trained and with divergent career paths; they squared off essentially as Traditionalists and the Avant-Garde. For the commitment to a continuum on the part of the conservatory composers, along with the need to produce music for consumption by the public, kept them in a conservative stance; at the extreme they were rehashing musical materials that had proved safe, forgetting to move forward as the goal of the traditionalists had always been. An equally strong commitment to theoreti-

8

cal innovation characterized the university composers and led them to an opposing position: at the extreme they were so concerned with new musical language that they forgot that a language exists only for the expression of ideas. The conservatives considered the most radical to be a lunatic fringe, while the avant-garde found the most reactionary of the conservatives to be musically moribund. But in the large middle area were composers whose strengths transcended ideology: conservatives with something new and vital to say, and avant-garde with the ability to communicate beyond the circle of their colleagues.

In 1925, conservatory musicians were safely in control of music as a cultural expression. By 1975 control had switched to the universities. The training of composers went with the switch.

The story of the two traditions and the reversal of musical dominance during that half-century is a fascinating one. Like most such shifts it was a reflection of general cultural changes, a complex of factors that serve to augment each other reciprocally.

Conservatories were privately owned, profit-making institutions; the Great Depression, followed by the second World War, weakened most of them. They survived only by re-incorporating as non-profit-making institutions; in the East particularly, this brought them under the aegis of university examination--either by submitting to the curricular scrutiny of academic evaluation (through university-staffed professional teams) or by becoming a department or school of music within a university, in either case coming under direct university control.

The universities were well equipped to deal with change. The enormous strength of the academic areas of music within the Liberal Arts tradition provided arenas for debates concerning the nature of musical thought in general and of "modernism" in particular. Musicology, uncongenial to the conservatory mind as an artificial extraction of scientific method from living art, found support in the universities.[5] The universities proffered havens to the displaced European intellectuals seeking harbor in the United States, which the conservatories had no money to do. The federal agencies, so vital in the arts under the Roosevelt administration, took over many of the groups of the public sector, but these were shattered by the second World War, which claimed both their personnel and their moneys.

After the War the final blows descended upon conservatories in the United States. The government and the great Foundations both turned to universities and university faculties to rebuild the intellectual community and to absorb the continuing influx of foreign talent. European scholars tended to italicize the importance of the intellectual elements in the university music departments of which they became members, most often at the expense of performers. By 1950 the failure of music schools was visiting the burden of producing professional musicians upon the universities. Still, as late as 1958, the National Association of Schools of Music was seen largely as conservatory-dominated--a group of music schools "whose orbit includes some college music departments among its galaxy of conservatories."[6] Over the next two decades an increasing number of conservatories merged with universities, and by the end of the 1970s, conservatories in the old sense were no longer of measurable significance in American secondary-school education. The National Association of Schools of Music had turned itself inside out in two decades, and in 1982 contained more than five hundred schools, of which only ten were non-accredited, non-university institutions.[7] Their faculty were absorbed by the universities, often uprooted from their traditional work and thrust into university music departments already established and functioning in the Liberal Arts tradition, apprenticeship musicians suddenly waking up in Academe. Faculties were often divided into two camps, of the conservatory-bred teachers of performance and the university-bred academics. The composers, already bound to academic interests and eager to prove the intellectual viability of their discipline in university terms, went with the academic side.

The three great financial arms of post-War musical endeavor,--the G.I. Bill, the Fulbright Act, and the projects of the great Foundations,--were all controlled by university faculty and administrators. Universities, with accreditation by academic professional societies on the one hand and cheaper tuition on the other, drew the bulk of students under the G.I. Bill. University committees adjudicated requests for funding, controlling the decisions of both government and private sponsoring agencies. The private patron, whose confident personal taste had determined the focus of patronage two centuries earlier, finally yielded to the university committee.

Before and during World War II the question of Americanism in music was a lively issue. Examination of the possible roots of Americanism, with a gamut of projected answers, led to a number of fine works of all stripes--from the Western and folk ballets of Copland to the supra-mathematical concoctions of emerging computer know-how.

But composition students after the second World War felt pulls quite different from those of their predecessors; those who served in the War were aware of the plurality of music, and many had had direct experiences with Oriental or other arts. As ideals of nationalism gave way to hopes of internationalism, composers turned from the desire to express themselves as Americans to the need to seek supra-personal, supra-national meanings. The university community itself served as a matrix for the consideration of inter-related studies in philosophy, literature, anthropology, the fine arts, and the new interdepartmental concerns that included types of computer science and ecology. University composers studied oriental philosophy, developed systems of composition (and non-composition) from new mathematical theories (probability theory, stochastic and statistical formulations), and began a serious study of American iconoclasts of previous generations. They were not helped by the European academics imported as refugees; these musicians, on the contrary, looked down on American music and taught a whole generation of students to belittle it.

The young American composers of the post-war universities did not move diffidently among their European counterparts as earlier Americans had done: the Fulbright Act sent many young men (and precious few women) abroad, but now the United States was in a strong position. Europe was slowly returning to educational norms, but the United States was developing a new system of educating composers, and was in the forefront of change and experiment. American universities could afford to establish electronic studios, and they had lectureships and visiting professorships to which European composers were regularly invited. And of course there was no important American university music program without a European faculty member, so the American universities were international as their European counterparts never had been.

The universities enjoyed extraordinary health and influence for the thirty years after the War, so this study ends with the apex of post-War flowering--the end of an era.

The Music

Fleshing out this short history with composers to represent its forces is essential; looking at the music is equally essential. In choosing composers to be the life of this study, I sought neither the most conservative nor the most radical; the scope of style can best be experienced in its extraordinary richness through the musical life itself, though a searching-out of the entire spectrum.

Rather, I have sought representatives of the institutions, composers with a full commitment to the ideals which those institutions stood for, but with larger views that enabled them to transcend the limitations of any one view. The choice of Irwin Fischer and George Crumb to represent the conservatory and the university shows the forces of those institutions in a conscious choice. Fischer's youth included a breadth of interests unusual in a musician of his school, while Crumb's youth included the strong influence of his conservatory-trained father. They form a fascinating pair of opposites in their attitudes toward the ideal schooling: although Fischer attended a university, as soon as he decided to become a musician he turned from the university absolutely and entered the conservatory: although Crumb attended a conservatory, as soon as he decided to become a composer he turned from the conservatory absolutely and entered the university. They form an incorporation of the switch, with these decisions just a generation apart. Their incorporation of these ideas goes further: Fischer's music is experimental and reaches into realms of theory beyond usual conservatory concerns; Crumb's music is humane and reaches into realms of communication beyond the ordinary university audience. Each is a powerful musical presence, and each has composed works of music that deserve to outlast the era that their music summarizes. In their string quartets--for each just one, written within two years of each other, and both about death--they are fascinatingly close, yet they approached this mid-point from opposite directions and remained true to the commitments which defined them.

12

The choice of the fulcrum could be none other than Ross Lee Finney. With his upbringing crammed with both conservatory and university influences, with his tremendous energy and creative drive, his style that reaches between conservative and avant-garde, his superlative gifts as a teacher, and his devising of the definitive university doctoral curriculum in composition, he is a man of tremendous importance to American music. And interestingly, he is in one sense the most American in style of the three. Fischer was trained in the early years of the century when obeisance to European inculcation was still unquestioned; Crumb was trained in the post-War internationalism. Finney had a strongly rooted American component from the beginning, and from the Pilgrim Psalms in the 1930s to the opera Weep Torn Land in the 1980s he has remained both strongly individualistic and strongly American.

There have been other times in the history of Western music when two styles have risen up in opposition. It is not important to adjudicate the battle, to side with the modernists (to keep Carissimi and suppress Victoria, keep Telemann and throw out Bach) or with the conservatives (to keep Brahms and suppress Wagner, keep Lanier and throw out Ives). From outside our profession that seems as defeating as to suppress Van Gogh or Vermeer because of an aesthetic stance, and as wrong as the suppression of opposing political or religious beliefs.

It is wiser--and more pleasurable--to enjoy the full palette, to welcome each course in a good meal.

To study and to enjoy the strong musical production of these three men is to savor that extraordinary banquet of styles which has characterized the music of the United States in the twentieth century and which is the central concern of this book.

Notes

1. This change is peculiarly an American phenomenon, but it is only one stage in the longer history of education; this stage began in seventeenth-century Europe. See the the author's monograph, Liberal Arts: History and Hope, the State University of New York Press, 1979.

2. At fifteen I was sent to my mother's piano master, Louise Robyn. For my first lesson with her I brought Brahms's Opus 118, and began with the G minor Ballade. Miss Robyn stopped me at the bridge into the B major middle section and asked me to recount the harmonic means of that unusual modulation. I was unable to do so, whereupon Miss Robyn came to the piano, closed the music, handed it to me, showed me the door, and said that I was free to return at any time that I had completed the harmonic analysis of Opus 118.

3. But it was a slow process. At Harvard, even after the second World War, the only instrumental group maintained by the University was the marching band, conducted by a conservatory musician within the Physical Education Department.

4. Fine works by apprenticeship masters, such as Adolf Weidig's Harmonic Material and Its Uses (1923) and Ernst Toch's The Shaping Forces of Music (1948), though published, have, so far as I know, been ignored in university curricula.

5. The first chair in musicology in the United States was established in 1923 (at Cornell University), but dissertations on musical subjects had preceded. In The Evolution of the Modern Orchestra (Harvard, 1905) Coerne sought to prove that laws demonstrated in the science of biology held also in music.

6. G. Wallace Woodworth, in a report reprinted in the New York Times, January 18, 1959, and in the history of the College Music Society, in Symposium, Vol. X, Fall 1970, pages 9ff.

7. Report from NASM's Robert Glidden, by phone on October 15, 1982. Used with permission.

Chapter 2
IRWIN FISCHER

The generation of American composers born just
after the Civil War were all apprenticeship trained;
but they can be observed as having begun the specialization which would eventually separate composition from
performance. Kansas-born Harold Henry (who studied in
Europe, with Moritz Moszkowski and Leopold Godowsky)
was more pianist than composer, his output limited to
piano pieces and songs. Charles Ives, New England born
and trained at home, opted out of performance but
expanded the means of composition, chiefly through
layered techiques long honored in the popular sector.
Rubin Goldmark and Amy Cheney Beach were more traditional, maintaining both vectors strongly. Both
branched out as composers from compositions for piano
to other mediums, chiefly those with greatest status--
chamber and orchestral music. Goldmark's music was
more exclusively instrumental, and, in becoming the
head of the Composition Department at the Juilliard
School of Music, he became a leader in the bringing of
American apprenticeship musicians to our conservatories.

Consummate apprenticeship careers are best represented by such musicians as Henry Hadley and Alfred
Robyn, both many-faceted and both fine composers.
Hadley was close to the European ideal (as were New
Englanders in general), was trained in piano and
violin, and centered his performance thrust in conducting, in the United States and abroad. (As conductor of
the Mannheim Symphony Orchestra from 1929 to 1932 he
would be one of the first Americans to make turnabout
fair play.) But he composed for the theatre as well as
for the orchestra to which he had ready access, and he
left a substantial amount of chamber and vocal music.

Robyn was representative of midwestern musicians,
who had full and often successful careers but without
the help of the eastern job network and supporting
critical apparatus. He was born in St. Louis, the son
of two professional musicians (his father was an
important musician in the growth of American music
and also the founder of the St. Louis Symphony), and he
was trained at home. At nine he was the pianist in a
trio, at ten he took the console at St. John's Church

(the pedals had to be raised for him) and was never without a position thereafter. By the age of forty he had composed a great many works that were "praised alike by the exacting critic and the untutored lover of beautiful harmonies."[1] His output included a considerable scope: a symphony, a piano quintet, four string quartets, a piano concerto, at least two operas, a symphonic poem, two oratorios, plus operettas, musical comedies, and well over 200 songs. Throughout, he maintained many jobs in St. Louis, remaining loyal to that city except for a concert tour in 1878. He was a fine example of the __Kapellmeister__ tradition, rare in his generation and even rarer in the next.

The popular tradition (the total apprenticeship art) yielded, as it often does, a few exceptional composers who seek training to work in the concert field. The black singer Henry T. Burleigh, of Erie, Pennsylvania, represents this group well, for, as critic A. Walter Kramer wrote, he was a man of "extraordinary gifts . . . and fine mental equipment, . . . a composer by divine right."[2] Through associations with established musicians (notably Teresa Carreno and Antonin Dvorak), he was able to study with Goldmark; he played bass in an orchestra, and he worked as a copyist (he copied parts for the "New World" Symphony), as well as singing on the stage, at St. George's Church and at Temple Emanu-El (both in New York City). His work as a composer was almost entirely in what Kramer called the "art song," though he composed other music as well (including a violin sonata). After Burleigh, few apprenticeship composers came through vocal training, which was one of the first areas of specialization.

The next generation, men and women born around the turn of the century, was to include the last of the apprenticeship-trained composers. Their careers for the first time were pursued in parallel with others being trained in the universities. The work of the musicians remaining in the apprenticeship venues formed an intensification of the directions taken by their predecessors. Some, like Roy Harris, Howard Hanson, and Bernard Rogers, turned to the universities (and accredited conservatories, now called schools of music). Others made their way in theatrical venues of varying status: Samuel Barber and Aaron Copland, though active in a number of mediums, achieved their biggest successes in the theater--opera and "modern dance," distinguished from "musicals" and "popular

16

dance" and hence of superior rank. Gershwin attempted to live in both worlds, but this was not successful.

This was also the first generation of film composers; these were for the most part European men (this venue is one of the last to open to women) of impeccable training and great gifts, like Max Steiner, Erich Wolfgang Korngold, and Ernst Toch, whose association with films made them critical step-children.[3] Radio, like films, required the versatile and many-faceted skill of apprenticeship musicians. (And radio, unlike the films, in that day hired many women composers and arrangers.)

The pianist-composer was now rarer. Marie Bergersen and Abram Chasins, both superlative pianists, composed marvelous music for their instruments and received European recognition for it (Chasins's concerto was featured by Leopold Stokowski in European concerts; Bergersen's Theme and Variations earned her entry to the Imperial Conservatory's Meisterschule in Vienna by acclamation). But they could not compete with European imported stars; both went into radio, Bergersen as organist/arranger/composer, Chasins as music director.

Apprenticeship composers who were innovative in theoretical aspects of music, such as Harry Partch and Alan Hovhannes, maintained the traditional apprenticeship avenues of experimentation: instrumental technique and folk (and exotic) idioms. Their work became popular with American youth, who were, especially after the second World War, interested in oriental cultures; Partch received occasional support from university grants.

But the Kapellmeister tradition was sparsely populated, and this generation would see its last practitioners. Leo Sowerby was one of many American-born church musicians (organist/director/composer/-teacher) who increasingly took over from European imports; the church musician still can rise out of apprenticeship. But the "compleat" Kapellmeister, the total musician, was a dying breed. Many musicians who in earlier days would have aspired to this culminating position turned from that path to avoid the financial insecurities which now characterized it; others were content with orchestral chairs and other lesser positions left to Americans after the imported stars had taken the best jobs.

Yet there were a few marvelous musicians who were culminating figures in the history of American apprenticeship musicianship at its best.

Perhaps the finest of these--and among the finest in the long history of such musicianship--was Irwin Fischer. He was born on July 5, 1903, in Iowa City, but his early years were spent in a number of Iowa towns, where his father tried a variety of occupations, from farmer to shopkeeper. He had one sister, a year his junior, who would become a milliner (and, in retirement, a painter and ceramicist). The children grew up in hard days, often in need. The son was musical, but learned music at church and in school rather than in the home. In 1914 the family moved to Chicago, where the boy sold newspapers after school, starred in high-school productions of Gilbert and Sullivan operettas, and studied piano with Kathryn Leslie Williams. She was a remarkable woman, teaching him for nothing, encouraging him intellectually and musically, and leading him at once to the heritage of the traditional European masters. Under her care he became a fine pianist, with an impressive repertoire by the time he finished high-school.[4] She also encouraged him in composing piano pieces and songs in that tradition.

As Fischer was finishing high-school his father died suddenly, after a brief illness, leaving the son free to pursue the education of which the older man had disapproved. He was the first in his family to go to college, entering the University of Chicago financed by a scholarship and by outside jobs. He was not comfortable in the university atmosphere, in spite of his voluminous appetite for learning and his eagerness as a student. Without the acceptance of intellectual interests by his family, his education always seemed to him more exceptional than natural; his wonder at intellectual pleasures remained strong throughout his life.

Fischer found that his intellectual appetites made it difficult to know what he wanted to learn, or more precisely, it made him want to learn everything. He majored in English and French, and he was a fast and insatiable reader; he had no sense of specialization, but read all kinds of literature in and out of school; he wrote a good deal, and he was more and more drawn toward the study of drama. He became active in the University Theatre, playing the ghost of Hamlet's

18

father and alternating with Will Geer in the title role
of <u>The</u> <u>Truth</u> <u>about</u> <u>Bladys</u>. He also had a short piano
piece--a musical commentary on Housman's "From Far,
From Eve and Morning"--published in the school magazine.

At twenty-one, when he was graduated from the
University (Phi Beta Kappa, third year), he had still
not decided what his career would be: his musical
activities had expanded and his gift for acting had
defined itself; it was chiefly between these two
professions that his decision would lie, a decision
concerning which Fischer maintained an attitude
compounded of a somewhat restive willingness to wait
and a passionate desire to get started. His autobiography, written at nineteen as a university assignment,
tells of his desire to learn, of his ambition, and of
his determination to better himself, all entirely
American in its outline, but personal in its detail and
in its omission of the issue of money:

> . . . I entered the University, and this was an
> entirely new life for me.
> Sometimes I am rather glad we have known
> privations. It may help me to stand them some day
> again. Some people say it builds character.
> Heaven knows I need it.
> At any rate I am glad I am here now. I am
> where I want to be and where I feel I ought to be.
> How much good I get out of it depends upon myself
> alone.
> Why did I go to University? I do not
> know. I had the opportunity to do so, and I
> grasped it. It seems strange, but I have a
> curious mania for learning, wishing to know
> just for the sake of knowing. People ask me
> what I am "taking up," what I am studying
> for, what I am going to do when I get
> through. I do not know. Perhaps it is
> foolish for a boy like me with no means of
> support but myself to feel so unconcerned,
> but I cannot make myself be worried over the
> future. I must wait till it gets here. . . .
> I shall cross no bridges until I
> come to them. Once over perhaps I shall burn them
> behind me. This I know: I shall throw myself
> heart and soul into the thing I decide upon. If I
> fail, I shall "go down . . . foaming in full body
> over the precipice."[5]

Fischer considered himself too raw-boned and facially angular for leading roles, and he had great difficulty with make-up because he was color-blind (he had minimal yellow-purple color vision). More important, music was becoming indispensable to him, and in the end he could not conceive a future without it.

In the fall of 1924 Fischer entered the American Conservatory of Music in Chicago, seeking his musical education in the tradition of Miss Williams. He studied piano with Louise Robyn, a remarkable musician and educator (she was the niece of Alfred Robyn); organ with Wilhelm Middelschulte; and composition with Adolf Weidig, a chief proponent of the valued German Kapellmeister tradition. Fischer readily absorbed Wiedig's musical ideals; he won the Gold Medal for composition and became an excellent organist as well as pianist; he was graduated in 1928 summa cum laude. By the time he received his Master's degree in 1930, his life pattern was set: he was a member of the Conservatory faculty; he had married (and would have two sons); he held the console of the First Church of Christ, Scientist, Chicago; he was active as a pianist; he was composing enthusiastically; and he was beginning to train seriously as a conductor.

Fischer's compositions in the 1920s consisted chiefly of songs and piano pieces, plus two or three more substantial works, most of them lost or later withdrawn. A few songs are still available, along with the Burlesque for piano (1927) and the Recitative and Aria for organ (1928). Although strongly rooted in European tradition, always tonal, and often diatonic, the early works just as often ranged freely in chromatic materials, and some melodic elements are nearly twelve-tone. Above all, they are idiomatic; both the Burlesque and the Recitative and Aria have something original to say to the performer.

Fischer's further study, in the 1930s, was divided between composition and conducting: in composition he had a year in Paris with Nadia Boulanger and a year in Budapest with Zoltan Kodaly; in conducting he worked under Eric De Lamarter as one of the Chicago Civic Orchestra apprentices; then, on an American Academy Fellowship, he studied at the Mozarteum in Salzburg with Nicholay Malko and Felix Paumgartner; and later he worked briefly with Pierre Monteux.

The decade from 1932 to 1942 was one of growth and

considerable recognition. By the mid-thirties Fischer
was firmly established in the musical life of Chicago,
where he remained for the rest of his life. He was
prominent equally as conductor and composer, chiefly of
orchestral works, and he had ready access to orchestral
performances through his conducting--the Chicago Civic
Orchestra, the Illinois Symphony, and the National
Youth Administration Orchestra.

In 1936, when he was in his thirty-third year,
Fischer's talents were combined in an unusual concert
of the Chicago Civic Orchestra: he conducted the
program, save for his own Piano Concerto, in which he
was the soloist. "Irwin Fischer appears in 3 concert
roles," the Chicago Tribune headlined, and the article
called him "a man with ideas." The reviews were
unanimously favorable: "The shining talents of Irwin
Fischer were given a suitable setting; (the concerto
is) singularly remarkable for the maturity with which
it delves into, utilizes, and even expands the pianistic idiom" (Daily News); "Entirely modernistic, but
not cacaphonic, . . . (revealing) talent and inspira-
tion that teachers alone cannot give" (American);
"Genuine originality" (Herald Examiner).[6]

By the time he took the podium of the National
Youth Administration Orchestra (NYA), Fischer was a
highly respected figure. "Clarity" and "eloquence" are
the words that described him in reviews. Even the
redoubtable Claudia Cassidy hauled out some unusual
adjectives: "crisp and lyrical" for his baton technique in general, "mettlesome" for contemporary work,
"beguiling and fluent" for Schubert, and "superb" for
Mozart.[7] These assessments did not change over the
years; Fischer was a superlative conductor, and had
there been any hope for American conductors during his
lifetime, he might have risen to the top in that field.

Throughout the 1930s Fischer continued in his
teaching and his organ positions; he began work on his
Harmony text, and he expanded his organ technique
substantially, appearing in recitals in the Chicago
area, which he would continue until his death.

The compositions of the early 1930s were not
unlike those of the late 1920s, the songs and short
pieces tightening craft. More importantly, the young
composer began a series of orchestral works, such as
the overture Marco Polo, which initiated his work in
larger forms. His growing orchestral competence raised

issues for him in matters of both fabric and meaning in his music. Tonality and structure posed problems for a composer based in the conservatory tradition, but Fischer also had a personal problem of meaning. In the Piano Concerto he reached to his own directions, beginning his experiments in two-level pitch structure that he called biplanal, and he began to re-explore tonal forms in new terms. The triadic language Fischer considered to be still viable, and he expanded that language now through combining triads of two levels, often a tritone apart, and often adding a third layer (as, in the Concerto, A major, E-flat major, and d minor), thus making the term biplanal insufficient.

The Concerto was successful in Chicago, but Fischer's mentors at the Conservatory told him that the music was "too Nordic, cold, intellectual." Since for him the music was emotionally informed, he was shocked; but he was confounded after he played the Concerto for Nadia Boulanger, to be told that the work was "beautifully wrought but over-emotional" (trop chargé). These contradictory judgments had far-reaching effects on the composer at a crucial period in his development: from that time, he said, he was his own judge; the authoritarian concepts and their guardians, however respected, were no longer to hold power over him. Fischer was to come to his own terms with the issues of tonality, chromaticism, and form; he was a conservative in the true sense of wanting to carry tradition into new unfoldings.

Tonality for Fischer was not so much a center as a fulcrum against which melodic and chordal oppositions could pull. His work with Kodaly in Budapest coincided with Bartok's time there, and expanded his sources of musical materials to include the Hungarian/Bulgarian folk idioms, melodic and rhythmic, that Kodaly and Bartok were discussing, idioms made vital to the young composer in the folk music concerts that the two older men were directing in Budapest at that time.

In many ways the pre-War years were Fischer's most hopeful. He had a number of successful premieres, he was highly valued in the city where he had chosen to center his life, and he had created in the NYA Orchestra a fine and unique group.

The War changed Fischer's life forever, derailing his promising career as a conductor with the disbanding of NYA in 1942, and limiting his audiences to church

22

and school groups. In 1944 he took over the South Side
Symphony Orchestra, his first community amateur group,
succeeded by the Gary and Evanston Symphonies. Also in
1944 he became the organist of the Chicago Symphony
Orchestra and was soon featured in such works as the
Saint-Saëns Third Symphony. He continued to be
extremely active, but at the end of the War he found
himself engulfed on the one hand by foreign conductors
rescued from Europe and valued ipso facto over Americans, and on the other hand by a freshet of young
composers whose confident radicalism was encouraged and
confirmed by nouveau-riche university music programs.
In three years' time Fischer was plunged from the
younger to the older generation, and, hardly forty,
found himself a kind of musical elder statesman without
portfolio.

His biplanal experiments culminated in the First
Symphony (1943) and the suite for string orchestra and
celesta based on tunes heard in Budapest, called The
Pearly Bouquet (later recorded as Hungarian Set).

But the composer, in addition to seeking answers
to issues of tonality, chromaticism, and form, had also
been searching for new ways to integrate certain
techniques of the German tradition into his style,
particularly the learned contrapuntal techniques.
(Variation was always a French technique to Fischer.)
He turned increasingly to the German chorale, to the
chorale-prelude, to the fugue, and to such techniques
as canon, inversion, and the combining of elements--but
as layers of activity rather than as double or triple
counterpoint.

After 1950 Fischer's life reached a steady
plateau, and his professional life, always vigorous,
continued at a high level in its several elements, but
without the national and international success for
which he had hoped before the War. Organist from 1950
at the First Church of Christ, Scientist, in the
northern suburb of Evanston, organist of the Chicago
Symphony, conductor of the Evanston Symphony and then
of the West Suburban Symphony Orchestra, Fischer
nonetheless continued more than a full-time schedule at
the American Conservatory, teaching piano, several
theory courses, composition, and conducting. He wrote
texts in counterpoint and composition, and he developed
an extremely successful method for the teaching of
conducting.

With decreasing access for performance of large works, and busy with such special efforts as the 1955 performance of the Poulenc Concerto for Organ, Strings and Timpani with the Chicago Symphony (as always to enthusiastic reviews), and serving as Guest Organist at the Mother Church of Christ, Scientist (Boston) in the summer of 1956, Fischer's productivity as a composer slackened in the 1950s. Most probably this was related to the difficult (if not impossible) position in which he found himself as a composer. To the radical avant-garde, who by now controlled the funding and performing of the New Music, he was old-fashioned, but to the performers and audiences with whom he had contact he was, if anything, too modern. His music fell between.

Nonetheless, the 1950s saw a group of substantial works. Above all, it was a decade of songs, the sacred texts now overbalancing the secular, a new balance that would remain. Because of his early work in language and literature and his sensitivity to words and meanings, Fischer not surprisingly found in vocal music a particular fruition of his gifts.

The sacred songs were written for performance in the Christian Science Church (though entirely suitable for performance anywhere), which uses soloist and organist but no choir. The toleration of Fischer's church, whose music committees are chosen not for musical competence but to pass on the texts selected for performance, in general did not extend to new sounds, and in the need to make his work accessible to congregations of limited vision, Fischer simplified the harmonic language of his sacred songs.

In the second half of the decade, beginning with the Legend (for organ, 1955), Fischer began a twofold expansion in instrumental works: one in American folk idiom (with the symphonic Mountain Tune Trilogy, 1957), and the other in chromatic integration (with the Piano Sonata, 1960).

The 1960s and 1970s would see a reverse of the 1950s: a slackening of professional activities and a growth of creative power. Fischer reduced his teaching to full time and resigned as Organist of the Chicago Symphony (after twenty-two years) in his sixties, but maintained his directorship of the West Suburban Symphony Orchestra and his tenure at the console of the First Church of Christ, Scientist, Evanston, in both of which he remained fully active

24

until his death. His directorship of the Orchestra centered in a policy of balancing standard repertoire with new works (and an emphasis on American works), the ideal with the practical (that is, a preference for works using the entire orchestra to avoid idleness and boredom at rehearsals). In 1973 the orchestra received the ASCAP Award for performing the highest percentage of twentieth-century and commissioned American music of any orchestra of its category in the country. In the church services and recitals, Fischer maintained another kind of balance, of French and German, eighteenth-, nineteenth-, and twentieth-century music, and a smattering of British, seventeenth_century, and other types, including American. In the last few months of his life, over seventy, Fischer was presenting substantial musical fare.

In 1974 Fischer further cut down his schedule: he reduced his teaching to about half of a full load. In the same year he was disignated Dean of Faculty of the American Conservatory, an honor which pleased him.

The last fifteen years of his life allowed Fischer the time to explore the new directions in composition toward which the Piano Sonata had turned. He also reached a culminating power in the solo song, in a lyric intensity rare if not unique in twentieth-century music. From 1960 all of Fischer's instrumental music was serial, and like his concept of tonality, his concept of serial technique was of a fulcrum against which organic musical form could pull. The Piano Sonata had focused in and out of both tonal and serial function; the Overture on an Exuberant Tone Row was concerned conjointly with being serial and tonal, while also making witty (at times irrepressible) comment on the forced division between them.

Fischer's sense of humor, always strong in his personality, entered his instrumental music with renewed zest in his last works, beginning with the Overture; it informed both the clarinet Concerto Giocoso (1971) and the Symphonic Adventures of a Little Tune (1974). Even the String Quartet (1972), a lament, contained a counter-balancing carnival element. As he developed his serial technique he bacame increasingly concerned with the abstract and philosophical implications of both serialism and atonality.

The songs of the 1960s were a counter-pull against the increasing complexity of the instrumental works.

25

They represent the ultimate simplification of writing in Fischer's output, both in basic triadic harmony and in melodic form--everything is stripped down to the simplicity of the texts, which generally incorporate a direct and uncompromising statement of faith. From that time the songs took a new direction, toward a non-tonal fabric in an over-all tonal structure that resembled Guidonian modality in its phrase mirroring of text without tonal commitment until the end--and then often to an unexpected conclusion.

With these songs Fischer transcended the capacity of his congregation, leaving himself doubly stranded as a composer. His tolerance of composers to his left was not reciprocated by them, and those composers of the avant-garde who controlled performance used their positions to blackball the conservative element, returning a favor of the unyielding traditionalists of a generation before. Fischer's orchestral music was too traditional for the avant-garde (who retained their opinion from the 1940s without having heard the later works). The double bind at first confounded, then depressed Fischer. In 1965 he set the last of the hymns by Mary Baker Eddy, and sent all seven of her hymn poems in his settings to the Christian Science Publishing Society. The insensitivity, both musical and personal, of the Society was perhaps Fischer's bitterest pill: they replied that they already had a setting of the hymns and that he should use his setting for some other texts. To Fischer this was an aesthetic blindness beyond fathoming, and it was a blow from which he never fully recovered. He sent the seven to an independent publisher in 1977, as soon as the texts entered the public domain, with the hope that they could be published as a set; he died before the publisher replied.

That experience influenced Fischer in a way similar to Nadia Boulanger's comment that his Piano Concerto was over-emotional. From that time he again sought his own path, this time without reference to any reception that his work might receive.

Many of his earlier works had been unperformed (and some have not been performed to this day; many others--the works of the 1960s and 1970s--would be mounted through the aegis of admiring performers and former students, whose love for the man and the music made them loyal and enthusiastic proponents. For Fischer this was enough, in part because he was a philosophical man who remembered that in his youth his teacher, Kathryn Leslie Williams, had told him that if a single person were raised up by his art he would be blessed, and in part because it had to be.

As in the earlier instance, rejection was a means to freedom, and the last fifteen years of creativity evinced a new musical power and fulfillment. Several remarkable works served to summarize Fischer's musical philosophy and incorporate his lifetime interests at a time when he had so mastered his craft that he could transcend technique: the Meditation (for band, 1970), the Concerto Giocoso (commissioned by a fine clarinet player in the West Suburban Symphony Orchestra, 1971), the String Quartet (commissioned by his club, the Cliff Dwellers, 1972), and the Symphonic Adventures of a Little Tune (for narrator and orchestra, to his own text, for a children's concert, 1974). In 1975 Fischer was commissioned by the Steven Avery Pearson Foundation to compose a work for choir and orchestra that would have a text suitable to the Bicentennial and to performance by the forces of the United Church on the Green in New Haven, Connecticut (where the premiere would take place in 1976). For Fischer, whose religious and patriotic feelings were strong and sincere, this was a welcome assignment. Recognizing its importance in his own interior life, he called the work Statement: 1976.

In February of 1977, the Newberry Library in Chicago produced a fifty-year retrospective concert of Fischer's work: piano works, including the Sonata, three groups of songs, and the String Quartet provided an evening of remarkable range. The concert was extremely successful and was a welcome confirmation to a composer who had enjoyed little recognition since the War; but the critic "forgot to come," and the announcement which Fischer had sent to the Alumni Magazine of the University of Chicago was not printed-- a letter from the editor explained that the University professor of composition was "not much impressed" by Fischer's music (he had not heard any of the works of the concert) so they declined to print it. (One wonders if the Economics Department rules on the economic or political ideas of business executives before announcing a promotion.) But Fischer never knew of the rejection: the letter was in the mail when he died.

His death came suddenly (probably from angina pectoris) on the evening of May 7, 1977, at his work

27

table, while he was copying a completed portion of the piano score of the Piano Concerto No. 2, of which he had completed about half.

Fischer produced over 140 works, including about 65 songs. He was not prolific, but he was fairly consistent in output and his works were spaced over a period of just over fifty years. Few of his works were published, though he was a member of both the American Composers Alliance (where his works are still available) and Broadcast Music, Inc. Only two works appeared on commercial recordings: Hungarian Set (The Pearly Bouquet) and the Overture on an Exuberant Tone Row (in the Louisville series). As always, the reviews were excellent: Oliver Daniel in the Saturday Review called Hungarian Set "delicious;"[8] the American Record Guide said of the Overture that "musically, this is among the best of the Louisville releases. . . The Fischer opus is Scherz, clean and clear, healthy 12-tone music-- effectively nullifying the argument that dodecaphonic style can apply only to neurotic subject matter."[9] High Fidelity was equally enthusiastic:

> The Overture on an Exuberant Tone Row by Irwin Fischer is a perfect example of its genre--the sparkling, lively, brief, and exhilarating overture of which the archetype is in that to The Marriage of Figaro. The lineage of Fischer's piece is long, but it stands up very well in the procession.[10]

Fischer's career exemplifies splendidly the Kapellmeister tradition, of which his music represents a culminating excellence. In his passing one sees the end of that tradition, treasured in its modern form by many professionals through more than two centuries, and still valued in retrospect by the few. Of that tradition, and of Fischer's place in it, musicologist F. Joseph Smith wrote:

> I regret I only met him once, twenty years or so ago as a student. . . . I'd have had very much to gain from contact with such a man. . . . There are too few such "professors" of the full spectrum of musical experience these days, with all the narrow focus on a small technical area or over-specialization even in performance techniques--few able to play Mozart, Brahms, Stravinsky, and "avant-garde" Boulez equally. Fischer was a

Plate I
Fischer in his late twenties

Plate II
Fischer in his early forties

Plate III
Fischer at seventy
(Stuart-Rodgers Studio)

unique musician--a kind of 20th-century Bach-
-intent on solid craft and conserving the
common ground between old and new.[11]

The Music

When Fischer "threw himself heart and soul" into
the study of music, his compositions began to appear
systematically, as both a series of works composed
uncer the aegis of his teacher, Adolf Weidig,[12] and
additional works conceived on his own. Weidig took him
through a number of traditional instrumental forms,
assuring him of a rounded craft, but Fischer explored
the vocal art for himself. This twofold course established instrumental music as the discipline through
which he would yield himself to tradition, and song as
the musical expression of an emerging personal style.
The difference was a subtle one, for it was never
Fischer's desire to be absorbed into tradition, but to
learn his craft, pursue a career as an active musician,
develop, and become a forwarder, working for the future
of his art. It was an important element of the young
man's projection that "tradition" was not static; he
saw the attainment of mastery of traditional forms as
exordium to the work to come, the Western art tradition
as in a state of flux, and his own role as active,
exciting. While not unmindful of the past, he was
working in the present to shape the future.

Fischer's background in literature made song of
special importance in his work; song was at the heart
of his personal style from the beginning and was a
particular fruition of his gifts. The texts that
appealed to the composer were often by women; chief
among them was Patience Worth,[13] whose work was published in 1927. These were short prose-poems, often
about death and the transcendence of death, a subject
of deep concern to Fischer throughout his life. Other
texts of hers dealt with less recondite subjects, but
were nonetheless based in religious--even mystical--
feeling.

An example is "A Lullaby" (composed in 1927),
which speaks not the outward reassurances of mother to
baby but the inward wonder of the mother at this new
life, both "flesh of me" and "breath of Him who watch-
eth." The poem rises in an arching excitement and
then subsides to the more usual reassurance: "nestle
warm, And rest and rest and rest." This parabola is

mirrored by an arch of tonal and non-tonal materials within a rocking rhythm: voice and right hand in 6/8, left hand in 2/4, though notated in 6/8 (Example 1); the song begins and ends in F major but quickly diffuses into an integrated, non-tonal, ornamented but still triadic language. Return to F is achieved through the roots D-flat, E, A, and finally C, which becomes the dominant and then resolves.

The song presents Fischer's diatonic style, with two strong characteristics, both deriving from a sensitivity to the text and its musical potential: first, the tonal basis, with each chord derived in relation to a key but with few resolutions so that the references are lost; and second, a collaboration between the two performers that stems from the meaning of the text and which is always conceived as a dramatic interaction.

Example 1

"A Lullaby" (Patience Worth), first seven measures

The chords themselves are not always traditionally structured or related, and are enriched by embellishment; embellishment for Fischer was almost structural, able to clarify or to blur the harmonic progression according to need. The opening figure, for example, uses appoggiaturas to accent the midpoint of the measure and create the rocking rhythm; variations in accent are subtle and support the reading of the text virtually beat by beat. But most important is the tonal plan itself: the only clear statements of F roots appear in the first three and the last three measures; between these points of rest are spun a restless and reaching series of chords, with F in the bass in only three other measures, each one at major points of textual division. But these are not related to the key of F: as dominant of B-flat, as leading-tone of G-flat, and as a pivotal submediant/mediant (f minor) in a passing from A-flat to D-flat. The root F is used not as a tonal basis operandi, but as a bracket of stability, the "sleep" and "rest" with which the poem is concerned as its point of departure. The tonal pull is thus symbolic as well as functional.

Collaboration of the two performers is based in idiom and in dramatic function. Everything serves the musical fulfillment of the text. The piano part is difficult but pianistic, and it supports the voice in large and small elements. As would be true of Fischer's song style in general, piano and voice present two vital components, in this case complementary. The vocal line is a heightened declamation of the text, yet it is also lyrical and dramatic, difficult in idiomatic rather than arbitrary ways. Although the part seems essentially diatonic, it is in fact integrated, calling for seventeen different pitches, including five enharmonics (a progression from C-sharp to D-flat in the final section, is difficult to sing). At the climax, the voice leaps up an octave, to sing sotto voce the dramatic climax of the poem; the piano supports the voice in the traditional (harmonic and rhythmic) sense while also providing the psychological frame of the rocking motion and the tonal security of the mother's arms.

Another prose-poem of Patience Worth, also set in 1927, was "Predestined Love," a mystical text suggesting the eternal nature of love, present for a life--time, in sorrow or joy, absence or presence. Fischer called it "Can I Then Hope" (its opening words). The song is the chromatic complement of "A Lullaby,"

31

although it uses only three additional pitches (twenty, as against seventeen) over-all, and is actually more conservative vocally (fourteen pitches only, with one enharmonic progression, for the voice).

Here the tonal function and the chord structures prefigure Fischer's mature style: tonality (not unequivocal, for E, the supposed tonic, is approached most often as a dominant, and resolution is never total) is a fulcrum against which the musical ideas pull in opalescent reflection of the textual subtleties, and the chords are expanded and diffused in chromatic embellishment. As before, the nature of the tonal pull is symbolic, a musical counterpart to textual meanings; and the piano must bear an equal emotional freight, suggesting the inner parabolas of the heart as the poet-singer delineates the indwelling emotion.

The opening phrase (in E/A) catches the voice in medias res, as though in continuation of the emotion (Example 2); the third phrase (Measure 7) seems to begin in C, but in fact begins a long peregrination to B-flat minor. Like "A Lullaby," this song uses the tonic as a tether rope; the bulk of the song rides freely through integrated materials--and in part roughshod, reflecting a young man whose passion was greater than the gentle text would suggest. Decoration becomes abrasive--the singer at a climactic moment must hold a tone against both upper and lower neighbors (C against C-sharp and B-natural). After references quite far afield, then to roots closer to home (C and a minor), the final phrase seems to settle into E rather than resolve to it as tonic.

Although "Can I Then Hope" is easier to sing than "A Lullaby," it is no less lyrical or dramatic. The song is couched as a monologue; a large range (the opening phrase spans a tenth) leads to a declamation more associated with opera, and the pianist must be co-equal, providing inner commentary as well has harmonic and dynamic furtherance of the musical meaning.

In many early songs the piano provides an essential dimension: in "Song of Shadows" (Walter De La Mare, 1931), it presents slowly shifting chords that mirror the candle-light shadows of the text; in "Ay, Gitanos!" (Velma Hitchcock Seeley, 1936) it suggests the guitar music of the canto hondo evoked in memory in the poem.

Example 2

"Can I Then Hope" (Patience Worth), first nine measures

Exceptional in its unity of keyboard and voice is the setting of William Alexander Percy's "A Sea-Bird" (1933), a song that in many ways sums up Fischer's early style. The poem is an intense, stark invocation of melancholy, alienation, and, finally, madness-- subects seldom approached by Fischer, who was happier with affirmation and subtlety.

Both keyboard and voice set forth the bird's haunted flight and cry (Example 3), D minor is the fulcrum, used in a full scale including the Hungarian double leading-tone and other alternate inflections. The flight over the "mad" sea calls forth a number of exceptional effects, including stochastic rhythm, clusters (all notated traditionally, though not without problems),[14] and a parenthetical _ad lib_ passage, marked _pppp,_ in the high register of the piano. At the climax, the voice re-enters in a difficult enharmonic (on D-flat above high C over a piano C-sharp); the effect is strident.

Return to the opening creates the hope of a rounded ABA form, unusual in Fischer songs, but the return is truncated, the full statement is not granted, and the keyboard lets a blurred reverberation die away without a cadence.

Example 3

"A Sea-Bird" (William Alexander Percy), first ten measures

As a whole, the early songs are secular and mystical. The majority of the later songs would be on sacred texts: Biblical passages, poems by Mary Baker Eddy used as hymns in the <u>Christian Science Hymnal,</u> and religious lyrics from a variety of sources. Most of these were sung in Fischer's church; this meant a containing of materials with a view to the limited aesthetic capacity of the music committee and of the congregation, which at first resulted in constraint. But at the end of the 1950s the desire for his songs to be heard and savored led Fischer to accept the constraints as a challenge, and he refined his style into a spare fabric that could satisfy his audience without loss of integrity. In the late 1950s and in the 1960s, Fischer produced a number of remarkable songs, variable in form, that were traditional and simple in materials, but often innovative in the use of them. They range from simple alternation of elements in a sectional format, through a number of more subtle shapes, to expository songs that delineate a continuing text with no repetition at all.

Fischer solved problems of his own tendency to become complex by stripping down to a basic chordal/bass structure that seldom proceeds according to traditional tonal progressions, yet is coherent and dramatic. A song could be lyrical and grow steadily in tension to its final vocal phrase, shaped with exactitude by the text and by its inner meaning.

Another method used by Fischer to achieve structural validity with simple materials is through alternating sections of recitative and aria. This technique proved useful especially with Biblical texts, which the composer selected and juxtaposed with care and often with stunning effect. Fischer's religious thought was constantly changing, finding new emphases in the long unchanging (but very private) Christian commitment that he had made in his twenties. In his fifties the issues of religion coalesced into large, ever sweeping areas: recognition of God as Creator, wonder at Creation, Praise, Joy, and transcendence of Death. Two songs of 1959 represent his own religious feeling and his power to enlarge religious statements in musical settings.

"Delight Thyself in the Lord" alternates verses from Psalm 145 and Psalm 137. The first is of praise: "I will bless thy name forever and ever." This is treated as recitative (Example 4-A), but repetition of "forever and ever" forces a metric regularity after

Example 4-A

"Delight Thyself in the Lord" (Psalms), first
   eighteen measures

the first few measures. The second text is of joy,
"Delight Thyself in the Lord," and it is the complementary aria in a lilting rhythm with a restless
accompaniment, diatonic, and all motion (of pitch and
rhythm) an activation of a static E-flat root. The
aria is developed, with long roots on G (minor), C
(minor), and G (major); the voice stops finally on a
high E-flat fermata (over a converging knot of left-
hand f-g-c-flat and right-hand e-flat-g-c-flat). Then
the recitative returns, this time extended by a new
phrase, "Thou openest thine hand, and satisfiest the
desires of every living thing," an extended sentence
mirrored in a phrase which opens like a flower to the

Example 4-B

"Delight Thyself in the Lord" (Psalms), Measures 61-71

full <u>G</u> major chord of Measure 62 (Example 4-B). The
word "openest" is taken in an upward octave leap by the
voice, and the ensuing phrase extends itself first by
taking two notes for some syllables and finally by a
hemiola (Measures 68-69). Resolution elides with a
short codetta which begins with the activated <u>E</u>-flat
sonority, but descends almost at once to low chords
over an <u>E</u>-flat pedal, while the voice repeats the
opening phrase (but reserving <u>G</u> for "Lord").

The second of the songs of 1959, "There Is No
Time," is perhaps even closer to the composer's religious thought and its ultimate simplicity; at the same
time, it is his most moving statement about the transcendence of death. The fair copy of this song (kindly
given to me for study) shows a great many changes, most
of them further paring down and simplifying, as though
Fischer wanted to leave nothing but the very core of
his thought.

The text, by Verne Taylor Benedict, comprises two
short statements, the first, "There is no Time;/
Eternal winds are blowing / About thee now;" and the

37

second, "There is no death;/ In God we have our being."
The two ideas of the song are brought in at once
(Example 5), the first a four-note motif in thirds
presented imitatively in the piano or organ; the
second is the opening phrase of the voice, immediately
repeated in an extended form. The first statement
completes a tonal circle of traditional tonal progression, slowly winding through supertonic, subdominant,
dominant, and resolving to tonic as the voice completes
the section with repetition of "There is no time,"
now with the opening motif of the piano and answered by
imitations at new intervals.

    The second section, a parallel poetic structure,
is vocally a repetition of the first, a third lower,
using the C major scale but harmonized in A minor,
in a new format. Again the section ends with the
opening figure on the repeated text.

    A new imitative idea begins in the piano (derived
from the second vocal phrase), and institutes a new,

Example 5

"There Is No Time" (Verne Taylor Benedict),
    first nine measures

38

expanded texture: the voice re-enters, repeating the first section exactly, over a new piano part. This time the final repetition of the opening motif on the text "There is no time" initiates an extended section which develops the opening motif in thirds, now with imitations more extensive--the figure expanded, the range extended, the harmonic motion once more circling the tonal ambitus of C to the final cadence. Over this coda the voice recapitulates the phrase, "In God we have our being," a fifth higher (and with the high E extended to three beats), and then adds the text "So rest in Love," from the first section (a change from "And rest in Love") augmented and inverted so that it rises rather than falls.

Thus the voice presents an ABA form with a coda derived from elements in the body of the work, while the piano is through-composed. The symbolism of tonality here is the serenity of faith; there is little harmonic tension, but the interaction of the performers is so precisely drawn, and the fabric so direct, so reduced to essentials, that the singer can present the long-limned phrases with dramatic thrust. The instrument and voice project their different ideas, but join in the final phrase of each section, an apposition yielding to unity in another type of resolution.

This song was a courageous one for a composer in 1959, when such comfortable tonality was unstylish even when it was symbolically right. The complexity of structure is in large part made possible by the tonal simplicity, which parallels the simplicity of faith upon which the believer can ramify its meanings.

The Songs of the 1960s

The songs of the 1960s returned to a more specific subject matter, becoming more evocative of particular rather than generalized feelings. "There Is No Time," for example, had presented the deep and tranquil recognition of the composer's total absorption into the Godhead, the "eternal winds" reflected in long lines, in the slow unfolding of a complex but unruffled form; melodic parabola reaching over steady rhythmic motion and grounded upon tonal security was the musical embodiment of the text--and as serene and ineffable as the feeling behind it. Simplicity could go no further.

"The Walk in the Wilderness," a text by Doris Peel
(perhaps the favorite poet of Fischer's last years),
followed in 1961, and shows an immediate reversal of
direction. It is a marvelous musical fulfillment of
the text, which presents Jesus's walking in the desert
as affecting its elements--the thorntree, the stones,
the birds, the sky, the motion of the air, the darkness
of the night, and, at dawn, asking if a small creature
might stare out "from split of root . . . at footprints
left on sand like light?" The piano (or organ)
presents the rhythm of striding footsteps, with
restless unresolved harmonies and shifting meter, and
the voice enters in the low tessitura, dissonances on
the accents, so that the singer must enunciate at
almost a stage-whisper to effect the appoggiaturas in
the lowest register. The opening is in d minor but
with no cadence structure traditionally set up, and
with the double leading-tone (and both leading-tones
sounding against the unraised tones). Melodically the
song opens as a series of short (one- or two-measure)
descending figures.

     The form of the song is extremely subtle. Tonally
the long D minor opening is the only unequivocal mode:
the restlessness of the harmonic structure soon enters
the tonal structure and the piano then leads through a
series of tonal areas, clearly implying specific key
centers but never cadencing to any: D minor/major, F
minor/major, G minor/major, A minor/major. At the
half-way point (arrival at the brighter materials of A
minor/major) the voice inverts to rising phrases, and
from that point the slowly-winding harmonic progressions begin to work toward a tonal focus, now blurred,
and now reaffirmed, until the final phrase begins
(seventeen measures later) and the voice climaxes on
the word "light," a high F-sharp, the highest and
brightest note in the song. The piano joins the voice
in the upper register and feints toward B minor/major,
but ends in D minor/major (an F-natural against the F-
sharp of the voice). The opalescence of D minor/major
is savored in the accompaniment, which uses C against
C-sharp, F against F-sharp, and abrasions of B-flat
against an assumed B and E-flat against an assumed E;
these eventually clear, leaving an unfettered D major
chord, thickly voiced and, in a climactic opening of
instrumental range, spanning five octaves.

     The form can be perceived in two ways. First, the
tonal and melodic materials progress from D minor
through an unstable tonal wandering to a mid-point,

40

Plate IV
"The Walk in the Wilderness" (Doris Peel), complete

and in the dark-est dark of night did far- off stars quite close ap-pear? Did lit- tle winds, up-blown at dawn, Touch with ten-der-ness his face; and ev'ry crea-ture, shy and small, That dwelt in that for-bid-ding place

FISCHER: "When in the Wilderness" p. 2.
125

did it with won-der-ment peer out from sun-dered rock, from

split of root, at some-one more than us-ual tall, at foot-prints

left on sand like light? like light?

like light?

June 3, 1961

8m bassa - - - - - - - -

from which they turn and slowly rise to the end:

Measures	Tonal materials	Melodic materials
1-11	D minor; open cadences only, achieved untraditionally	falling motifs
12-27	Restless succession of feints to minor/major centers never realized; all centers dark	falling motifs
28-53	Slow turning via bright-	rising motifs
Measures	Tonal materials er centers (not realized) toward achievement of D minor/major.	Melodic materials

This is most probably the way in which the accompanist would hear the song. The singer perceives it differently, for the voice presents less tonal and modal ambivalence. In the second half of the song, after the accompaniment begins the long pull into focus and the voice introduces the inversion to rising motifs, the continuing tonal wandering leads through D minor, and at that point the voice is given an exact inversion of the opening phrase. And in the final phrase the voice sings the final words of the text ("like light") three times in a strong and tonally unequivocal assertion, which subsumes the question as rhetorical, a rising motif expanding from fourth to fifth to sixth. The accompaniment here (as elsewhere) is tonally at odds with the voice, in B minor under the fifth A-E, and modally unstable at the final F-sharp, when the singer can perceive no shadow of minor from the vocal line. The singer's part thus resembles a miniature sonata form:

Measures	Tonal/melodic function
1-10	D minor--exposition
11-33	Tonal peregrination--development
34-45	D minor/G minor--recapitulation
46-53	D major climax and resolution-- coda, with new melodic motif

Both perceptions of the form reinforce the meaning of the poem, each in a different dimension. The essential elements inhere in the hushed mood and the unfolding triumphant light. In fabric the accompaniment is seamless, while the voice presents a dramatic declamation of the text, carefully punctuated for clarity, above it. The ambivalence of form and the

achievement of the clear authority of "light"/D_ major
in the voice combine in a final fruition of the text,
making of those footprints the symbol of that Light
which is an essential metaphor of Deity.

The Late Biblical Songs

Like many composers before him, Fischer interpreted his faith by juxtaposition of scriptural texts so
that they could take on new meanings. In "Praise Ye
the Lord," a forthright accumulation of statements in
praise of God (from Psalms 148 and 150), Fischer
created a litany of iterative phrases that are cumulative and which give rise to a long crescendo ringing
changes on the essential meanings of praise.

Example 6-A

"Praise Ye the Lord" (Psalms),
    first ten measures

In technique it is tertian, but not triadic: the opening builds on thirds a tritone apart (Example 6-A), and much of the interior builds with thirds in odd pairs, making untraditional as well as traditional sounds. The "standard" chords, however achieved, often behave untraditionally: seventh or ninth chords change association by musical puns; but traditional progressions also enter, at unexpected places. The song is not a vocal melody with an accompaniment but a collaboration in penetration of the meanings of the text. The opening suggests the pealing of interior bells; the singer presents the text as a rising level of tensions; the organ or piano provides an interior swelling of the heart that is vital to praise. A more specifically imitative reference comes at "Praise him with the sound of the trumpet" (Example 6-B), which initiates the final crescendo. The final cadence (Example 6-C), with the vocal F-E-flat-D-flat, would suggest a final D-flat

Example 6-B

"Praise Ye the Lord" (Psalms),
    measures 45-52

Example 6-C

"Praise Ye the Lord" (Psalms),
    last phrase

or A-flat but not G, nor would such a progression suggest the key of F. The voice is in fact a bell tone over the forceful F root, which rings out joyfully in the accompaniment. As in many of Fischer's works, everything is connected, everything interpenetrates--the musical concentration is intense.

Some of the songs are clearly akin to the French petit motet of the early eighteenth century--short microcosms that expound a depth of religious thought. The Psalms in particular drew from Fischer some extensive lyric statements, generally in juxtapositions of his own. "Let the Beauty of the Lord Be Upon Us" would seem to be a song of growing wonder, climaxing in the awe-struck "O Lord, how great are thy works!" But it ends in a short coda: "And thy thoughts are very deep." The six sections of this song use elements of harmonic stability and instability, contrasting melodic types, dynamics, rhythms, and textures.

In fact, the simple language and complex form, the subtle and yet clearly mirrored religious intention, the remarkable concentration and musical integrity, are highly personal, and represent a coming together of commitment and craft in a mature composer of great skill.

The songs represented for Fischer a separate creative channel that remained to a large extent independent of the developments of his instrumental music. It may be that the simplicity of the songs was dictated by necessity, but in the end it served him well, providing a narrow discipline within which a master craft could be channeled with remarkable containment, concentration, and thrust.

Music for Piano Solo

Fischer was an accomplished pianist by the time he began his composition studies with Adolf Weidig in 1924; his intensive study of that instrument culminated in his undergraduate music study (his graduate work would emphasize the organ), and coincided with the systematic investigation of traditional forms of composition. A substantial number of early works have been either lost or withdrawn.

The earliest of these investigations to remain is the Introduction and Triple Fugue (1929), a work with formal heritage in the German fugue but with both fabric and over-all form in the heritage of French works, notably the large sectional forms of Franck. It is a youthful work, delighting in both the intricacies of its form and in the virtuoso demands of the instrumental writing, while taking the tradition of its type and expanding it with elan in naive and individual means. It is almost a leisurely work, with a discursive Introduction and three subjects (of the Fugue) that are forthright and not especially pianistic in themselves; but the eventual working-out of the triple fugue develops the subjects with imaginative and pianistic know-how. The culminating triple counterpoint may have begun in Weidig's studio, but it ended in a free exuberance that owed not a little to the stage.

Example 7

<u>Burlesque</u>, first nine measures

In instrumental work as in the songs, Fischer carried on experimentally with additional works not assigned in his composition work. The early <u>Burlesque</u>, a parody of certain Viennese musical confections, is probably as early as any Fischer work still in the repertory. The <u>Burlesque</u> is lively, as supple as a waltz, full of capricious expanding and contracting bits of melody, often resulting in augmented sonorities that are characteristic of Fischer, though achieved in non-traditional ways (Example 7). The form of <u>Burlesque</u> is simple: <u>ABA</u> with a concluding one-line coda of new materials which nevertheless share a concern with convergence, with which the whole work is infused. The piece is extremely difficult to play with the necessary insouciance, and, like most of Fischer's early piano music, was written for his own large hands.

The piano music of the next three decades remained basically tonal and idiomatic. Representative of Fischer's humor are the <u>Scenes from Childhood</u> (1937), with its evocations of organ grinder, swing, and scissors grinder. These were written for his children and were pianistically simple; but he later orchestrated them.

Ariadne Abandoned (1938) was a conscious tribute
to the sensibility of women, toward which Fischer was
always sympathetic. (He dedicated this work "To the
cause of women in music.") It is unusual in having a
program, extremely rare in his work:

> Ariadne sighs and weeps alone, searching
> the rim of the sea for the ship which does
> not return.
> At night the gentle winds of the garden
> caress and vainly try to soothe her as she
> sleeps, dreaming still of her faithless
> lover.

Example 8-A

Ariadne Abandoned, first sixteen measures

Example 8-B

Ariadne Abandoned is modal (in E without signature and the F-natural exploited), grounded on E rather than tonally in E. The form is ABBA, A being a heroic theme which comes first in an open statement (Example 8-A), without harmonization, and then in full panoply (from Measure 9). This material is developed at leisure and culminated in stentorian chords ending with E major; the G-sharp is then allowed to carry over to become the A-flat of the next idea (B section).

The B section (evidently parallel to the second paragraph of the program) is as mysterious as the A section was clear and melodically delineated: it moves slowly and indistinctly from a grounding on C (Measures 50-55, Example 8-B) to D-flat, A, and beyond. The B section is repeated, developed differently, and eventually reaches a climax before returning to the A section with the opening melody on B and eventually on the original E. The recapitulation is slightly extended by additional stentorian chords, which seem to become fierce at the end.

This is a highly impressionistic work, especially in the soft, indistinct, hovering B section, with its una corda designation and its whole-tone scale imterpolation (Measure 53, Example 8-B), unique in the compo-

ser's work. Although it is difficult to play, its
difficulties are the kind that pianists enjoy: it is
idiomatic and effective, using the color and resonance
of the piano to produce both the ambiance and the scope
essential to the concept.

Fischer's work with the expansion of tonal materials took five directions:

(1) increased chromatic diffusion
through embellishment and through non-traditional root progressions;
(2) static basses, producing music on a
tone rather than in a key, with upper parts
thus released from tonal obligations and free
to express themselves independently;
(3) simultaneous reference to more than
one root or key;
(4) modality and bimodality, most often
in connection with other elements;
(5) projection of basic chord structures
built of fourths, large thirds, or tritones,
and demanding expansion of scale materials,
sometimes within a tonal frame.

The last of these had already appeared in a few
early works, and in particular, those structures which
were systematized in the song, "A Sea-Bird" (pages 32-
33, Example 3) continued to intrigue the composer. He
turned to them in 1952, twenty years after conceiving
the song, as a basis for the Etude in A minor. A
falling motif (with hemiola across the third and fourth
measures) and quartal chord structures characterize the
opening, establishing its basis operandi. In an
extended elaboration (104 measures) of this single
premise, the Etude can be heard as a series of variations, as an extended crescendo, or as an ABA form in
which the last section is the Finale, the longest and
most driving of the variations. As usual for Fischer,
however, even this dual perception does not fully
reveal the subtlety of the structure: the second
section (or central group of variations) is so ordered
that a seeming recapitulation of the opening at about
the midpoint (Measure 69) is not a recapitulation at
all, but a bridge to the penultimate variation, in
simple terms a lull before the final storm or energy.

The work demands both agility and brute strength;
it is percussive and relentless, full of tension. The
tension is never resolved; and it is difficult to

52

shape perfectly because of its duality of form. The
expanded tonal materials (A minor with B-flat and a
second leading-tone, to the lower rather than the upper
dominant--C-sharp rather than D-sharp) and the free use
of two forms of a scale degree in a single sonority (G
and G-sharp, B and B-flat) produce a strident and
importunate sound that dominates the work. The basic
harmonic structure contains one perfect and one augmented fourth spanning a major seventh; this chord pounds
against the doors of constricting tonality.

The Piano Sonata of 1960

Already restive with tonal composition, at the end
of the 1950s--at the same time that the songs were
being stripped down to the barest simplicity Fischer
turned to more and more fully integrated materials, and
then, in the Piano Sonata of 1960, to serial techniques.

Example 9-A

Piano Sonata, I, beginning

The Sonata begins in the key of G, but almost immediately expands from a brusque diatonicism to a freer fabric, chromatic but neither integrated nor serial (Example 9-A). The second subject, with a repeated bass return to D, is tonal as well, but it extends further and further into chromatic diffusion until a melodic entity appears which is totally integrated: it contains all twelve pitches of the piano octave in twelve successive quarter-notes (Example 9-B, Measures 39-41). This subject, initially in the bass, is repeated in the treble (Measures 42-44), then it is given precipitato to both hands in broken octaves, the right hand inverted in mirror image (Measures 45-47). The action subsides, and the integration is reduced, in preparation for the development section to follow. The integrated theme appears in that section and in the recapitulation, but does not dominate the movement.

Example 9-B

Piano Sonata, I, Measures 36-50

Example 9-C

<u>Piano</u> <u>Sonata</u>, II, beginning

Example 9-D

<u>Piano</u> <u>Sonata</u>, II, Measures 61-70

Example 9-E

Piano Sonata, III, beginning

Example 9-F

Piano Sonata, III, the "carnival" element

The slow movement, _Lento,_ is one of the most compelling in Fischer's music. The opposite of many movements in which a simplicitiy of fabric is wrought in a complex form, the _Lento_ is, at its height, a complex fabric wrought in an extremely simple form. The movement begins as a forthright statement of treble melody and chordal accompaniment (Example 9-C). The melody is made of simple figures, a three-note unit of rise and fall, which begins three times on _E,_ rising each time by a half-step; and a longer unit (five or six notes) which dips and rises (Measures 4-5, 9-10).

The melody continues` to expand, passed back and forth between the hands; it finally returns, in octaves, to its opening form, but now it leads to a new sectioned marked _Maestoso,_ based on the integrated theme of the first movement, inverted, transposed down a minor third, and couched as a development of the preceding materials. The _Maestoso_ moves more smoothly and is fairly short, reaching toward a return to the _Lento_ with increasing demands. Return is to a _Quasi lento_ (Example 9-D), a more highly motivated version of the _Lento,_ in 3/2 instead of 5/4, with triplets forming a hemiola against the melody, and the melody now in a canon at one quarter-note at the upper fifth and with both voices in octaves. This fabric is intricate and deftly deployed; it must be precisely negotiated in performance, but it is marvelous to play. The third section is the same length as the first, but the tension is much greater, and it builds to a towering climax. The conclusion is a settling resonance, a reverberation that does not resolve but rather evanesces as a decrescendo _a niente_ whose details must be redetermined in each performance according to the acoustical and psychological actuality. Thus it maintains its energy into nothingness.

The ensuing _Allegro_ is a highly activated reply to the intensely sustained _Lento:_ it starts with a broken staccato version of the integrated theme in retrograde (Example 9-E, Measures 1-2 and 3-4), and then in its original form under sliding major thirds (Measures 5-6, and, transposed a major third upwards, from Measure 7). The movement is integrated, developing the retrograde version of the theme and expanding the treble dotted-half-note theme (in octaves and without the added thirds) in a long bravura section of double octaves. The left-hand octaves develop the integrated theme, finally joined by the right hand octaves in a falling pattern which uses the last two notes of the theme

sequentially, closing the section and leading into a
Capriccioso. The Capriccioso (Example 9-F) is a
"carnival" element in an otherwise unrelenting work:
it is tonal, delicate, rhythmically en pointe; it
equals the main second of the movement in energy but is
virtually its mirror image in everything else. It is
the gaiety of a masque, not false perhaps, but rendered
askew by its context. It is a concept found elsewhere
in the composer's music: a sudden appearance of the
antic that becomes an ironic comment, the tragi-comic
spirit of motley. The first three sections of the
movement (ABC, the Capriccioso as C) leave the listener
open to a number of structural developments; a bridge
leads to return of the double-octave materials (B) in a
new form, an Allegretto built on the retrograde inversion of the integrated theme (D), an Allegro non troppo
comprising a diffused triplet variation of the double-
octave materials, which slips into the Capriccioso in
the middle of its activity, a minor third higher; this
is followed by still another version of B and a
concluding variation of the opening.

The over-all form, like many of the composer's
structures, is heard in superimposed possibilities.
Its section analysis (though with very little exact
repetition) is ABCBDBCBA, a nine-part movement that is
possibly a rondo of the B element, a palindrome or
mirror form reversing itself from the central D, an
off-kilter sonata form, or a long macho movement
relieved by two kittenish encounters--an interpretation
which is, no matter how non-academic, helpful to the
pianist, for whom any one interpretation might rule out
the others and deny the essential ambiguity and
multiplicity of the design.

The Sonata was an important work in Fischer's
development, opening the door for his mature style and
to work in serial techniques. The integrated serial
theme intrigued him, and he used it in the second and
third movements to provide unifying force in the
integrity of the work. The Sonata, interestingly, does
not emerge as cyclic, since the unifying materials
never appear as an opening subject: the effect is one
of interior materials of the first movement becoming
overt in the mid-section of the second, and then
emerging as dominating in the third.

That progression, which is audible, parallels the
composer's process of working with the materials: a
theme which injected itself into the first movement and

58

then would not let him go, in spite of the strength of the concept of the <u>Lento,</u> but insisted upon being interpolated there; at that point, the composer recognized its nature and its demands, wrote it down, and objectified it as four forms of a tone row. The nature of the row is cognate with its origins as a series of small melodic gestures and harmonic configu- rations; its rising (and, in inversion, falling) lines and its harmonic augmented forms (augmented triad sonorities 1-2-3 and 5-6-7, tritones 8-9 and 11-12, but 1-2 and 4-5 in the retrograde forms) are close to Fischer's predilections regardless of context, and as important to the songs as to the piano music.

The Organ Music

In the early years, Fischer's work centered in piano music and in song; in his training at the American Conservatory of Music, he became an excellent organist, and gradually composition for the organ equalled the other avenues in concertration and, in the 1940s, surpassed them. Fischer's first permanent console, to which he was appointed in 1930, led to the further sharpening of his skill as an organist and eventually to his exclusive public performance as an organist (save for his own piano works). Thus the organ works took two paths: first, through his attain- ment of virtuoso skill as an organist, the composition of concert works, including an organ concerto (the <u>Chorale Fantasy)</u>; and second, the association of the organ with Fischer's religious life, and the composi- tion of many chorale preludes (my estimate is that there remain well over a hundred of these in manuscript in addition to the seven in the catalogue)[15] used during Fischer's forty-four years as a church organist.

The early works are of particular interest because, unlike the piano, the organ lay outside the purview of composition study, so that the works for organ began as expressions of Fischer's personal style, and remained so. If the German literature was strong in the piano heritage, the French was fundamental for the organ. Not surprisingly, perhaps, Fischer's early organ works, through 1940 at least, vacillated between German and French types.

The French tradition is apparent at once in the <u>Recitative and Aria,</u> composed in 1930, in its free sectional form and in its melodic and harmonic details.

An opening Recitative concentrates upon augmented intervals, and creates a unified fabric in which the melodic elements produce the harmonic language. The ensuing Aria, _Andante con moto,_ is a complement, with interest not in an expository melody with chordal punctuation but in a pliant and arching melody in interaction with other melodic elements, creating harmonic interest that is more colorful than functional, its sonorities derived through _la marche des parties,_ the independent progression of lines basic to French technique since the seventeenth century. A second Recitative is followed by a variation of the Aria that is purely a melodic efflorescence in the top line; but it is melodic embellishment that transforms the material rhythmically. The flow and freshness of the variation make it the centerpiece of the work. The final Recitative and the codetta, based on the Aria, are full of high color over a static bass and are quintessentially French. So is the work's intimate relation to the nature of the pipe organ and its technique.

The chorale prelude _Liebster Jesu, wir sind hier_ is as German as the _Recitative and Aria_ is French. The tune and the sentiment of the hymn are both direct and simple; the uncomplicated tonality of the chorale is taken by Fischer in a metaphor of unwavering faith and of the serenity which is one aspect of religious commitment. The setting is in four parts: a steady pulsating bass line that seems to infuse the work with inner life; a sedate statement of the chorale tune in the top voice, decorated with gentle turns and passing-tones; and two contrapuntally intricate voices between them. The inner voices are twice the speed of the tune and introduce a poignancy through dissonances and strong counterpulls. Thus although the work is simple in structure and general harmonic frame, it is neither placid nor lacking in shape--a slower harmonic motion at the start of the final phrase signals the stretching of an ornamental leap, previously a fifth, to a seventh, now a dissonance, and an extended final descent to the tonic. It is noteworthy that the composer at thirty-five was able to turn from his intensely chromatic style to produce a diatonic work, a model of traditional form, yet unlike the works that inspired it. It is fresh, personal, unapologetic, and satisfying.

The later works based on chorales, especially those after 1960, were more complex musically and

symbolically, often parallel to the songs: a straight-
forward presentation of the chorale within a context
complementary rather than unified; suggesting peripheral or apposite meanings rather than ramifying the
central one. The Prelude on Franconia is exceptional,
a larger free form presenting the tune in a series of
variants, alternating with an original tune, also
varied, and ending in a spacious final section combining the two.

About 1950 Fischer composed an organ Toccata, a
work of substantial size and difficulty, stemming from
his own virtuosity; it is marvelous to play. It
represents the organist at the height of his power.

Example 10

Toccata, first twelve measures

The work is in the French tradition. It opens (Example 10) with a forceful subject in the pedal organ alone, which leads directly to a long theme, also in the pedal organ, but now with shimmering chordal accompaniment specified for the choir manual. The long development of this material pits the dotted figure of the opening against the pedal subject, but it finally calms and is succeeded by a theme for the choir manual, quietly at first and then in a quickening fabric: the melody, in quarter-notes in one manual, comes in increasingly shorter values in another; this section is without pedal organ.

Both subjects return, rising to a new climax, then descending to a final section in major in which the pedal organ presents an augmentation of the opening. The section's exuberance is italicized by sweeping arpeggios and an accelerando in which the references are so profuse that it is impossible to hear a dominating thematic element. The Toccata ends in a slow double-chord version of the second idea (traditional structures in the left and and quartal structures in the right)—the chords not in progression but in parallel motion, an orchestration, in crescendo to a final _ffff_.

Both the fabric and the form of the Toccata are intricately worked; but the tonal fulcrum and the overlapping elements that interact against it, along with a steady rising of the activity of the fabric, give the work a greater unity to the ear than to the eye: when performed with elan, the Toccata presents a single rise, punctuated by changes of texture, characterized by increasing urgency and unbroken in its expressive line.

The Chamber Music

Fischer's chamber works were few and were for the most part unperformed. The early Piano Trio was performed several times; it is a lovely, Brahmsian work of solid craft, which shows the hand of Weidig. The Fantasy with Fugue Plain and Accompanied (1958) and the Divertimento (1963) are products of the composer's mature style, individuality, and humor. The Fantasy, for solo violin, flute, oboe, clarinet, harp, and strings, is a double work: the fantasy begins it, the fugue follows and then both recapitulate together as two layers, the fantasy taking on new meaning as it

62

overlies the fugue, now askew, now antic, now strangely opposite. The Divertimento, for flute, clarinet, bass clarinet, horn, trumpet, violin, cello, and string bass, is in the zestful tradition of its progenitors two centuries earlier; it is Fischer's neo-classical work--of high texture and instrumental color. But the work is of symphonic proportions, of four long move-ments (24 minutes): Allegro moderato, Andante tran-quillo, Allegro scherzando, and an Allegretto alternat-ing with two contrasting Pomposo sections. The Divertimento is a spacious work of unusual balances and probing development, in which the instruments are actors in an essential way; their color and technique energize the materials and inform the whole.

The String Quartet of 1972

When Fischer was in his seventieth year his club, the Cliff Dwellers, commissioned from him a memorial work to be performed the following year. Fischer took the opportunity to compose a string quartet, a medium previously closed to him (the Conservatory had no resident groups, no faculty or other concert series, and no venue for chamber performance). In addition to the exploration of this medium, Fischer welcomed the commission as a chance to create a highly mystical work dealing with death and the transcendence of death, and, strangely, leading through that to a statement about brotherhood.

Ostensibly a memorial to members of the club, it became, in Fischer's hands, equally a memorial to the club stewards. He wove names of three of them into into the fabric (see Example 11-B and D) through the Renaissance technique of soggetto cavato or "carved subject" (in German, H is B-natural and Es--pronounced "S"--is E-flat). By extension, the statement is racial as well, since the stewards were black men; the brotherhood thus cuts across race as well as class. And interestingly, it is an exclusively male symbolism, unique for Fischer, who was unusually sensitive to women's lives and feelings.

For Fischer the intellectual techniques were always associated with the emotional elements of music: the traditionally "respected" worked elements, such as inversion, canon, or double counterpoint, and forms such as fugue and passacaglia, took their real meanings not as pedagogic exercises but as musical and emotional

Example 11

Row structures and carved subjects for the
<u>String</u> Quartet

intensifications. By 1972 Fischer's craft and personal
thought had gone beyond mastery and realism to musical
and philosophic reconciliation.

The <u>Quartet</u> is extremely dense and complex, but in
general it is cumulative rather than cyclic or simply
discursive. It is a three-movement serial atonal work
(though it ends on a major triad) that presents a
multi-layered fabric and introduces references to
well-known tunes. Each movement has its own row, and
the rows interact with the carved subjects and cited
tunes. In this work, Fischer thought of the row in
multiple ways: in earlier works the row had been
primarily a melodic element, a series of gestures.

Here his notes on the Quartet show that the row changed
shape in its various forms--the inversion and the
retrograde statements reshape the row. More important,
Fischer saw the row as worked in a number of significant harmonic divisions: tetrachords, trichords, and
dichords (Example 11-B and C), all of which are structurally important in the work.

It opens (Example 12-A) with an intense harmonic
statement of row tetrachords, reiterated in different

Example 12-A

String Quartet, I, beginning

Example 12-B

String Quartet, I, Measures 142-156

Example 12-C

String Quartet, II, beginning

67

Example 12-D

String Quartet, III, beginning

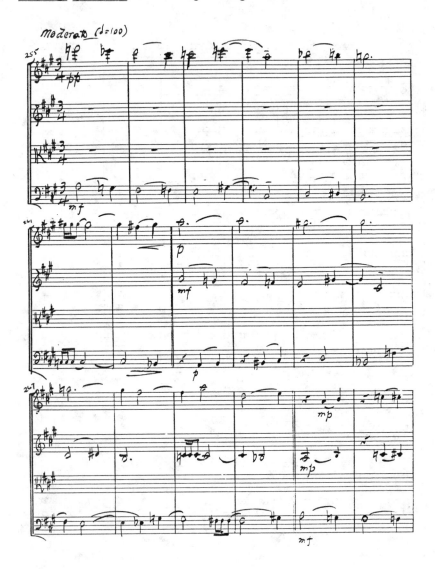

deployments and established as basic material. As the material extends, it is thinned, to trichords, in wheels, and finally to a single, very soft line. After a pause, a slow, peaceful statement of the spiritual Swing Low, Sweet Chariot appears in octaves in the violins over a permutation of the row, pizzicato, in the lower instruments (Example 12-B). The violins are to be almost without vibrato and the high C-sharp of Measure 153 is to be taken low and then gradually pulled up into a true octave. In the remaining section the texture thickens again, and elements of the spiritual are used against elements of the row, but are finally subsumed into the chromatic diffusion.

The second movement is a ghostly fugue played sul ponticello, pianissimo (Example 12-C), whose row is its subject. Each instrument works out its own destiny until the new row develops still another carved name, when the instruments join in stating it, then arrive at a cadence which is in reality a doorway to the third movement.

The third movement is the culmination, a Passacaglia longer than the first two movements combined. The ostinato is the row of the movement, and the initial presentation is in dynamically controlled parallel minor sixths (Example 12-D); the composer has given the movement a three-sharp signature, but if the row in the cello creates a magnetic pull towards A, the statement in the violin then of necessity creates an equal pull towards F. The set of variations projects a continuing series of textures over and around the ostinato, which appears at various pitch levels and in alternating original and inverted forms (or both); materials from the previous movements are introduced in countersubjects, and increasing importance is given to the sixteenth-note figure that had appeared, at first incidentally, in the ostinato. After excursions to extraneous materials, the sixteenth variation, marked Tempo I, returns to the row of the ostinato, the violins in quick triplets; in the seventeenth variation (Example 12-E) these triplets take on the configuration of the triplets in J. S. Bach's setting of "Jesu, Joy of Man's Desiring;" the chorale itself follows in the eighteenth variation, the ostinato in its original form in the viola. Association with the spiritual in the first movement is emphasized by the key (A) and by its statement Tranquillo in octaves in the violins. The chorale extends through four statements of the ostinato, which is variably deployed: the regularity is broken and the hushed statement of the chorale brings the emotional life of the work to a descent into the knowledge of death, a long recognition not peaceful, not acquiescent, yet not stark or ugly.

The rousing from this intensity comes not with divine comfort or heroic reassurance, but with humor and with the affirmation of life in the "carnival" element. Interruptive fragments of Sousa's Stars and Stripes Forever and of The Daring Young Man on the Flying Trapeze break in upon the reverie, finally yielding to the song, "Zivio!" (Life!), which was sung at club dinners. It is the final quotation of the work. A Coda ensues, again pulling towards both A and F; F predominates but the final chord is on A.

Example 12-E

String Quartet, III, seventeenth variation:
    preparation for entrance of "Jesu, Joy of Man's
    Desiring"

Example 12-F

String Quartet, III, eighteenth variation:
        entrance of "Jesu, Joy of Man's Desiring"

The _Quartet_ is an intense work: finally, it leaves the impression of its intricate fabric as a matrix for the two melodies (the spiritual and the chorale), set as two pillars spaced within it, and all else deriving from and commenting upon them. The gestures, though conceived in varying fragments of the row, appear large; the outlines are clear and the colors vibrant. The static diatonic melodies superimposed upon the tesserae of the integrated material take on unsuspected depth and meaning, and while the spiritual and the chorale are never sounded together, they are made one--the consummate statement of brotherhood. The work is personal, original in concept as well as in sound, and it stands, unique in Fischer's output, as a work of confrontation in the depths. It is a rare combination of sharp mature craft and philosophic purpose by a master at the end of a half-century.

Works for Orchestra

The earliest of Fischer's orchestral works were tone poems or fantasy overtures; in a number of such pieces he learned the management of larger forms and the art of orchestration. In these works he was first Germanic and later, as in the organ works, he arrived at an odd mixture of the Teutonic and Gallic that would define certain elements of his style.

It was not until well into the 1930s that Fischer found his own orchestral voice (his early works have been withdrawn); this meant not only achieving maturity as a composer but also becoming a skilled conductor and working with orchestras on a regular basis. Fischer's view of orchestration was never separate from his sense of interaction between conductor and the individual men and women at the music stands: he dealt with personalities and with technical demands, as well as with instrumental color in the abstract.

In 1938 Fischer produced _Lament_, a short work for solo cello and orchestra (written for the artistry of Jenska Slebos, a young cellist in the Illinois Symphony). It is a remarkable work of compelling emotional force, in which a tight canon produces abrasive and demanding tension, yet it is tonally and formally simple: an _AABA_ form with a short _B_ coda, almost _AABAB_.

72

The first <u>A</u> is for a solo cello alone; it is basically diatonic, characterized by large leaps, and harmonically obscure; the second <u>A</u> passes the theme to the violins, now with a chordal accompaniment made of moving voices that introduce sharp dissonances and prod the melody into restiveness. The contrasting <u>B</u> section is a chordal, dissonant idea characterized by a driving hemiola rhythm. The opening theme then returns in a canon at one beat, whose stretto effect and overlapping dotted-quarters intensify the abrasiveness and the dissonance of the previous statement. The coda recalls the chordal, hemiola-defined idea of <u>B</u>, with the melody in parallel fifths, and the work settles slowly to a final cadence that is not so much resolution as surcease. A work of great passion, it is short, pithy, and a perfect mixture of elements: too emotional to be "classical," too finely worked and intellectual to be "romantic," too static tonally for the modernists, too dissonant for the tonalists. Forceful, clear, and coherent, it is a work of extraordinary power.

Symphony No. 1

The <u>Symphony No. 1</u>, completed in 1942 and scored in 1943, after the War had forced Fischer's orchestra to disband, was modern when it was written but conservative by the time it was finally performed, two decades later. The composer projected a systematic bitonality; earlier works--notably the <u>Piano Concerto</u>--had explored simultaneous roots but not simultaneous tonalities. The fabric is, over-all, complex, but breathes in a motion from duality to multiplicity. Fischer called the technique <u>biplanal</u>, which was doubtless its basis of departure, but the prefix "bi-" should not be construed as limiting the planes of activity to two.

The <u>Symphony</u> is interestingly constructed, of two pairs of movements, each pair comprising a long, highly developed <u>Allegro</u> followed by a shorter afterpiece:

  I. <u>Larghetto/Allegro</u>--extended sonata form
 II. <u>Alla marcia maestoso</u>--arch form
III. <u>Allegro grazioso</u>--extended scherzo
 IV. <u>Adagio/Allegro</u>--interrupted rondo

The opening movement combines <u>D</u> major and <u>A</u>-flat major in a forthright, almost innocent group of themes

73

that stretch into a clear form much more standard than
is usual for Fischer; it is probable that he wanted
his listeners to be unobstructed by difficulties in
hearing the form and to concentrate upon the fabric.
It is a lyrical movement.

The second movement is an other-worldly march, a
short multi-layered movement perfectly conceived and
achieved--an exact conjoining of fabric and form with
intention and musical idea. The tonal pulls are closer
together, with the planes of E minor and D-flat major
starting the march, the lower strings pizzicato and a
solo bassoon above--bare bones, like a wry marionette
in an awkward strut. Successive entries rise a minor
third: G minor and E major; B-flat minor and G major;
and finally, at the mid-point, where five lines have
accumulated, C-sharp minor, A major, and B-flat major
in a multi-voice triplanal section. From the mid-
section (which is extended) the process is reversed,
voices drop out, the fabric is simplified, until the
hushed low flute and horn state the opening theme in
canon (in E minor) over the pizzicato basses (in D-flat
major), with interruptive comments in muted trumpet (A
major, then E-flat major). The movement ends with a
dreamlike evocation of the march in tambourine and
cymbals.

The last two movements develop what I have called
the "carnival" element in Fischer's work. The Scherzo,
in B major and F major, is broadly conceived, outgoing,
expansive, and cheerful, but with a charming awkward-
ness, like a simple, honest peasant; it is as intensely real as the march was unearthly. Its earthiness is
answered in the finale, a delightfully urbane rondo
that returns to the polarity of D major and A-flat
major. The opening subject is a repeated rising figure
that seems to throw itself against a wall of tonal
confinement, but is deliberately foiled; release is
attained all the more significantly in the contrasting
theme, which is the carnival proper, a perky tune,
busy, wide-ranging, and rhythmically off-balance. The
theme is assertive, saucy, and engaging, but it is
never free or exuberant; it is the clown mask over a
sorrowful face, the antic as denial of tragedy rather
than as true comedy. It unfolds as variations,
as truncations managed through the combining or
overlapping of materials, as intensifications, and
finally as a complete identification of the two
elements, which ring forth in the final section like a
victory.

74

The Pearly Bouquet (Hungarian Set)

Immediately after completing the Symphony in 1942, Fischer began work on a set of variations on a group of folk songs which he had heard in Budapest. It is a suite of seven movements, each dealing with a single song, except the last, which deals with two songs and is extended (it also incorporates references to songs from other movements). Fischer conceived the work for strings and celesta; he called it The Pearly Bouquet (but it was recorded as Hungarian Set). It is one of his most genial and successful works: a lovely fabric, luminous sound, with great energy and constant inventiveness. It ranges in mood from piquant to rip-roaring. The versatility of texture and the use of biplanal techniques occasionally rather than systematically, along with the power of the native materials, give the work an exhilarating freedom. If a pair of fragments must represent so long and various a work, the start of one of the variations in the fourth movement can serve as well as any (Example 13): here the original tune is presented straightforwardly in the first violins; the second violins present a complementary motif deriving from the tune; the violas and cellos (the basses double the lower notes of the

Example 13-A

The Pearly Bouquet (Hungarian Set), IV, Measures 19-22

cellos, pizzicato--there is no celesta in this variation) proceed in lumbering motion in C minor against
the A-flat major triad outlined by the tune, then a D
major seventh followed by an A major seventh and a
return to the D major seventh, all under the E-flat
seventh of the tune. At the end of this variation, the
tonal forces come together for a final statement of the
tune in the celesta with sliding chords in pizzicato
(pianissimo) in the upper strings, and a slow linear
descent (arco but still pianissimo) in the high
register of the cellos (no basses); but the unanimity
is short-lived and the movement ends with a splaying
outward, sudden, and on an unstable sonority.

    The free biplanal technique could be poignant as
well as sturdy: in the ensuing Adagio, the tune is
given to the violas and turned into a throaty, implor-
ing, resigned theme through its harmonic context
(Example 13-B). Alone, the theme simply presents D

Example 13-B

The Pearly Bouquet (Hungarian Set), V, Measures 19-22

minor and A minor chords, with melodic grace but
without harmonic or tonal tension; the simplicity and
security of the added harmonic component, neither
pitted against the tune nor yielding to it, provide a
union that is indeed greater than the sum of its parts.

    The Pearly Bouquet is an interesting amalgam of
folk and worked elements, of natural strength and
sophisticated structural techniques, of native Hungari-

76

an themes and American creative skill. Fischer made no
attempt to create a "Hungarian" statement as Liszt and
Brahms had done in the Rhapsodies; the work is sure
and unselfconscious, yielding readily to its eclectic
sources but never sacrificing its own vision or its
own integrity. Fischer would have asserted that that
is in fact an American statement and that the work is
as entirely American as its author was entirely
American.

Mountain Tune Trilogy

More obviously American, the Mountain Tune
Trilogy, composed in 1957, is a short symphony on
American folk tunes. Its three movements incorporate
the moderation of the work, which abjures extremes of
all kinds:

> I. Little Sparrow--Andante cantabile/Allegretto
> II. Jack O'Diamonds--Allegretto giusto
> III. Bird Song--Poco allegro

Although the Trilogy is for full orchestra, the
tone painting is unusually delicate for Fischer, with a
lovely parallel between melodic, harmonic, and orchestral forces. The work is tonal, even at times employ-
ing tonal harmonic progression, but more often using
key centers as either areas of magnetism or as static
grounds over which other kinds of activity can play.

Example 14

Mountain Tune Trilogy, II, conclusion

77

The concurrence of forces is evident in the strings-only fugal statement of the tune Little Sparrow in the first movement, then its fragmentation in a variation for winds; the layered elements of the finale laid out by orchestral choirs; or a subtle cadence that closes the second movement (Example 14), whose three elements converge upon G major. A fragment of the tune, now in augmentation, is on top, with biplanal triads in the middle; and a stepwise progression comes up from D-flat to G on the bottom. These opalescent elements sound in the trumpet (on top), winds with string harmonics (presenting the chords), strings and brass (on the bottom), harp glissandi and cymbal with soft stick--orchestral deployments based in traditional techniques but crossing choirs to create an ambiance of sound at one with the nature of the cadence.

Later Orchestral Works

The Short Symphony for Full Orchestra (1960) is an orchestral version of the Piano Sonata. It is an effective work, and it provides an interesting comparison. Like other orchestrations of virtuoso works, it must switch means: the effects of intricacy and personal force, both significant in the piano version, are sacrificed; but the orchestral version gains the dramatic tensions between sections in addition to expanded range, color, and dynamic scope. The use of brass in the serial elements of the first movement, for example, suggested by the long notes in the left hand, gives those notes the bite and sustained tone which the pianist achieves only in illusion. The poignant second movement's complex climax must be effected almost by sleight of hand by the pianist; in the orchestral version the tension is built through dramatic confrontation of strings and winds. And the final movement benefits particularly from the percussion and from the woodwinds in the insouciant "carnival" theme. The music is almost the same, but the effect is very different; it seems more dense, and darker. I would not like to have to choose between the two forms of the work.

The Overture on an Exuberant Tone Row (1964) is Fischer's last work for orchestra alone. It is of irrepressible good humor, a tonal serial work--or a work which departs from a tonal base and is content to dip back for brief touches, yet is free of the need to do so. The row is conceived as gesture and is treated for the most part as an entire twelve-note melodic unit. The delight of the work was recognized to lie in its high surface texture, which is more authentically classical than merely neo-classical, especially in its bassoon obbligato, characterized by arpeggiations, pianissimo, in staccato notes.

But its charm lies even more in its wit, and here Fischer is absolutely wicked: the title suggests a spoof of serial technique, but it is not that at all (the critic had called it "healthy 12-tone music")--it is a spoof of sonata form and the "learned techniques" which lay close to Fischer's own musical centrality. Somehow he made the form itself risible, devising the means of announcing the sectional divisions and under-scoring them: seven chords before the exposition and twice-seven chords before the recapitulation, and a coda that has a fugal stretto section, a final crescendo which ends with a musical exclamation point.

Beneath the obvious but effective use of the row, the equally obvious cavorting in learned techniques, the lightsome textures which make the materials easy to follow, and the humorously italicized sonata form lie layers of subtlety that keep the work from becoming a coarse joviality. It is so tasteful, so beguiling, so innocent of any hint of cruel derisiveness that it succeeds almost without reference to its source or its form, though the carefully delineated form superimposed on so blithe a fabric is a particularly enjoyable relationship. Within the context of Fischer's work, the Overture takes on added glints: a passage full of parallel fifths speaks to the pedagogue; the obvious sonata form is a real thrust from a composer whose use of form was so often ambiguous; the genuine exuberance is not the "carnival," but is equally true to the personality of the composer.

Works for Band

Fischer's works for band were all commissioned. In the 1960s he wrote a march for the National Concert Band of the Salvation Army, at whose special summer band conference, at Camp Wonderland, he had been a guest lecturer for over two decades. He named the work the Wonderland March; it is not quite traditional. The work is scored for the army's British all-brass instrumentation.

In 1970 the Cambridge Citadel Silver Band (of Cambridge, Massachusetts) commissioned Fischer to compose a virtuoso concert work. The result was the Meditation; it is a work difficult in all areas—fabric, form, and meaning. It too is for the British all-brass band. It was a work in which Fischer was free both to plumb the depths of his religious feeling and to couch his work in terms that would equate the group's virtuosity with the grandeur of the inner life. He subtitled it "The Strength of God's Love;" the suggestion of quiet certitude and comfort is at once denied by the active, soaring fabric, richly worked, and in part using the chorale "Lobe den Herren" (which he had used earlier in the Chorale Fantasy), a hymn of praise. This work, more than any other of Fischer's, is majestic.

In 1976 Fischer composed the Fanfare for Brass and Percussion that was his last instrumental work to be completed. It is a short work—Fischer intended it to open the first concert of the 1977-78 season—that presents four separate groups as independent entities: three trumpets, four horns, three trombones and tuba, and percussion of snare and bass drums, triangle, and cymbals. The planes of activity seem related to the biplanal techniques of thirty years earlier, but the work is not made of clear key levels; it does combine triadic sounds with varying roots, and takes them in directions both seemly and surprising. But the purpose is that of a fanfare: to flourish in a clamorous announcement or display. Fischer's is an ebullient splash of sound, stirring and strong.

The Concerto in E Minor

Fischer's first concerto was the Concerto in E minor for Piano and Orchestra, which he completed in 1935 and performed in 1936. Interestingly, he was captured by musical ideas which at first he thought were purely orchestral, and it was only as the materials insisted upon expanding pianistically in his mind that he realized he was dealing with a piano concerto.

Like many of the composer's works, the first Piano Concerto can be heard in more than one way—in this case as a cyclic multi-movement work, or as a single long movement combining elements of fantasia, variation, and sonata form.

80

The work opens with a string of five chords in the piano which are integrated, though not serial, and which point to a concentration on B. This pitch is confirmed by a tattoo on the kettledrum. A dialogue ensues, with the same chords, a tritone higher, in the strings (without basses), the F also confirmed by a kettledrum. The result is a tonal/harmonic fabric characteristic of Fischer's early style: the double fulcrum of tones a tritone apart within an integrated fabric that produces both a diffusion of the tonal elements and a strong suggestion of the Phrygian mode. At the same time, the harmonic structures, never triadic in traditional terms, move freely between suave augmented and brusque perfect-interval components.

The two main thematic elements of the Concerto are presented from the bases of E and G, though both expand reference freely and in the whole are supratonal. The first is deliberate and is both mysterious and stately; it is highly ligamented, polyphonic, and even in steady quarter-notes with an undiscernible meter. The second is a complement: a single melody energetically sounded with accented chords as punctuation. Both have remarkably long projections, reaching forth again and again; it is this nature of the themes as extended, organic entities of compelling force, which characterizes the Concerto.

These themes in the solo instrument become intensely pianistic. The first becomes a fantasia; the second eventually becomes a bravura etude. A cadenza is central in the Concerto: it unites the two themes and their two moods--and it also creates the earliest surviving biplanal fabric in Fischer's work. The next-to-last variation (or closing group of the recapitulation) reveals a kinship with jazz rhythms. The final variation (or coda) moves toward a virtuoso conclusion.

The Concerto was a highly original and very successful work, difficult but idiomatic and exciting to play. This is the work that sealed Fischer's mastery and his individuality, the work that Robyn called "Nordic" and "intellectual" and that Boulanger characterized as "over-emotional." In its splashes of color, its use of augmented intervals and intervallic pulls, it is close to the French aspect of Fischer's musical personality.

81

The Chorale Fantasy

It is surprising that the Piano Concerto should have evinced so much gallic influence; it is even more surprising that the organ concerto, which followed in 1938, in spite of the virtuoso French tradition for organ, should have been so Germanic. Its Germanic nature lies in its contrapuntal language and in the nature of its melodies, for the organ concerto is a free form, a series of variations and worked combinations of three chorales (plus one original theme); Fischer named it the Chorale Fantasy. The three are all used as tunes in Protestant hymnals: St. Anne, Old Hundredth (the Doxology), and Lobe den Herren, all of them associated with Praise.

The chorales are the essence of hymnody, with regular phrases in duple measure; to these Fischer added, as a fourth thematic entity, an original melody which (after a slow introduction that expands from a pedal D with fragments of the chorales) is the first theme to be heard complete (Example 15-A). It is stated by the organ in G major in 5/4.

A series of sections follows: Lobe den Herren presented in the orchestra, then in canon between organ and orchestra; a development section, fragmenting and

Example 15-A

Chorale Fantasy, Measures 15-20

presaging St. Anne; a scherzo of the original theme
with the complete St. Anne over it in augmentation. A
great climax leads to the midpoint of the work; the
organist presents St. Anne in E, as a toccata, first
alone, and then (Example 15-B) with string doubling
(from Measure 213) and the horns sounding Old Hundredth
(from Measure 214), an exuberantly virtuoso coupling
that culminated in a pedal cadenza. Two fughettas
follow, separated by a sectional dialogue: the first,
on the original tune (in B), is given to the organ;
the second, on the first phrase of Lobe den Herren (in
E-flat), in the orchestral winds, leads to a fragmented
developmental section that builds to the final statements, all in G; an Allegro combining the original
tune (organ) and Lobe den Herren (orchestra) in a
chordal Marcato fabric; an Allegro sostenuto with the
original tune (again in the organ, but now in a fast
figuration) against Old Hundredth (in the brass choir
of the orchestra); and a combining of Lobe den Herren
(organ) with Old Hundredth (full orchestra) in a
majestic climax (Example 15-C). This climax wanders
afield tonally and retards with a hemiola to prepare
for the final statement: this is an Allegro marziale

Example 15-B

Chorale Fantasy, Measures 212-218

83

Example 15-C

Chorale Fantasy, Measures 390-396

combining the original tune up a third and Lobe den Herren, also up a third but also followed by a canonic statement at the normal pitch. The sound suggests the pealing of bells and the mood is triumphant.

The Chorale Fantasy is a series of interactions. First, of course, it is a concerto, an interaction between two forces of equal power, but power of different kinds--the corporate strength of the orchestra countered by the virtuosity of the soloist. Second, it is an interaction of the tunes, pulling between the traditional and the experimental, with layers of tonal and less traditionalharmonic components--sometimes gracious, sometimes rough. Third, it is an interaction between the sacred and the secular, of paean and dithyramb, of the mind and the emotions, and of design and color. It has been called the finest organ concerto of this century.[16]

Other Concertos

Fischer also completed violin and clarinet concertos. The _Idyll_ for violin and orchestra (1949) is a work of such gentleness and serenity that its opening is more a meditation than an exposition; yet it grows and presents an exciting culmination. It is idiomatic, and its long cadenza combines the sense of the instrument (and its mastery) with the contemplative mood of the work. It is a single long movement, in an unequivocal sonata form at one with its simplicity of mood. It is in C_ major and the most nearly traditional in its tonal usage of all the orchestral works; it is close to central in the composer's years of work, and thus it forms a fulcrum between his early and late compositions, a gentle pause before the redefinition of style that would take place beginning in the 1950s.

The _Concerto Giocoso_ for clarinet and orchestra (1972) is as representative of Fischer's late style as the _Concerto in E Minor_ and the _Chorale Fantasy_ were of his early style. Integrated and serial, it is, as the title indicates, a brace of jovial movements, but they span a quiet movement that the composer called an _Intermezzo._

All of the movements are built on two tone rows, with a third entering in the expansive finale; the Allegros also feature glissandi parenthetical to the rows. The pairings of the solo instrument, now with strings, now with woodwinds, brass, or percussion, provide major interactions. The opening movement is energetic, good natured, and at times funny. But it is beautifully structured, and the extensive development of materials is emphasized by a slightly slower tempo in which interlocking thirds, latent in the second row, are allowed to emerge. The coda is a faster version of the introduction.

The _Tranquillo_ is based on the interlocking thirds which had emerged in the first movement, a mysterious ground in muted violin and flute, over which the solo clarinet presents a version of the first row. As the mysterious interlocking thirds expand to more and more members of the orchestra, the solo clarinet reaches further and further in one of Fischer's long lines, soaring at last in the high register; the movement is an arch, and the last section falls in thickness, dynamics, and register.

The Finale is more complex, a sectional elaboration of the rows in an idiom which shows the composer to have been clearly aware of the jazz history of the clarinet. The interlocking thirds appear in the Allegretto sections, in a complex maze of shifting intervals. In the long final Allegro the cellos introduce the new row, which is picked up by the solo instrument and featured in the cadenza. The work ends with long runs and a glissando in the clarinet. The work explores the solo instrument with a joyful and generous hand, yet the work is as serious as it is expansive, as meaty as it is giocoso. With its basic insouciance and the counterpull of the lovely, sorrowful second movement, it reverses the "carnival" element in earlier works. It is interesting that Fischer was led to such a statement in his seventieth year.

In fact, humor was a vital component of both the man and the music, and as he grew older that element flowered in him more specifically. In 1973 Fischer conceived a children's work of substantial scope, for narrator and orchestra; he finished the text in 1973 and the score in 1974; he called it The Symphonic Adventures of a Little Tune.

Although there is no musical soloist, the work demands a skilled actor/narrator and the coordination of two forces by a conductor. The text deals with a short melodic element that suddenly appears at a rehearsal, is swallowed by the orchestra, and embarks upon a series of adventures.

Fischer chose a musical element that is short, characteristic, and easily perceived, so that the manipulations are clear and to the point. The narrator combines the duties of story-teller, magister ludi, and teacher. But the work is not systematic or soberly didactic; it is rather a loose concatenation of musical techniques, types, and styles. In its free-wheeling itineration through musical ideas (including some very funny indications that other composers have swallowed the same tune), as well as in its genuine wit and pleasure in musical discourse (without condescension), the work seeks dramatic rather than musical form, though the score alone, as variations, would form a musical unity. It is a joyful and at times zany piece--with jokes in both the text and in the music.

The Second Piano Concerto, on which Fischer was working when he died in 1977, represents the composer's

use of the row in its most developed personal form.
The first movement (Maestoso/Allegro) was finished but
not scored. The introduction is based on what Fischer
called the "New Row," a series of large gestures, which
he used as melodic cells and variable harmonic sets
(Example 16-A). The Maestoso takes the row systematically through harmonic deployments of hexachords,

Example 16-A

Piano Concerto No. 2, the "New Row"

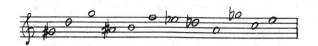

tetrachords, trichords, dichords, and finally single
notes. The Allegro (Example 16-B) begins with presentation of the row melodically in the orchestra over a
slow bass permutation, while the piano presents a
figuration of trichords in retrograde. The movement is
long and, like so many of Fischer's highly developed

Example 16-B

Piano Concerto No. 2, I, Measures 37-40

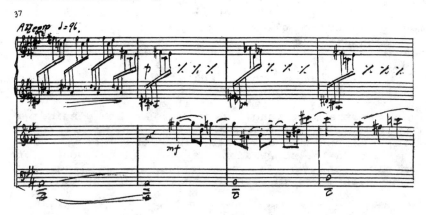

forms, can be read in more than one way. At the climax it introduces the chorale "Jesu, Joy of Man's Desiring," as an almost dissociated layer of activity--as far from its use in the String Quartet as can be imagined.

The second movement, of which only two pages and a sketch were completed, is based on a row that Fischer called the "Can I" Row, derived from his early song, "Can I Then Hope" (Example 2, Page 33), composed exactly fifty years earlier. The sketches of the row (Example 16-C) show the easy derivation--the first ten

Example 16-C

Piano Concerto No. 2
Selected sketch materials from the "Can I" row
    a. original form derived from the song
    b. inversion, with new shape
    c. retrograde inversion, with new shape
       (used at start of the second movement)
    d. transposed inversion , with E and C starred
    e. sketch with four-note groupings, E and C
       reversed

notes of the vocal line became the first ten notes of the row, and the remaining two complete it.

The second movement begins with a vigorous rhythmic version of the retrograde inversion (Example 16-D); a chordal version follows. The copy stops shortly thereafter, but evidently Fischer was about to incorporate the vocal line of the song itself, for a sketch of that lay on the page. The connection was partially laid out and was evidently already clear in Fischer's mind.

Example 16-D

<u>Piano Concerto No. 2</u>, II, beginning

No sketches have been found for the third movement, though Fischer had mentioned that the <u>Concerto</u> was to be a three-movement work. Use of a chorale in the first movement suggests a balancing reference--to the same chorale, or, more probably, to another-- in the last movement. Knowledge of such a plan would be necessary to clarify the intent of the first two movements or, especially, to deal with the philosophic intention of the work as a whole.

The Choral Works

In spite of his having no access to choral performance, Fischer remained interested in choral composition, and had he had hopes of publication or performance he would probably have been more productive in this genre.

Two early choral works were written for choir and piano, the piano parts essential and difficult--almost orchestral. He Is the Gentleness, to a text by Patience Worth, is multi-sectional, developed, and demanding; it follows the suggestion of the text, which has several lines detailing the "gentleness," each of which is given a section. These lines make up a substantial Poco allegretto, supple, warm, and lyrical. The final line, "Yet He in His strength hath poured the universe across His ever-space!" is an Allegro that begins with a strong imitative point; rising octaves present "hath poured," and augmented patterns "His ever-space!" It is a work of breadth and effect but with no clear performance venue: its use of a piano, along with its considerable difficulty, keep it from most church choirs, while its religious text keeps it from the repertoire of choruses more suited to its difficulties.

In the 1940s Fischer wrote a number of easier anthems, some of which were published. This was one direction in which to go from the early style. The other was to write for large choir and orchestra, a direction closer to the composer's heart.

The Symphonic Psalms

The Symphonic Psalms, completed in 1969, is a five-movement work for solo soprano, chorus, and orchestra (the fourth movement omits the choir), which was an elaboration--and transformation--of five of Fischer's songs:

1. Psalm of Thanksgiving--Andante con moto
2. God Is Our Refuge--Andante
3. Delight Thyself in the Lord--Poco allegretto

4. If I Take the Wings of Morning--Adagio
   misterioso
5. Psalm of Praise--Molto moderato

Fischer turned to four songs of the past (spanning the fifteen years 1951 to 1966), and composed a new one (the fourth movement) to complete the concept. In keeping with the more accessible music which Fischer provided for his church, the Symphonic Psalms are elaborated in ways associated with the symphony at its height: the result is the same mixture of simplicity and opulence found in the Brahms Requiem, though in a very different style. The parallel is not simply one of fabric and mood; for the two works are both highly personal religious affirmations, individualized through selection and juxtaposition of scriptural texts, couched in a conservative language, on a broad canvas, and in a style that uses traditional elements freshly, resulting in works of originality and purpose. Fischer never heard this work; it was given its premiere performance in 1980.

Statement: 1976

When, in 1975, Fischer was awarded the Pearson Foundation bicentennial commission, he was already caught up in the exploration of a row which, he had noted to a friend the year before, "has been keeping me awake nights." The row, typically for him, was both melodic and harmonic in its hold upon him; his summary of its potential (Example 17) presented the row (the inverted and retrograde forms were explored on other sheets), and below it the di-, tri-, tetra-, and hexachords with which Fischer was concerned; a cadence of mixed trichords and hexachords; a melodic enuncia- tion of the row and its inversion; and, to the right of the row, a group consisting of the six dichords derived by sounding the row forwards and backwards at the same time (1 and 12, 2 and 11, etc., ending with 6 and 7). These provided the essential pitch materials for two layers of the new work: the orchestral layer, really itself multiple, and a solo vocalise. The third layer is the choir, whose materials were derived from familiar choral pieces: the chorale "Jesu, meine Freude" (Jesus, My Heart's Treasure, in the translation he used) by Johann Crüger; the patriotic song, "O Beautiful for Spacious Skies," composed by Samuel A. Ward; and the hymn tune "St. Agnes" (used with the text "City of God), by John B. Dykes.

Example 17

Sketch from 1974
The material would be used in Statement: 1976

The orchestral layer of the work is a "ground of being," a fabric of life which is the matrix for all other elements whether derived from it or from other sources: the achievement of the work is that all elements seem to derive from this orchestral layer.

The layer of the vocalise serves to present the row in its melodic enunciation and to function as mediator between orchestral and choral elements. Its wordlessness suggests a relationship between that which words can project (choir) and that which is beyond their reach (orchestra).

The choral layer is that of literal statement, to speak to the double charge of the commission: patriotism and religious commitment. For Fischer, who abjured chauvinism as much as public piety, the work could address two concerns that lay between: first, the need for religious commitment at the deepest roots of national concern; and second, the hope to transcend the national basis of brotherhood to attain the universal kinship of the children of God.

To do this, Fischer directed the text in an outward spiral from the highly personal sense of union with Godhead of the chorale, through the national song that ends by stretching the nation "from sea to shining sea," to the transcendence of nation which he achieved by changing "City of God" to "Kingdom of God." And to ensure the clarity of that expanding thought, Fischer introduced that text first as "city of God" and then inserted new textual material: the first three phrases of the Lord's Prayer ("Our father which art in Heaven, Hallowed be Thy name: Thy kingdom come") plus his own line, "Kingdom of God where all men are Thy sons, Thy beloved sons, now!" The concluding "Kingdom of God" is thus clarified. The interpolated text is the only choral section based on independent materials: it is given a separate row.

The work begins with a form of the dichords in two trumpets (Example 18-A, Measure 1-3). The dynamic level drops down; chords spread out in the strings, pianissimo (from Measure 9); and the vocalise enters with the melodic form of the row (from Measure 17). Its juxtaposition of perfect and augmented fourths was a characteristic of Fischer's late style as it had been of his early style.

An orchestral elaboration of the row materials, emphasizing the brasses, builds to a climax; return to pianissimo string chords heralds the entrance of the choir with the chorale tune. A shimmering integrated string accompaniment of augmented sonorities (which he had used twenty years earlier in a chorale prelude) forms what Fischer called a "water wash" behind the intense, quiet unfolding of the chorale; the bass is tonal until it becomes static while the row material returns. The last phrase combines all the layers: the tune, now in augmentation; orchestral row materials, as dichords; and the vocalise with the first hexachord.

94

Example 18-A

Statement: 1976, first page of the reduced score

Example 18-B

Statement: <u>1976</u>, Measures 178-189

Example 18-C

<u>Statement</u>: <u>1976</u>, last sixteen measures

97

A short orchestral section leads to the introduction of the patriotic song, first in the orchestra, then in the vocalise, the song in traditional rhythm and four-part harmony (though not traditionally harmonized), the solo voice with song fragments above (Example 18-B). A substantial development follows, in the orchestra, in an articulated atonal fabric, which finally pulls to a bass B-flat, clarifies as dominant, and prepares for a clear tonal choral setting of the song in E-flat. The notes of the vocalise, though row-derived, coincide with the harmonic structures of the choir.

A short bridge and a single phrase of "City of God" lead to the core of the work, the choral setting, in its own row, of the added text: this is atonal polyphony, with independent voices and some (but not systematic) imitation. The opening trumpet dichords then herald the complete hymn, "Kingdom of God." The last stanza ("Patriot's dream") of the patriotic song, then the final stanza of the hymn (ending with the text "in boundless freedom flow")--both over continuing orchestral serial development--conclude the work. The coda (Example 18-C) recalls the initial appearance of the patriotic song (now transformed by the power of God's "boundless freedom") in vocalise and orchestra.

The orchestra presents the row materials, melodic and chordal, in a condensed form, and the chorus completes the work with a rising "Amen" (Measures 357-361)--on a C major chord (a key rare for Fischer) that once more symbolizes the strength that Fischer found in steadfast faith.

As a philosophic statement that affirms national brotherhood only as a responsibility for a much broader (and deeper) commitment, and as a musical statement that makes peace between tonal, traditional, serial, atonal, and layered materials, the work is an excellent representation of its author: spacious, reconciling, strong, and above all faithful to the goodness--musical and spiritual--to which he was centrally committed.

Notes

1. The National Cyclopaedia of American Biography (New York, 1897), VII, 425f.

2. Musical America, April 29, 1916.

3. The earliest movie score, to be synchronized with the 1915 Fall of a Nation (D. W. Griffith's sequel to Birth of a Nation), was composed by Victor Herbert.

4. The letters sent to Fischer by Kathryn Leslie Williams can be found in the Fischer Archive at the Newberry Library, Chicago.

5. From Autobiography, c. 1922. I do not know the source of the quotation. This manuscript also is in the Fischer Archive of the Newberry Library.

6. All quotations are from February 26, 1936.

7. Chicago Journal of Commerce, March 10, 1941.

8. November 29, 1958.

9. Signed "A.C.," in the issue of July 1968.

10. Signed "A.F.," in the issue of May, 1968.

11. Letter to the author, July 22, 1978. Used with permission.

12. Weidig was the son of Brahms's copyist and himself a violinist/conductor/composer/teacher/author, thus incorporating for the young man the ideal of the "master."

13. Patience Worth was a celebrated poetic voice of the 1920s, the purported work of an eighteenth-century woman dictated to a twentieth-century woman through psychic means from 1913. Arguments about authenticity centered not on fraud but upon the alternative possibility of "dissociation of personality." See Walter Franklin Prince, The Case of Patience Worth, Boston Society for Psychic Research, 1927. This book was in Fischer's library.

14. A discussion of these problems, as well as the general structure of the song, appears in "Spelling and Intention," an essay by the author in <u>Notations and Editions</u>, Edith Borroff, ed., Da Capo Press, 1978.

15. These chorale preludes were in the music cabinet of Fischer's church when he died. Two letters to the church about them have remained unanswered.

16. Organist Paul Jordan, in an interview of April 24, 1976, when he appeared as soloist in the <u>Chorale Fantasy</u> in New Haven, Connecticut.

Chapter 3
ROSS LEE FINNEY

As musicians were staying the course of Kapellmeister musicianship in ever-dwindling numbers, the
universities were beginning to subsume the services of
more and more composers. Universities undertook to
provide courses in composition, but without any of the
practical training which had been both ground and seed
for composers in the past. In the universities
composition was unrelated to performance; it was an
adjunct to the theoretical studies which had been the
core of Liberal Arts schooling for over a thousand
years.

Two points of interest characterize this new
academic concentration. The first is that it came to
America with stunning celerity: John Knowles Paine, a
Berlin-trained musician from Maine, took the first
chair in composition, at Harvard in 1875. This was
less than forty years after Boethius' De Musica had
been used at that school--that text had been used
there for over two hundred years, and for almost six
hundred years before that. There was not time in that
hiatus to change the traditional view, of both university and tutorial venues, that the highest musical art
is criticism, and, not, as the apprenticeship venue
would have it, performance. "It is more meaningful
and profound," Boethius had stated, "to know what
someone else does, than to demonstrate onself what one
knows." Performance, he said, is a physical skill and
associated with slaves, while criticism is intellectual
and associated with masters. "That man is a musician,"
Boethius concluded, who "possesses the ability to pass
judgment."[1] That, of course, was the fiat of Prince
Esterhazy, whose confident judgment acquired the skill
of Joseph Haydn, who was considered a high type of
servant. Residues of this attitude can still influence
the careers of musicians.

The second point of interest that characterized
the new academic concentration in composition is that
it was, because of its new context, conceived very
differently from the studies of the past. In Medieval
terms musical performance, insofar as it was associated
with the Liberal Arts at all, was a kind of rhetoric.
Singers and composers, as late as the seventeenth
century, were called rhetoricians.) Thus its essential

philosophic place lay in the Trivium, and a work of music was viewed as an utterance, a statement of musical Idea couched in a musical Grammar, presented as audible expression through Rhetoric, given coherence and shape through musical Logic or form. The rigors of the apprenticeship disciplines could clearly be seen in such a schema. Music was no more capable of separation from its audible reality than were oratory and drama.

As part of the Quadrivium, however, music was ratio, in its most rarefied form virtually at one with its sibling sciences of arithmetic and geometry, so defined and so displayed from Pythagorus to Newton. Ideal music within this concept need not be heard, but should be philosophically lovely, theoretically vital.

During their first century of university studies, academic composers proposed (and did their best to effect) a turnabout: the old view was that if a piece of music was wonderful to listen to, it must be worthy of theoretical study; the new view was that if a piece of music was theoretically "right," an audience was obliged to like it. Theory thus preceded the music; the theoretical rectitude of a work of music was to determine not only its nature but its critical success as well.

The first generation of university professors of composition were of necessity apprenticeship trained, and they responded to academic careers by leading two lives; they continued in the usual apprenticeship venues while also teaching at a university part-time. Paine at Harvard, Horatio Parker at Yale, and Edward MacDowell at Columbia, all maintained essential avenues of their careers in non-academic areas.

Their musicographer confreres, men like Waldo Selden Pratt, Henry Finck, and Henry Krebiehl, were more completely university men; Pratt studied anthropology and aesthetics at Williams and Johns Hopkins, and lectured at many schools, including Smith College; Finck studied at Harvard and then worked in psychology in Germany; all were thoroughgoing Germanophiles. University criticism became a German colony, so strongly so that the long line of composition students who would emerge from the French courses of Nadia Boulanger had little effect upon the strong commitment to German music, and particularly to German music theory, in American universities.

Two early university products can represent two new developments on the American musical scene. The first is Arthur Foote, our earliest composer graduate (MA, Harvard 1875), who can be said to have incorporated the twentieth-century phenomenon, the "private music teacher," as much of a specialist as the performer and composer. Foote was active in the Music Teachers National Association and the American Guild of Organists (both still viable and still only loosely connected to the university system), and attempted to vitalize that profession, which retained its strong apprenticeship leanings. This profession in fact is very often the only avenue for a gifted child not living in a musical household (which will probably always constitute the best incubation of musical talent); study with a local music teacher is most often the first training even for a university music student. Foote worked to see that private teachers could have college or university training and be accredited, a hope not yet realized: MTNA still grants accreditation to music teachers in the old way, by proof of competence and not by transcripts (that is, not by proof of training).

Oscar Sonneck, from Jersey City but educated in Kiel, Frankfort, and the University of Munich, had two careers: from 1902 to 1917 he was Chairman of the Music Division of the Library of Congress (he was the first Chairman); from 1915 he was the editor of the Musical Quarterly, and from 1917 until his death in 1928, the Director of Publishing at G. Schirmer. His interests stood athwart the German/American poles: he was founder of both the Beethoven Association and the Society for the Publication of American Music. Thus many university music graduates worked in publishing and criticism; composition was to become but one specialty among many in the next generation.

That generation, parallel to Fischer's--that of people born about the turn of the century--produced the first "genuine" university composers, those trained in the universities and pursuing their careers in academe. These were men like Walter Piston (Harvard) and Milton Babbitt (Princeton), Carl Ruggles (Harvard, University of Miami), Henry Cowell (in part conservatory trained, but a strong university proponent, teaching at Stanford, the New York School of Social Research, and Columbia, among others), and his student John Cage (whose career in many ways paralleled that of Harry Partch, appealing to radical university

103

intellectuals often not in the music departments, and not affiliated permanently with one school).

Exceptions are composers such as William Schuman, a graduate of Columbia but a conservatory teacher by choice; George Rochberg, conservatory trained, a teacher at the Curtis Institute and later at the University of Pennsylvania, whose espousal of apprenticeship values (interpreted as renegade conservatism) turned criticism against him; and Ruth Crawford (later Seeger), a product of the American Conservatory of Music in Chicago (she studied with Fischer's teacher and mentor, Adolf Weidig), who later accepted university radicalism, yet as a female was as unwelcome in that territory as she had been welcome in the conservatory. Elliott Carter and Roger Sessions, in many ways the quintessential university composers of their generation, and certainly the repository of both kudos and financial support from university channels, have been more restless—Sessions in a succession of chairs, and Carter with no permanent university affiliation.

This was the first generation to speak of themselves as "composers" rather than "musicians," a change that speaks eloquently of specialization, but also of separation—even of alienation—from performance. Women tended to be exceptional. Only a few women made it into the college teaching of composition; these tended to take college degrees in something other than composition, study that privately, take college jobs later in life (often in their forties) and then teach something other than composition. Louise Talma and Miriam Gideon can represent them. Talma, a New Yorker, studied at New York University and Columbia, but also with Isidor Philipp (piano) and Nadia Boulanger (composition), won a Guggenheim Fellowship at forty, and then taught at Hunter College. Gideon, born in Colorado, studied privately in piano and composition (with Sessions, in New York), took a degree in musicology at Columbia, and taught finally at Brooklyn College.

Blacks also tended to have mixed careers. Enormously gifted, Ulysses Kay is an ambassador for all groups judged on bases other than competence. Born in Tucson, he studied at the University of Arizona, then went to the Eastman School of Music and studied with both Hanson and Rogers, emerging to compose, study with Hindemith, and do editorial work

104

for Broadcast Music, Inc. His work reflected his apprenticeship leanings--his film score for The Quiet One (1948) is hauntingly beautiful. Only after a distinguished career did he enter the academic fastness.

Composers of the popular sector who tried to enter this venue had a much harder time than Henry T. Burleigh, who could superimpose lessons with Goldmark and informal sessions with Dvorak upon his continuing activities as a professional musician. George Gershwin, for all his pianistic and creative vitality, could not take time out for a university degree; and he was denied both the production and publishing venues available to lesser talents with more acceptable credentials. Performances of his concert works were sponsored through theatrical and popular avenues, most specifically the "symphonic jazz" orchestra of Paul Whiteman, a self-supporting group founded after the first World War in California but active throughout the country.

Whiteman was born in Denver and represents one type of mid-western composer of that generation. He was born into a musical household and his first strong competence was as a viola player; he did not go to a university at all, but remained an essentially American product--an apprenticeship man in every respect. Rosseter Cole represents the other type of mid-westerner, those who were German-trained and returned to their native climes as European musicians. Cole was born in Michigan, studied in Berlin, and returned to a distinguished career as teacher, organist, and composer, in Iowa, Wisconsin, and Illinois (where specialization as a composer was still impossible). He found the university system his natural habitat.

Ross Lee Finney is, in a sense, a hybrid. Living virtually all of his life in the university world, he was nonetheless, for his vital early years, apprenticeship trained. With a deep understanding of both traditions and a natural gift for teaching, he was the ideal man to create the post-World War curriculums that would bring composition into full university status.

Finney was born in Wells, Minnesota, on December 23, 1906. He was the third of three sons: Theodore, the eldest (1902-1978) was to enter the profession of music (his text, History of Music, of 1935, would be an important influence in the emergence of American

105

musicology); the second, Nathaniel, a year younger, would become the Washington correspondent for the Minneapolis Star-Tribune (and win a Pulitzer Prize, for a series on government proposals on peacetime censorship, in 1948). Their father, a sociologist/writer, centered his career in his university professorship.

Like Fischer, Finney formed lasting impressions during what he calls the "tender years" and then came to a large city--Minneapolis--at the start of his teens and entered the environment that would be decisive in his musical formation. But unlike Fischer, Finney was comfortable in an academic setting and easy with the intellectual life; and he was familiar with university machinery even as a child, through his father. While he was still in high school he entered the University of Minnesota, studying with Donald Ferguson, a gifted musician, historian, and educator; Ferguson's was a vital influence on the young composer, opening his mind to a spectrum of historical and philosophical as well as creative aspects of music.

Although Finney was born in Minnesota and returned to that state while in high school, his "tender years" (1912-1919) were spent in Valley City, North Dakota. Music was a primary part of both town and family life in Valley City, and Finney recalls the years there with affection. His father disclaimed any substantial interest in music, but he was tolerant (even encouraging) of the musical activities of his wife and children. His wife (Ross Lee's mother) had earned a degree in piano from Upper Iowa University, and the piano was always a domestic focus; the mother was musical and her love for and participation in performance was definitive for the son. She played the melodeon at church and the piano in the family quartet, Theodore played the violin, Nathaniel the trumpet, and Ross Lee the cello. They also played in the community orchestra. It was an American-style musical apprenticeship.

Finney also played the guitar, particuarly as an accompaniment for folk songs, for singing was a family custom and one of his great joys. As late as 1960, Finney would tour as a folk singer in Europe and in Greece for the State Department.

And of course Finney played the piano. Even before the family moved to Valley City, he spent considerable time at the piano, improvising, and he was highly competent at the keyboard. Thus the homespun apprenticeship was close to its traditional prototype. There must have been some theory study, or else Ross Lee was keenly observant (which is likely), for the boy "made up tons of music" in which he was never discouraged), even devising a method of sketching out some of the sounds on paper. The system of notation was not successful, but it suggests the imagination and energy which have characterized Finney and his music throughout his career.

Doors into the university life opened easily for the student, and his connections deepened. After one year of degree work at the University of Minnesota, Finney was invited to become a student/teacher at Carleton College, where he completed his baccalaureate studies while teaching cello and playing in the school string quartet. The second violinist in the quartet was an English instructor, Gretchen Ludke; she became Finney's wife in 1930 (they have two sons).

Finney's further studies strengthened the university commitment: he worked with Nadia Boulanger in Paris in 1927-28 under a Johnson Fellowship (and financed his trip abroad by playing in a jazz band aboard ship); with E. B. Hill at Harvard University in 1928-1929; with Alban Berg in Vienna in 1931-32; and with Roger Sessions in 1934-35.

In 1929 Finney joined the music faculty of Smith College, Northampton, Massachusetts (his wife later taught English there), an association which allowed him creative freedom while bolstering the pedagogical and scholarly aspects of his wide-ranging musical thought. Smith College was an unusual undergraduate environment, with resident musicologists (including Alfred Einstein in the last decade) and a program of publications; Finney founded the Smith College Music Archives and the Valley Music Press in 1935, and contributed editions of Geminiani, as well as his own compositions. (He worked also on music by Legrenzi, Tartini, and Cassati.)

Finney was on leave in 1931-32 when he studied in Vienna, and again in 1937-38, when he held both Guggenheim and Pulitzer Fellowships. These were vital years for the deepening of craft and for determining direction. The tremendous fecundity of the young composer leveled off into steady work, always substantial; but little remains from those early years--a few songs, piano and chamber works, and settings of poems by Archibald MacLeish (Poems, 1935; Bleheris, for tenor and orchestra, 1937).

The early works are vigorous and promising, couched in strong, often driving rhythms, using both diatonic (sometimes tonal) and chromatic materials; in these works form is achieved less often through thematic deployment than through extension and contrast, techniques that would be developed uniquely by Finney.

Finney had been a quintessentially American musician in Valley City--energetic, versatile, experimental, practical, cut off from authoritarian culture centers and making do with whatever was at hand, becoming steeped in many kinds of music, including folk song. The unselfconscious Americanism became conscious when Finney encountered the intellectual interest in defining Americanism that concerned Boulanger. For many American composers musical heritage and nationalism were a problem: some became European composers with American passports; others-- like Fischer--felt that the European heritage was the pith of their identity as Americans, in music as in everything else. But Finney seems to have taken neither course. He responded to his European tutelage by absorbing whatever he found useful, but he was never to embrace the view of Americans as musical foreigners as most other European-trained composers did. Much more deeply Americanized than Fischer, Finney added the older tradition to his own sturdy and confident musicianship, whereas Fischer dutifully asked to be indoctrinated in the European tradition and only later added American elements to a basically traditional musicianship.

Finney's Americanism surfaced in the 1930s in a more conscious use of American folk melodies; the violin concerto of 1933 made use of the folk song "Pretty Polly" and a fiddle-tune as well. In the years before World War II Finney worked on Poor Richard (text from Benjamin Franklin) and Pilgrim Psalms (based on tunes from the Ainsworth Psalter)-- both were to be completed after the War--and on the Third String Quartet, which is largely based on folk songs.

The style was tonal and diatonic, but with free

sections of chromaticism that occasionally strained tonal reference. The rhythm was steady, reinforced by harmony, and always, in the vocal works, a direct and simple reflection of the verbal rhythms. The Pilgrim Psalms contained the tunes of the Psalter, but Poor Richard is composed in the style of American song—Hopkinson, perhaps—without direct quotation. Yet it is impossible to say that these works represented a departure from Finney's "normal style," or even that they are "American" works in contradistinction to other works, for aside from direct quotation, the works are typical of Finney's style as a whole: vigorous, robust, of a natural simplicity—a deceptive simplicity which is not naivety but a scorn of pomposity and of complication that is not organic. These qualities, coupled with a lively interest in issues of construction (particularly the life of the phrase), are simply qualities of the man, who is, among other things, American.

In the 1930s Finney's conscious Americanism turned as much to pedagogic as creative channels; he was a participant in the creation of an interdepartmental major in American studies and he was one of the first to teach a course in Music in America. The pulling of knowledge together from a broad base is one of the great strengths of the university tradition. For Finney such an endeavor provided a strong focus on issues related to American traditions that could percolate into creative work in less obvious ways. At Smith College, the composer lived in the center of the strong New England heritage, a complement to the Prairie country of the early years. The friendship with Archibald MacLeish was a vitalizing force in the New England years. The two couples lived only a few miles apart, and they were a couple with conforming interests and answering minds. "We used to visit them and hunt mushrooms in their woods," Finney said. "Archy would read his poems and Ada would sing my songs on lecture engagements. She was a fine artist."[2] The influence of MacLeish came at a crucial time and was important.

The pleasant academic life was destroyed by the War. From 1943 to 1945 Finney served with distinction in Europe with the Office of Strategic Services, earning both a Purple Heart and a Certificate of Merit. The War was reflected in the Symphony #1 (Comminiqué, 1943), which was less directly American in context, but which represented a conscious synthesis

109

of influences into a mature personal style.

Issues of national style were subsumed for Finney into issues of personal style, and very quickly his concern turned to problems of structure. He had confronted what he calls "the chromatic phenomena" in his first lesson with Alban Berg in 1931, but his study in Vienna caused him to react against dogmatic serialism, and probably against the extreme concentration on pitch materials and organization as well; for Finney never has renounced his essential commitment to rhythm and to the "emotional structure of a work." Thus Finney began a long search for "freedom within a new complexity," and for a redefinition of the concept and the techniques of tonality. For Finney, tonality is "grounded in polarity," and the means lie not in triad-based vertical structures, however extended, but in pitch oppositions, not in successions but in contrasts, in magnetic pulls and counterpulls.

This was a period in which Finney was ready to be influenced by non-musical writers, particularly physicists and humanist philosophers. The work of Niels Bohr and Robert Oppenheimer interested him, as did certain aspects of Newtonian and quantum physics; these Bohr viewed as mutually necessary, as complementary (rather than as contradictory), a term Finney adopted and was to ramify musically.

The fruits of Finney's long thoughts included the clarification of two ideas that would remain vital elements in his work: that the small means (the factors of fabric) and the large means (the factors of form) are not the same; and that the pulls and counterpulls could be savored, structured, and used in composition; this important principle he called complementarity.

Finney was awarded a second Guggenheim Fellowship in 1947. He focused on chamber music during his year's leave; he was at the cusp of a significant change in direction.

In 1948-49 Finney served as Visiting Professor of Composition and Musicology at the University of Michigan, and from 1949 to 1973, when he retired, was Professor of Music and Composer in Residence at that institution. (He is now Professor Emeritus.) He introduced a seminar in American music and others in twentieth-century literature and analysis. But above all, the appointment was crucial for the establishment of composition programs in the American universities, for Finney, at the height of his power, was ready to bring to this position the many facets of his creative and pedagogic energy.

The doctoral program in composition which Finney established and honed became a model for virtually all subsequent programs in the United States. Within the first five years he developed a powerful curriculum, with strong if demanding classes and seminars that provided background of literature and analytical techniques, along with a full and rigorous discipline in the craft of composition itself. Finney realized that a group of young composers had much to learn from each other, and central to his program was the Composers Forum, where students could hear their own works and discuss them. His home was often a meeting place for the composition students; lively coffee-pot dialogues were perhaps the American counterpart of European beer-stein get-togethers.

Finney also believed in exposing students to a broad scope of influence, and he initiated a series of visiting lectureships which brought composers of many stripes to the campus for interaction with students-- men as different as Luigi Dallapiccola, Ralph Vaughan Williams, Karlheinz Stockhausen, Elliott Carter, and Roberto Gerhard. In addition, Finney realized the importance of an electronic studio; he himself went to the Columbia-Princeton electronic laboratory, where he studied with Mario Davidovsky. Returning to Michigan, he organized the laboratory there, and then brought Davidovsky to the campus for a semester to teach the faculty. Thus his conception of a complete composition study was realized in a well-balanced program unique but soon to be emulated in many universities. Finney recognized the need for students to explore the gamut of styles, from traditional disciplines to radical techniques. It was by Finney's students (and with Finney's blessing and counsel) that the Ann Arbor ONCE Festival was founded in 1959.

In addition, Finney developed composition courses for students not majoring in composition, elementary courses open to students with no background in music theory.

As a teacher Finney was unparalleled: first, his own craft was secure and thoughtful; second, his

expansive mind and his enjoyment of discussion put him
in the role of <u>pater familias</u> and gave his students an
<u>esprit de corps</u>. But also he could sense the exact
degree of involvement and authority that would most
benefit his students;   he knew how to encourage
without undue or unstructured praise;   he could
support, surprise, and even confound his students;
and above all, he could foster each one's particular
gift. The list of Finney;s students is long;   it
includes William Albright, Leslie Bassett, George
Crumb, Donald Harris, Sydney Hodkinson, Gerald Humel,
Roger Reynolds, and George Balch Wilson.   It is not
the length of the list that is remarkable (though it
is long), nor even the many distinguished names upon
it;   what is so remarkable is the scope of style
represented in it.

During the 1950s Finney composed many works for
the performers and groups of the School of Music of
the University of Michigan, while also working on
increasingly frequent commissions. The decade was
thus one of chamber works, a period of absorbing and
consolidating. Again toward the end of the decade
came an expansion: fantasy and variation, both close
in means to extension and contrast, came into particular prominence in Finney's output. The fantasy in
the tightening craft would come to fruition in the
remarkable <u>Fantasy in Two Movements</u>, for solo violin,
commissioned by Yehudi Menuhin and premiered by him at
the Brussels World's Fair of 1958.

The <u>String Quintet</u> with two cellos (1958) brought
Finney's seemingly contradictory principles--extension
and contrast--to an apex. The long work is made of
two large movements, each built of several short
sections. The formal means eschew thematic repetitions;   the musical memory is for tempo and mood.
Even the restatements are not of themes;   they are
ruminations upon a mixture of ideas familiar from
earlier sections of the work but varied and elaborated
in return. The important formal means is the creation
of a coherent structure through a dozen-odd sections
which are both spun out in a prose rhetoric and
ordered by contrast. I have called this technique
<u>elaboration.</u> Although the pitch materials are integra-
ted over-all, the ideas are often diatonic, a granite
force which emphasizes the direct, sometimes rough,
driving rhythms of the work, and at the same time
provides one more element of complementarity. Diatonic
materials, often with a pull towards certain tones (as

112

magnetic forces rather than as key centers), and chromatic, diffuse elements play off against one another; so do fast and slow, expanded and contracted (range), rough and smooth (textures). Above all, the work maintains a tension of active elements. Its relationship to traditional sectional forms, such as rondo or suite, is apparent, but the means are radically different, and the internal structures have little in common with older types. The work is less static than the rondo,, more organic than the suite.

Such a culminative work necessitates a shift to new sights; in the Fantasy in Two Movements Finney had already composed a serial work, and in 1959 he turned to serialism as a basic principle. The principles of complementarity led him to a highly individual concept of the row, as made of two hexachords that could provide the means of opposition, tension, and accomodation that Finney continued to find necessary. The tightening "small means" carried over into the "large means," particularly into forms characterized by elaboration. This shift in Finney's style had been presaged in the fifth and sixth string quartets, composed for the Stanley Quartet of the University of Michigan: the Fifth (1949) is tonal, cyclic, organic; the Sixth (1950) is serial, elaborated, emphatic. But they share the compelling rhythmic life, the dramatic juxtapositions, the marvelous actuality, the interactions not of "parts" or "voices" but of instruments played by persons, that potent vitality which is at once the most obvious and the most difficult to penetrate of the virtues of Finney's music.

As the 1960s began, Finney's work reflected anew that concern with humanist philosophers which had shown itself twenty years earlier (particularly in such symbolism as is basic to the Spherical Madrigals of 1947). Number and shape, evidenced both in acoustical number and in stage placements and interactions, can be found in works of the next few years, such as Three Pieces for Strings, Winds, Percussion, and Tape Recorder (1962) and Three Studies in Fours (1965), for solo percussion. The latter represents also a growing interest in percussion instruments in and out of the orchestra.

The decade 1962 to 1972 saw the production of a remarkable series of works, particularly in the joining of philosophical, personal, and musical elements. Still Are New Worlds (for chorus, narrator, and orchestra, with electronic tape, 1962), premiered at the Ann Arbor May Festival in 1963, is a synthesis of these elements, controlled through the selection of texts, through complementarity and elaboration, and unified by spatial metaphors that inform both text and music. In the end, the three become one.

Still Are New Worlds was pivotal in Finney's development--it was in a sense the culmination of the metaphors which had been so important to him in the 1940s;   but it was also the first of a series of extraordinary works which, though philosophical and personal, came close and closer to the purely musical statement.   Rhythmic energy, the marvelous actuality, and the deep care of the emotional life of his work continued to define Finney's style;   and within this continuity the oppositions--and appositions--were significantly expanded.   The range of materials enlarged, in time and scope, and included American and folk materials.   It was not a return to the Americanism of the 1940s, but a new kind.   In this music, Finney did not leave himself to enter the concern of nation-hood, but he began with his own memories, found them and himself American, and moved outward from this internal recognition.   Concepts of time and memory are basic in such works as Summer in Valley City (1969), Landscapes Remembered (1971), and Spaces (1971);   time and memory are equally verbal and musical ideas, in the unity of which the verbal is transcended and clarified by the musical.

Parallel to these was a series of more overtly abstract works, including choral pieces, which increas-ingly recognized long, even universal traditions, and in general evince more concern for less standard chamber groups and for orchestra and band (Summer in Valley City is for concert band): Divertissement (a piano quartet with violin, clarinet, and cello); Concerto for Percussion and Orchestra (1965); Nun's Priest's Tale (text from Chaucer), for chorus, solo-ists, folksong singer with electric guitar, and small orchestra (1965);   Symphony Concertante (1967);   Five Organ Fantasies (1967);   the Fourth Symphony (1972).

Since his retirement, Finney has continued to maintain his pace of creative work, responding to commissions that have led him to forms both large and small;   his work has become increasingly spare, pared of unessentials.   Since the Fourth Symphony, Finney has produced two concertos;   a work for five trombones;

114

Plate V
Finney at eight

Plate VI
Finney at forty

Plate VII
Finney at seventy,
at the University of Michigan

another choral/orchestral work (<u>Earthrise</u>, to complete a trilogy with <u>Still Are New Worlds</u> and <u>The Martyr's Elegy</u>); and an opera (<u>Weep Torn Land</u>) about the American West.

Thus in a span of over fifty years, Ross Lee Finney has contributed signally to American music as both composer and educator. His works have expanded in craft and musical reference while pulling against a tightening aesthetic discipline. The very youthful works, expressing a hardly disciplined creative energy, displayed a love of free imagination (Finney's earliest remembered title is of a piano piece, <u>Freaks of Fancy</u>), a joy in musical means, and a confidence in his own instincts that gave him a largeness of vision. This same confidence led him to become essentially his own teacher, in the sense that he listened well to instruction and then used what he wanted of it in building his own creative life.

Finney's music is difficult to analyze because in certain essential aspects of composition he has run counter to the accepted norms of the university group to which he nominally belongs: for Finney, pitch is a means, not an end; it is secondary to the rhythmic elements, to the essential energy of music, to the physical presence not only of sound but of the <u>means</u> of sound.

Many critics of the music of twentieth-century composers begin (and in some cases, alas, end) with a computation of pitch materials and organization of a work, and on the basis of this abstract conclude that the piece is structurally interesting and thus theoretically satisfactory. With Finney's music, one must begin, on the contrary, with the reality of the music, with the full-bodied satisfaction of the work, and then proceed to search for the pulls and counterpulls that make it live. Finney's craft is no less vital, but it is not the craft of a theorist; it is a means to the realization of the tensions and reconciliations that form music as a coherent energy, as a living and intensely human art.

The Music

Whereas Irwin Fischer began creative musical life
with a belief in the totality and validity of the
musical tradition of the conservatory, and sought to
define himself within an expansion of that tradition,
Ross Lee Finney began with an interior, unchallengeable
musical core "too strong," he later wrote, "to be
uprooted,"[3] and examined musical traditions in the
light of his own inner necessity. Finney has remained
remarkably his own man, welcoming and freely opening
himself to the various ideologies and systems presented
to him by his teachers, but never joining any group or
espousing any single system. In a time when composers
are classified by their "camps," their commitment to
one system over others, Finney has taken the courageous
stance of a non-joiner; as a teacher, his life is
centered in the university, but as a composer he is an
independent agent.

In this independence he joins Fischer (whose
teaching career centered in the conservatory but whose
life as a composer lay elsewhere), though his self-
determination came from impulses opposite to Fischer's.
The two men were also parallel in their questioning,
and their eventual embracing of twelve-tone serial
techniques. Before the second World War both perceived
a dichotomy between tonal and serial composition, but
both believed it to be a specious dichotomy. "In the
30s," Finney wrote, "the idea of combining a serial
organization with a pitch-functional orientation was
unthinkable. There was a split in the road and one
had to choose which one led into the future. I never
believed in this split and saw reasons for traveling
both roads."[4] By 1950 both men had begun to work out
the means of reconciling the two systems, combining
elements in highly personal ways; both emerged as
serial composers, Finney in 1950, Fischer in 1960.
They both experimented with divisions of the row
(hexachords, and, particularly Fischer, tetrachords,
trichords, and dichords), and remained serialists only
with a small s; they remained equally committed to
"tonal magnetism" (Fischer) and "pitch polarity"
(Finney). And neither man ever became an ideologist:
each was committed only to the individual work of
music and within that work to its "emotional life" (a
term used by both men) and artistic totality, of which
pitch organization was but one element.

Finney, however, was able to find companionship for the discussion of music, as Fischer could not, for Finney's university life gave him avenues through which he met and interacted with other composers. He sought out men who "showed in their music and talk a less ideological attitude towards style."[5] Notable among these was the Spanish-born Roberto Gerhard, ten years Finney's senior but of a similar independence. Gerhard had studied with the Spanish elder-statesman Felipe Pedrell, a conservative musicologist/composer already seventy when Gerhard was five, and with Arnold Schoenberg, the founding ideologue of the avant-garde serialist camp; further, he had grown up within the twofold musical traditions of Swiss parentage and a Catalonian childhood, a duality confounded by expatriation in 1936, when he moved to England (where he would meet Finney during the War). Such counterpulls, more extreme than those in Finney's formative years and a decade earlier, made Gerhard a strong intellectual independent, a man of constructive mind from whom Finney was ready to profit. Such a friendship, coming at the right time for the younger man, was a confirming benison.

The Songs

Finney has composed over fifty songs, among which were many early settings important in the composer's youthful formation of a personal style. The earliest songs--and the earliest music of any kind still in Finney's available works--demonstrate a highly individual use of basically diatonic materials.

The volume of Poems by Archibald MacLeish (completed in 1934, though published in 1955) contains five songs for soprano and piano. The first, "They seemed to be waiting," is representative in its focus on a tone (E) as a center or centrifuge rather than a key. The music is free of tonal function in the traditional sense; rather than upper and lower dominants and leading-tones, there are pedal tones, departures and convergences, within a basic ten-note definition of materials (E, F, F-sharp, G, A, B, C, C-sharp, D, and D-sharp) that do not duplicate any standard tonal scale. The root B, if not avoided, is at least not present in the cadence, nor is the tone D-sharp, which appears in some descending melodic lines but is not used as a leading-tone. The interval and chord roots of the piano are independent of the vocal line, while the final piano melody, over the settling E root, presents a melodic culmination traditional for the key of B minor.

A dual root structure is typical of Finney's early songs as a whole. "Salute," the fourth of the MacLeish songs, is based on the fifths C-G (in the piano) and A-E (in the voice). "These, my Ophelia," the last in the group, uses the fifths E-B and G-D, with a clear loyalty to E minor. This produces an alternation of D and D-sharp that becomes sensuous.

The songs share a love of prose rhythms and free phrases over a consistent eighth-note flow in the piano, the pitch organization of varying roots within a structure on a tone rather than in a key, and the twofold voice/piano fabric. The melodic gestures tend to be freely ranging, giving the impression of freedom even in phrases of restricted range; above all, they provide a declamation and musical support of the text.

The Three Love Songs to Words by John Donne (completed in 1948, published in 1957) are of interest equally for what they maintained from the early style and for what they changed. The opening song, "A Valediction: Of Weeping" (Example 1), begins as a sibling of the earlier songs, with a short pedal E, over which shifting roots in left and right hands do not coincide. The eighth-note flow in the piano supports a freely-ranging and rhythmically independent vocal declamation, whose opening leaps define a center of B. The second phrase expands harmonically and shifts from minor to major through the introduction of chromatic alterations. The vocal line is diatonic and retains the wide range and rhythmic character--derived from the text rhythms--of the earlier songs.

The second of the Donne songs, "A Valediction: Forbidding Mourning," illustrates a continuing formal definition in the piano, which presents both the tonal ground and the melodic form: The ABA structure proceeds in wide-ranging eighth-note patterns in the piano, which combine chords and melodic gestures, establish the mood, and provide the ground for the vocal declamation of the text (Example 2). Clashing roots still inform independent elements: the piano left hand presents G-A, and over it the right hand introduces a rising arpeggio that spells a B major triad. The right hand piano melody spins out a series of gestures that consume two and a half octaves in the

Example 1

Three Love Songs to Words by John Donne
1, "A Valediction: Of Weeping", first nine measures

Example 2

Three Love Songs to Words by John Donne
2, "A Valediction: Forbidding Mourning," first
   six measures

119

first four measures, then compress the same rise into two measures (4 and 5). The same piano materials end the song, omitting the opening G to allow the B root to energe unobscured; a plagal cadence establishes the long B pedal as tonic, and the opening materials, previously aggressive, become a coda, settling into a closing fifth. What makes the technique remarkable and the song successful is not only the functional pun, in which extremely subtle changes transform the meaning of the gestures, but, more vitally, the nature of the vocal declamation, which rides upon the piano materials as in the earlier works, but which now interacts with them, reflecting them or echoing their gestures, and joining the piano in a preponderance of eighth-note motion. Thus Finney achieved a greater unanimity of musical statement without sacrificing the independence of the two parts with which he had begun.

Music for Piano Solo

Music for piano solo presented an interesting challenge to a young composer most intimately aware of cello, guitar, and vocal technique. In his early piano music, Finney was concerned with more abstractlky musical dimensions, while in the later works he became deeply concerned with the physical presence of the pianist in a dramatic (rather than merely theatrical) sense.

The Piano Sonata No. 3 in E

The Piano Sonata No. 3 in E, composed in 1942, is a stunning example of a piano work which effectively defines its own idiom. The opening is almost tumultuous: an Allegro giusto, at top speed and fortissimo, barrels ahead in short, then longer metric motifs, in which single-note runs lead to two-note chord groups across the bar (Example 3-A). These sweep across the keys, upward or downward, in longer and longer gestures that force the pianist to achieve the chords as culminating emphases. After a final descent and pause, a second subject presents a very different incorporation of the same interests: this time, soft (piano) off-beat chords alternating with diffused eighth-note patterns (pianissimo, Example 3-B). The movement is hard to follow in detail, in part because of its headlong speed, which draws the listener's

Example 3-A

Piano Sonata No. 3 in E
I, Allegro giusto, first fourteen measures

Example 3-B

Piano Sonata No. 3 in E
I, Allegro giusto, Measures 44-49

Example 3-C

Piano Sonata No. 3 in E
II, Lento, first ten measures

Example 3-D

Piano Sonata No. 3 in E
III, Prestissimo, first fourteen measures

Example 3-E

Piano Sonata No. 3 in E
IV, Allegro energico, first twenty-two measures

attention to the pianist as athlete; but the E roots
of the opening and closing sections, along with the
clear sonata form (with the second subject on B and
recapitulating on E), make the movement extremely
clear in over-all structure. Much of it is diatonic,
with enough emphasis on fourths and fifths to give it
a quartal sound. As in the songs, the tonal centers
are achieved through a mixture of traditional and non-
traditional means. The focus of the movement is
strongly upon energy, with its variable phrase lengths
over a driving beat, its hearty consumption of range,
and its exploitation of runs and big chords.

The second movement is, in contrast, a lyrical
statement that separates the two hands and creates a
melodic top line harmonized at the start (Example 3-C)
and then, as the melody expands, accompanied with
substantial left-hand chords, and returning to the

simpler texture for the final section. The form of
the movement is a simple ABA arch, defined not so much
by its melodic materials as by its texture: the
center of the arch is a four-measure free fioratura
(over the continuing left-hand chords) of Chopinesque
elegance.

The two opening movements, in E minor, are
balanced as a pair by a third and fourth movement both
in E major: a Prestissimo toccata-like movement and
an Allegro energico that is in essential ways an
expansion of the opening Allegro giusto.

The Prestissimo offers a soft, fleet, non-legato
perpetuum mobile in a dialogue between the two hands
(Example 3-D);   the irregularity of the 7/8 meter is
given a slightly jarring propulsion heightened by
natural accents (of occasional chords and/or breaks in
register). The dialogue begins with the hands similar
in rhythmic motif but individually characterized as
being concerned with seconds and repeated notes (right
hand) and downward quartal arpeggiations (left hand).
The structure again is simple to hear over-all but
difficult to perceive in detail.

The last movement is the most complex of the
four. The opening section (Example 3-E) reveals at
once the similarities and differences from the first
movement. The concern with runs culminating in short
emphatic chord groups, the dramatic brilliance of the
fast passages done at great speed, forcing the pianist
to play the chords as dramatic achievements, and the
relentless pursuit of the gamut of the keyboard—all
are the same. But the means have expanded: not only
are the pitch materials basically chromatic (rather
than basically diatonic), but the tendency is to
develop rather than repeat materials; moreover, the
centrifugal first movement is answered by a centripetal
finale. Again the movement is richly detailed and
hard to grasp measure by measure, but clear and simple
to take in as a total form, ABACA. The B section is a
diatonic right-hand melody whose repeated notes and
turning figures derive from developmental extensions
of the opening but whose texture and mood reflect the
Lento. The C section is an alternation between a
simple quarter-note descending figure and a quick
right-hand running figure over left-hand quarter-note
harmonic accompaniment. This is drawn from the short
passage that connects B to the first return to A, but
it is reminiscent of the free fioratura that caps the

124

arch of the slow movement. The emotional life of the finale is thus not a simple one; the movement must balance and complete the Sonata, while at the same time presenting a strong presence of its own.

The Sonata is immensely zestful, full of direct, honest musical energy. Its strength derives in part from its strong pulls, rhythmic and tonal, but essentially from its kinesthetic vibrancy, which is so powerful that it dominates even the printed page.

It is of interest that Finney, not himself a pianist, has been able to create a personal keyboard idiom that, although not traditional in nature, is entirely successful. The two chief characteristics of the piano are its disinterested half-step equal temperament and its tone activation by hammers in an equally disinterested gamut of pitches. The central fact of piano technique is the physical structure of the hands of the executant, both the separation or joining of the two, and their twofold nature: the potential for intricate figuration of the fingers and for chords powered by arm and back muscles. Many twentieth-century composers have maximized the musical character of the instrument in dodecaphonic abstractions couched in percussive fabrics, but Finney reverses this, maximizing instead the reality of technique as informing the whole. Thus the sonata is not serial and is never percussive, however powerful, and never abstract. It lives as piano music and as piano music only, as a work to be played and to be heard as a presence--a reality to be of increasing importance to Finney's growing power as a composer.

Later works deepened Finney's commitment to his personal piano idiom. The Sonata quasi una Fantasia (1961), almost two decades later than the Sonata No. 3 in E, is fully integrated, more various in melodic and rhythmic materials (and hence more disparate), but its greater subtlety of fabric and form does not impede a continuing focus on the kinesthetic actuality. The third movement of the later work, an Allegro scherzando of imposing structure and variable materials, contains a climactic passage that in its basic outline could have been drawn from the earlier Sonata.

The reality of the pianist in Finney's piano music informs his children's pieces with special delight. In the 32 Piano Games, for example, the mirror image of the two hands becomes the performer's

Example 4

32 Piano Games
XXVIII, "Mountains," first three systems

mainspring: in the final section of a Mirror Waltz
the pianist is to play the central D with both thumbs
at once, while shaping arches of melody upwards and
downwards simultaneously. "Mountains" (Example 4)
presents a series of highly activated events separated
by rests. In this work, Finney becomes a teacher: a
chart on the inside front cover presents a key to the
notation, introducing young pianists to new symbols
and expanding their range of ideas about what music
can say. But the didactic aspects of the work are not
at all limited to items of notation, for the "Games"
themselves, like many games, in reality present a fine
course in meanings of the physical act of playing the
piano, that immediacy so vital in Finney's music.

Chamber Music

The move to the University of Michigan in 1947 gave Finney an unparalleled opportunity for the production of chamber music, for the School of Music contained a remarkable faculty of resident performers, and regular recitals and concerts provided a venue for works by their Composer in Residence. Finney built slowly, striving for a mutual confidence and never straining the institutional reciprocity; he also maintained ties with other universities and performing groups, accepting more commissions as his patronage widened.

The smaller groups provided a natural focus for Finney's creative mind and formed the area of experimentation that incorporated the crucial changes of style that were budding at the time of the move.

The personal style had already developed a rhythmic validity and idiomatic immediacy, as represented by the piano works as early as the Piano Sonata No. 3 in E (1942). The Second Sonata in C for Violoncello and Piano (1950) combines two musical personalities in a work at the cusp of a new view of form that, like the new pull toward series construction, would come into focus in the string quartets of the next decade.

The cello sonata establishes the two personalities at once in an Introduction (Adagio espressivo) in which the cello range and technique is demonstrated, the piano relegated to staid repeated chords (Example 5-A). The cello idea spreads into a freely expanding line (Example 5-B). The short Introduction yields to an Allegro con brio in which the piano shares materials with the cello; it is a long sectional movement that finds energy in shifting meter, with constant driving quarter-pulse but with alternating sections of duple and triple divisions. The lovely Adagio arioso ensues, a poignant movement highly worked, and proceeds in constant interaction of deeper significance than the dialogue of the Allegro con brio. A Prestissimo follows, beginning with a shimmering texture of E major and minor, pianissimo, with cello melody, pizzicato, arching above it (Example 5-C). In this movement increasing demands on the pianist balance the relatively undemanding earlier movements. It too is

Example 5-A

Second Sonata in C for Violoncello and Piano
I, Introduction, Adagio espressivo, first ten measures

Example 5-B

Second Sonata in C for Violoncello and Piano
I, Adagio espressivo, Measures 21-28

Example 5-C

<u>Second Sonata in C for Violoncello and Piano</u>
IV, Prestissimo, first fifteen measures

sectional, with variety of idea and continuing rhythmic
drive but without obsession. The movement ends with
the same sonority with which it had opened. The
<u>Sonata</u> is completed by a Conclusion (Adagio espres-
sivo), obviously a return to the Introduction, though
with cello lines reminiscent of a middle section of
the Allegro con brio. The piano chords, now a half-
step lower, are the same, and in the final phrase the
cello presents a memory of the opening phrase of the
Introduction.

This closure was to become more important in

Finney's mature style, to be defined with particular
clarity in the string quartets.

The turning point away from his youthful style of
composition came with the String Quartet No.
5, a
work of marvelous energy and emotional power that not
only sums up the musical personality of the young
composer but clearly demonstrated that a new path was
necessary.

Like the Second Sonata in C for Violoncello and
Piano, the String Quartet No. 5 is couched in four
movements and ends with a return to the opening. It
begins at once Moderato e appassionato with the figure
that is to dominate the work (Example 6), and retains

Example 6

String Quartet No. 5, opening motif (first violin)

its forthright driving presence in a complex and
compelling fabric. The individual lines are beautifully contoured and wide-ranging, and the movement,
though complex and highly worked, manages a rough
innocence. The second movement, Adagio ma non troppo,
is a discursive alternating form (ABABABAB) that is
quiet and expressive but restless. An Allegretto
grazioso ma misterioso (a scherzo) returns to the
opening of the first movement.

It is the tonal structure which led Finney to
something of a dilemma: the main figure of the work
(Example 6) is so powerful and so insistent that it is
almost inescapable, presenting E not as a tonal center
but as a magnetic field toward which the pounding
rhythms drive again and again. The second movement is
simultaneously pulled toward C major and A minor,
which serves only to bisect and ramify E and lend more
force to the central magnetism, which returns and
remains in the final two movements. Although by this
time the diffusion of pitch materials was complete and
thoroughgoing, it was not systematized, and, in the
cosmic metaphor that suffuses Finney's thought, E here
becomes almost a black hole, so strong that the music
must fight the danger of being pulled into it.

The <u>Sixth</u> <u>String</u> <u>Quartet</u> <u>in</u> <u>E</u>

The <u>Sixth</u> <u>String</u> <u>Quartet</u> <u>in</u> <u>E</u>, composed in 1950,
represents the final step toward pitch serialization.
It works out the serial technique without either
insistence or intensity, while maintaining fully the
essential melodic and rhythmic characteristics that
have remained a permanent aspect of the Finney style.
The Introduction (tranquillo, Example 7-A) opens with
a quiet violin solo that exploits both the row and the
nature of the instrument: the row is presented and is
immediately reversed, pivoting on the <u>D</u>-sharp (Measure
3) and presenting the fourth and fifth notes of the

Example 7-A

<u>Sixth</u> <u>String</u> <u>Quartet</u> <u>in</u> <u>E</u>, I, Introduction (tranquillo)

131

row (C-sharp and E) as a double-stop that forces the
tone of the instrument to a certain restraint. The
viola and cello each work out their own presentations
of a complete series (Measures 6-9), while the two
violins split the row between them (Measures 9-11); a
final statement of the series is compressed as a
reversal of the first violin melody (Measure 11), but
the final twelve notes do not "compute" in a regular
way, requiring use of the lower instruments in Measure
12 and ending with an extra B and E-flat, which, as B
and D-sharp, leave the Introduction with a theoretical
dominant emphasis.

The ensuing Allegro appassionata (Example 7-B)
demonstrates an equally free use of the pitch series:
the second violin and viola split the row between
them, presenting a pattern of repetitions and jagged
shapes that seem more important than the pitch relations, while the cello presents its own series, its
own less active statement. The first violin, when it
enters at Measure 19, does so with the row that the
viola had introduced at Measure 6. The movement
continues with alternation between marcato and legato
elements: the first are characterized by energized
textures, both in articulation and in worked separation
of parts (as in Example 7-C); the second by slower,
more chordal, steadier, closer sounds and by concern
with elements of the Introduction. The alternating
form is clearly delineated but without exact repetition, heightened in a number of inventive ways, so as

Example 7-B

Sixth String Quartet in E
I, Allegro appassionata, Measures 15-19

Example 7-C

Sixth String Quartet in E
I, Allegro appassionata, Measures 25-30

Example 7-D

Sixth String Quartet in E
I, Allegro appassionata, Measures 76-90

Example 7-E

Sixth String Quartet in E
I, Allegro appassionata, Measures 211-225

to quicken the listener's perception of their polariza-
tion (Example 7-D). The end of the movement (Example
7-E) is the final form of the quiet element, expanding
individual lines in range and dynamic level, but
limiting the melodic units to two three-note figures:
they appear in an essential form in the cello first,
rising from E to F and then falling to B (Measure
212), and then in an expanded rise from G-sharp to C
and G-natural (Measure 218). The final sonority, the
fifth E-B in the violins, with the two thirds, G-sharp
and G-natural, in viola and cello, pianissimo, is a
compression of the tonal center E that follows naturally upon the succession of rising trichords; but the
real fulfillment of the movement is postponed.

An Allegro scherzando (Example 7-F) seems to
reply to the rising trichords, presenting the row that
the cello had introduced in the opening (Example 7-A,

Measures 7-9), then running it backwards in a passage as obviously humorous as a reverse minute in a movie (Measures 3-5). This kinesthetic flair is increased by range, sudden huge chords in rhythmic unison at unexpected places, and dynamic juxtapositions. Intensification continues; the sections of slower motion (B elements in an AABABA form) are achieved through longer note values rather than through slackening of the pace. The final phrases take on the drive of a perpetuum mobile and clarify the importance of the tonal pull to A--the movement takes its departure from A and returns to that magnetic lower dominant, ending on A (not in it).

The third movement, an Intermezzo (tranquillo), returns to the row of the Introduction (as well as to its mood) and to the texture of the legato (B) element of the first movement; it is an ABCA form. As a

Example 7-F

Sixth String Quartet in E
II, Allegro scherzando, Measures 1-9

whole, the movement seeks clarification in F (which the Introduction had left unexplored), and it ends with the chord C-F-A-flat (the C approached from its Phrygian neighbor, D-flat); it is joined by an A-natural, a cello harmonic tone--a sonority cognate with the close of the first movement. The tonal magnet of F serves as a Phrygian neighbor tone of E. Memory of the E-B fifth of the opening movement creates the expectation of a return to an E-B polarity in the Finale.

A brief Adagio (Example 7-G) prepares the way with a reinforcement of the E-F idea, relating it first to the preceding cadence and then to the final section of the first movement (Example 7-E). The last movement proper is an Allegro decisivo (Example 7-H), which begins with a fugal exposition with entrances of the subject on the traditional tonic/dominant (E-B) levels. These entries, italicized by trills, satisfy the demand for the fifth that had been established in the middle movements in a far from traditional way.

Example 7-G

Sixth String Quartet in E, IV, Adagio (entire)

The subject continues with materials from the first movement Allegro appassionata. The forward motion of the movement is uninterrupted; motion is intensified by sweeping lines, augmentation, and stretto, and in the end the movement yields its polyphonic force to a section (marked Animato) which simplifies the texture, first to alternating statements in dialogue, and finally to unanimous marcato iterations. The movement ends with fortississimo slides in the cello (the second violin an octave higher) and the viola (the first violin an octave higher). The final chord collects the pitches emphasized in the slides (E-flat down to E and G down to G-sharp) in the most intensely ramified statement of E root in the entire work: the fifth E-B, with both thirds (G-sharp and G-natural)

Example 7-H

Sixth String Quartet in E
IV, Allegro decisivo, first sixteen measures

and the lower second E-flat (to balance the Phrygian second of the previous movement).

The Conclusion (tranquillo) follows at once (Example 7-I). It uses the row and mood of the Introduction of the first movement, putting the row to still another tonal magnetism. This time the row is used as a total shape spanning from first to last pitch a perfect fifth. The original form (again in the first violin) is suggested at the start, but its course from A-flat to D-sharp is interrupted, and the second violin enters imitatively on E. The lower instruments also enter a major third apart at the distance of one measure; but the minor third and half-measure between second violin and viola are exceptional, making the total two pairs instead of four separate entries. The relationships here are fascinating, both

Example 7-I

Sixth String Quartet in E, Conclusion (tranquillo)

enlivened and clarified by enharmonic puns, and then concluded as a fulfillment of all four movements. The viola answers the first violin A-flat with a C-sharp, then continues a perfect fifth below after three notes at the distance of a diminished sixth; the enharmonics become more obvious (at Measure 157) when the second violin G-flat becomes F-sharp and the viola E-flat becomes D-sharp. The upper three parts present one row each, the first violin beginning on A-flat and ending on D-sharp (the row thus spanning a double-diminished fifth), the second violin spanning the perfect fourth E to B, and the viola spanning the perfect fifth C-sharp to G-sharp; their final tones thus accumulate as D-sharp, B, and G-sharp. Under these three, which stretch out (Measures 154-158) and then proceed in parallel motion (Measures 159-160), the cello presents a double series, forward from A to E (Measures 153-160) and then in retrograde from B to E (Measures 160-163). To this instrument is thus given the complete delineation of E as the tonal center, in a long solo that balances the double series presented by the first violin to open the Quartet.

As a whole, the Sixth String Quartet in E is a remarkable mixture of stylistic elements, using both traditional tonal elements, newly polarized, and serialization, explored with mature and imaginative techniques. It is explorative of thematic content and tonal magnetism; of the diatonic, chromatic genre; and of the harmonic implications--in the largest sense of that word--of the serial unit. But it also lives in extraordinary rhythmic energy, associated strongly with the metric impulse. It delineates materials as "thematic," but characterizes them with coinciding elements of articulation and phrasing, dynamics and accents, the use of register and range, so that thematic character is savored and differences are strongly emphasized. This in turn means that the form can be heard (though yielding deeper layers to analysis), and that as an organic work it thrives upon the reality of performance. Many of the effects of the work--the attacks, slides, and even the niceties of intonation suggested by the enharmonic puns--depend upon the nature of the strings and bows. It is representative of the composer's ideals: while it lacks nothing for the eye and the mind, it offers the most to the ear.

The Seventh String Quartet

The Seventh String Quartet (1955) presents a more
selfconscious probing of the techniques of the row,
while defining a form that represents Finney at his
most characteristic and also at his most skillful.

What Finney seeks in a row is a means not of
theoretical procedure but of musical coherence; it is
not to replace tonal function in the old sense but to
facilitate tonal magnetism in the new sense. In the
Sixth String Quartet in E the serial elements were not
so neatly twelve as might be expected: G-sharp and A-
flat were separate entities, like identical twins who
switch places occasionally; the row in this sense is
a progression, organic from beginning to end, a shape
with some opalescence. But in the Seventh String
Quartet the fluidity yielded to the nature of twelve
as a fixed number, deployed not as a parabola of
pitches but as two balancing hexachords. Within a few
works, Finney became a hexachordal serialist, searching
for reciprocal six-note groups that relate in varying
ways, both technically and dramatically, and exploring
an increasing scope of form and meaning.

The hexachord serves a number of purposes for
Finney. But primarily it is a truly musical unit--
recognizable, rememberable, and therefore usable as
reference and capable of audible development and
manipulation. A series of twelve different pitches is
difficult to hear, and, in a fabric where the series
is manipulated, shared among players, and put into a
variety of timbres and registers, it is impossible to
follow; the hexachord presents a more realistic
musical element.

Hexachords that form a pair whose second dupli-
cates the first in some way (by transposition, inversion, or retrograde motion) create the opportunity for
tight tonal schemes with intimate gestures and forthright musical relationships. Less theoretical but
more expansive and dramatic, the two rows of the
Seventh String Quartet (Example 8, shown as Finney
presented them in the Preface to the edition of 1960)
demonstrate the possibilities of interaction among
forms of hexachords and summarize Finney's thoughts
on their points of reference individually and as a
total set. C and G-flat are vital in both sets and

Example 8

Seventh String Quartet, row of the work

provide tonal pivots, magnetic pulls that, interestingly, bisect the octave in that uneasy equality which is
anathema to traditional tonality. In addition, the
abstract, almost geometrical structure is aesthetically
lovely in its own right--not static, but en pointe,
incorporating tensions and balances of great potential.

The opening Sostenuto (Example 9) displays a free
striding through forms of the row, the cello starting
with a row lacking the second trichord (B-D-G), taken
as a commenting chord in the upper instruments;   a
retrograde statement begins (in Measure 3) on the low
E that ended the opening row, with the same chord
again extracted to the upper parts.   Interactions
become more intense;   after the cello once more
strides down the row alone, the climax of the section
(Measures 12-13) presents the row conjointly in all
four instruments. The last measures are free, ending
in a sonority comprising a transposition of notes 7-10
of the inversion of Row 2.

The gestures of the row are operative on conscious
and unconscious levels;   the opening trichord, for
example, seems to be expanded in the third trichord,
then expanded again in the final trichord though in a
different shape. The reference at Measure 6 begins
with reversal of the original trichord, audible
because the pitches are maintained;   then the reverse
figure is developed. The coherence of the section is
in large part responsible for the rich emotional life
of the Sostenuto.

The compelling content of the movement is crucial
to the Quartet because its shape is a double circle;

Example 9

Seventh String Quartet
I, Sostenuto, first nine measures

the opening Sostenuto, and two long movements, each
ending with a Sostenuto. The three Sostenuto sections
work out further ramification of the opening section;
the original trichord is never forgotten, and it
accumulates meanings until the final section is able
to maintain reference to it almost with a whisper.

As vital as the binding power of the Sostenuto
sections is the nature of the two long movements.
Finney had already created substantial movements
through sectional alternations; in the Seventh String
Quartet he created forms through a continuing, discursive series of sections that take their analogy not
from architectural form or ground plan but from prose
forms. The String Quartet movements are:

I. Sostenuto
   Energico
   (Slower section—longer note values)
   (Energico)
   Appassionato
   Accento
   Grazioso
   Sostenuto

II. Capriccioso
    Misterioso ma agitando
    Meno agitato
    Capriccioso
    Giocoso
    Sostenuto

There are cross references—the Meno agitato (of
II), for example, is related to the preceding Misterioso ma agitando; but the two Capriccioso sections are
related only in secondary ways. Letters are unavailing
in analysis of this work; it simply does not yield to
any "ABC' categories. The sections are more akin to
paragraphs or chapters in a continuing narrative.
Such a form is possible only in a mature style in
which musical characterization is secure and pungent.

Because the two long movements work their way in
the two large circles by various means within a
musical rhetoric, I have called the technique elaboration, a working-out of the trajectory in a logical
sequence of loosely related sections. The trajectory
is a line of motion, and the form is organic; it is a
shaping en route, as it were. Finney described the
Seventh String Quartet as being shaped as one skates a

figure 8; the central point is the Sostenuto which is the beginning, the middle, and the end of the work.

Within the elaboration, Finney's style shows itself clearly. The vigor and drive of unison dotted rhythms, repeated notes, and accumulating lines, are basic to the character of the Energico; the long rising line is still a compelling part of the style-- in the Capriccio restrained in pianissimo, for example, passed from instrument to instrument, finally in the cello alone.

In many ways the Seventh String Quartet is a strong and immensely satisfying work. It achieves both tight balance and exhilarating freedom, in its serial techniques, in its rhythmic organization, and in its formal elaboration. Its balance between expenditure and containment of energy is remarkable, enabling a work that avoids repetition of theme to work out references to and development of musical character. Its form, which eschews sectional repeti- tions as it eschews thematic repetitions, can nonethe- less make itself felt in motion as clearly as a choreography.

Fantasy and Total Serialization

Finney's work moved in two directions from the late 1950s: toward a more thoroughgoing mathematical process in the setting up of musical materials, and toward a more developed, tighter elaboration. The complementary nature of these directions is obvious: the one is before the fact, the pre-composition setting up of a set of abstract relationships from which the composer draws the materials; the other is after the fact, the ordering of material through which the listener is to perceive the musical reality.

In the conscious working-out of these two musical dimensions, Finney separated them as the mathematical and the psychological, as logic and function, rethink- ing and strengthening his concepts of craft and musical reality rather than seeking new ones. Finney was quoted in a thoughtful article on his music by composer Paul Cooper:

I began to listen all over again. The conviction that one must understand by listening--must accept nothing except as it

144

is confirmed by the ear--strongly influenced me and still remains the basis of my teaching. This concern for function does not preclude a mathematical logic (certainly not in electronic music), for it is obvious that everything in music can be explained mathematically except the psychological experience. To control this experience, the composer must work with functions.[6]

This division of music into science and art, acoustic and rhetoric, is an ancient one, but Finney drew it into a highly personal distinction between fabric and form, between the structuring of materials and their ordering in audible organic shape. These Finney recognized as different both in essence and in method. An acquaintance with the ideas of leading physicists (Bohr and Oppenheimer particuarly), who found a necessary complement in Newtonian and quantum physics, led Finney to postulate a musical complementarity, a formalization of the mutual necessity for the make-up of materials as essentially different from their elaboration, which in his own terms he defined as the "small means" and the "large means." In his insistence that the small means are not the same as the large means, Finney departed from tradition; in his insistence that process be audible he braved the wrath of the radical university group who preferred to work without reference to an audience.

These two concepts represent two ends of a polarity. Exploration of both poles is to be expected in the work of a man of such creative energy, and Finney did pursue both directions, in two sets of works that he produced concurrently from 1958.

Total Serialism

The works of increasingly pervasive serialism began with the Second Symphony (1959) and the Second Piano Quintet (1961). A tighter organization occurred in Three Pieces for Winds, Percussion and Tape (1962), which serialized virtually everything but dynamics, including spans and durations. The electronic tape maintains its own serializations, more completely arithmetical, as, in earlier works, the character and function of two instruments had been consciously separated.
Three Studies in Fours, written for the Poznan

Percussion Ensemble, and the Concerto for Percussion and Orchestra, both of 1965, represent the apogee of Finney's total serialization. The two are closely related and derive through similar processes. The work chart for Three Studies in Fours bristles with computations through which the various elements of the work were derived; perhaps easier to absorb is the work sheet for the first movement of the Concerto (Example 10-A), along with the opening of the work (Example 10-B). Such a structure can be as complex and its proportions as obscure as the composer relishes, and analysis can be as thorny (and enjoyable) as a difficult cryptogram.[7]

Within the polar considerations of complementarity, these works had gone too far toward the mathematical, particularly to the extent that they serialized over-all proportions of the pieces and hence attempted to make the large means the same as the small means. At their worst, such attempts are anti-listener, a composer's game played with elaborate schemata that are either mathematical or visual (but not audible), and even at their best they are, Finney in the end decided, artificial rather than genuine or natural.

No polar extreme is viable without the counterpull of its opposite; for Finney the tight structure too easily capitulated to its own inflexibility, and it proved a dead end for him. With the 1965 works for percussion, Finney's investigation of serial totalitarianism came to an end.

Example 10-A

Work sheet:
Concerto for Percussion and Orchestra, first movement

146

Example 10-B

Concerto for Percussion and Orchestra, first four measures

147

Fantasy

The counterpull against mathematical process lay in experiments with the psychological life of the work of music, and especially with the creation of extended forms through a series of sections, loosely related in a discursive rather than a thematic plan, a process that I have called elaboration.

The more intense exploration of the technique of elaboration began with the Fantasy in Two Movements, for solo violin, in which the polarity between mathematical process and elaboration was savored in itself. This work, composed in 1958 for Yehudi Menuhin, reaches the freedom of rhapsody, the delicacy of meditation, and the excitement of bold virtuosity, all based in a very tight, highly concentrated and prismatic row. This row, a hexachord and its exact inversion, is a subtle and compelling structure, simple and memorable; Finney has written of its unfolding in a revealing article that discusses the process of finding the right practical working-out of the original impetus of the imagination.[8]

The Sonata quasi una Fantasia, for piano solo, followed in 1961. Like the Fantasy in Two Movements, it depends on the freedom of the solo performer to pull against the tight structure of the materials in creating the free elaboration. The violin work is a double elaboration, two movements which balance like a diptych, of reciprocal nature, self-contained yet speaking together of one larger subject; the piano work is a single elaboration, a sectional prose form in the shaping of which the performer is vital. Both are compressed, pithy, and musically concentrated; the comfortable expansiveness of some of the early elaborations has been turned to a much more dense expression, a quickly turning and intense rhetoric different in degree rather than in kind.

The Divertissement (1964) and the 2 Acts for 3 Players (1970) are closely related to fantasia, but are based in nostalgia rather than abstract fantasy. The first was composed in Paris and is reminiscent of experiences as Finney recalled them from his sojourn there almost forty years earlier. The second he described as springing from his recollection of silent films, not the films themselves or the music that accompanied them: the work is to be performed theatrically (as "actors to be watched as well as heard") as though they are providing music for an imaginary movie, "reflecting the pacing, the humor, and the bathos." Here the kinesthetic element is strong, and the three players--pianist, clarinetist, and percussionist--present an active and varied fabric very close to fantasia.

The mathematical pole was fulfilled in works of total serialism; the exploration of that pole was an essential exordium to Finney's next stylistic development, though it came through the concentration of techniques of elaboration into the tighter fabric that Finney associated with fantasia. This further development would be fulfilled in larger instrumental works.

Large Instrumental Works

In his works for orchestra or band Finney paralleled the stylistic developments of chamber music, often expanding upon techniques of composition, occasionally prefiguring developments to be explored more thoroughly in works for smaller forces, but always using the orchestra or band as a separate medium.

One of the early characteristics of Finney's orchestral scores is pungency of fabric, a use of the strings, for example, to cut wide swaths of color, heightened by expanded wind and percussion sections; the effect is a strong, positive sound, well balanced among the choirs (as Romantic scoring was not), and well-suited to his music of those years.

The Symphony No. 1 (Communiqué 1943) begins with a strong modal theme of great beauty and organic growth, accompanied only by a drum roll (Example 11); it starts in solo English horn, but at Measure 8 the strings enter with triadic chords, and an oboe joins in the theme. The harmonization is modal, and the effect is Appalachian. The symphony has six movements:

        Introduction
        Dramatic Statement
        Elegy
        Scherzo
        Interlude
        Fanfare

149

Example 11

Symphony No. 1 (Communiqué 1943), opening theme

But in fact, the slow poignant Introduction sets up
the Dramatic Statement very much like a Baroque adagio
sets up an allegro.   The Elegy is a contrasting slow
movement;   and the final three movements, performed
without a stop, together balance the first.   (A twelve-
measure Interlude brings back the opening theme, at
the original key level and beginning in the English
horn alone.)   Both the effect of a last movement made
of shorter separate movements and the return of the
Introduction prefigure later elements of Finney's
style.

Likewise does the Hymn, Fuging and Holiday (1943)
prefigure later elements in his style, particularly
the detached articulation, the pointed brass interjections and active percussion section (which has a
rousing solo), and the rounded form.   This was one of
Finney's "American" works, with obvious references to
recognizable tunes (an Americanism of Billings and the
song schools rather than of folk music) that worked
readily within the tonal and quartal organizations
akin to the early songs.

The orchestral works of the next two decades
paralleled the developments in Finney's chamber music
style: works after 1950 were serial, and those after
1960 were hexachordal.   Both the Variations for
Orchestra (1962) and the Symphony No. 3 (1964) are
concerned with techniques of elaboration, for which
the variation form is particularly suited.   The
Variations seek new delicacy of color, which would
become of even greater importance in the next decade;
the robust and the delicate alternate as a complement
in this work.   Here (Example 12) a solo oboe with the

Example 12

Variations for Orchestra, I, Measures 25-35

flutes and bass clarinet below it, are joined by a
single muted trumpet, a trombone, then two horns, with
gentle punctuation from harp and lower strings (pizzicato); the short quiet gestures are so deployed that
the meter is lost to the listener. Thus rhythmic,
melodic, dynamic, and color forces are conjoined in a
quietness to prepare for the ensuing Allegro energico.

The Symphony No. 3 is more thickly and traditionally scored, and tends to maintain a high level of
energy throughout. It is in three movements, with
material of the first heard again in the third. The
contrasting slow movement begins with percussion--
snare and tenor drums, then timpani, cymbals and tam-
tam, all playing softly and joined after four measures
by the strings, playing glissandos, and by muted horns
and the piano playing softly in thirds. This sustained
quietude, reminiscent of the Variations, is used as
the A section of a delicious slow rondo (ABABA) in
which the B sections, more traditionally scored,
involve fragments of the first movement. The Symphony
is notable for its polar use of sustained prose and
short marcato rhythms, which are developed separately
and also brought together. In both the Symphony and
the Variations, rhythms, melodic gestures, and orchestral colors work together in delineating the form.

The increased scope of instrumental effects in
the orchestral works developed as a gentle expansion
of color. Finney was in the company of many composers
who were exploring color as a functional element, but
unlike many of them, he was not interested in substitu-
ting color for content. Color never became idea for
Finney; rather, he used color to enhance and to
sharpen ideas and to clarify contrasts.

Parallel to the expansion and sharpening of
instrumental techniques was the expansion of rhythmic
technique to include sections without meter, made of
freely overlapping wheels and other short elements
(often worked out with some freedom within tightly
specified parameters). Finney tended to associate
such sections with special instrumental effects and
with piano or even pianissimo dynamic levels, creating
suspensive, floating sections that served to present a
significant contrast to incisive metric sections.
Thus the new "statistical" or "stochastic" rhythmic
technique, like the expansion of orchestral color,
served to clarify contrasts.

Toward 1970 Finney began to think seriously about memory and to analyze its nature and process. Several personal and musical elements were at the cusp of definition and were about to coalesce: a desire to transcend the simple nostalgia of recent chamber works, rejection of total serialism in favor of the techniques of elaboration, and the increased scope of color and rhythmic technique developed in the orchestral works. The coalescence of these factors led to a group of works unique to Finney, works exploring memory as a musical phenomenon.

Memory

Three works centrally concerned with memory date from 1971, when the congeries of factors converged in a new reciprocity of idea and technique. The rejection of total serialism had caused Finney to rethink the "small means," especially as creating musical idea; he emerged from this period of trial more deeply committed to the value of the hexachord. The finitude and capacity of the six-note shape to be recalled made it a versatile element, productive for the composer and effective for the listener--an excellent basis for communication. At the same time the composer's long thoughts about memory brought about a new concept of musical idea in the sense of "large means." For Finney, memory was fascinating not as a patchwork quilt of remembered prints reassembled into new designs, but as a process; not as nouns but as verbs. Again, Finney was in the company of a number of composers exploring the value of musical reference, the weaving of allusions into a new fabric; and again, Finney went in a very different direction, rejecting the "patchwork quilt" and attempting to do in his music what the act of remembering does in the mind. For memory is not a new design of old elements; that would define it as a static ground plan in a traditional, architectural view of musical form. It is rather an organic process, a coming in and out of focus, a procession of complete and incomplete elements, now clear and now fuzzy; of bits and pieces overlying and overlapping with longer reminiscences; of unexpected lucidity and frustrating indefinition.

The processes of memory are the same as certain processes in music, and the congruence was eminently practical in the further development of elaboration. As early as the time of his study with Alban Berg,

Finney recognized that the process of musical variation was not simply a matter of repeating the theme but of re-experiencing it, approaching the material anew, from different directions, in transformations less of the materials than of ourselves in the perception of it. Finney's piano Variations on a Theme by Alban Berg, a belated tribute to his teacher composed in 1952, is a dramatic unfolding of experiences of the row of the Berg Violin Concerto. The Variations were published in 1977, when the intentions of the composer would not be as far ahead of his time as they had been a quarter-century earlier. In a review, the work was described as "beautifully conceived" and was praised for the "honesty of concept, the lyricism, and the drama. The integrity of the thematic material is never sacrificed for a mere exercise in virtuosic variety."[9] The Variations for Orchestra, a decade later, is more prismatic still, expanding both in its fragmentation and in its elasticity of thematic content. All variation is concerned with memory, and these techniques, too, entered the coalescence.

Space

The final factor was that of space, an emergence of ideas about space both as location and as expanse, cognate with musical fabric and form ("large means"). For Finney, memory is not only time-centered but also space-centered. Whereas the functional aspects of memory can be assessed readily as musical techniques, the value of the ideas of space is elusive and philosophical, perhaps mystical.

The very title of the orchestral work, Spaces, reflects the mystical component, and its three movements are only a bit more specific: The Valley, The Prairie, The Sky. These three establish a philosophical progression from the closed valley to the open prairie to the infinitude of space of the sky. The reference to an old hymn in the first movement, the wind sounds and statistical hoverings of the second, and the incisive trumpet solo over woodwind wheels in the third (after a slow yearning start of cello against the other strings) does produce an effect of expanding spaces, but it is difficult to say how much is a response to the programmatic titles.

A complement to Spaces, the shorter Landscapes Remembered is focused as a vortex whose center is D;

it is a fixed point around which the fabric wavers, blurs, hovers, and clarifies. "Oh, Bury Me Not" and "Barbara Allen" are recognizable, like pictures that momentarily crystalize and then melt; yet the work is not about allusions. It deals with focus and unfocus, with experiences turning on the single point--an introvert counterpull to the extrovert Spaces.

Summer in Valley City

Summer in Valley City, composed for the University of Michigan Concert Band, is another type of comple- ment, a festival recollection of happy days that unfolds in elaboration as a series of movements: Fanfare, Interlude, Parade, Games, Fireworks, and Night.

The Fanfare presents a series of trumpet motifs (repeated notes, triadic tattoos) interrupted woodwind glissandos that are as fuzzy as the trumpet motifs are clear (with instructions for the woodwinds that they be played "in differing ways by different performers. This diversity is desired"). Soft detached quarter- notes follow, a brief, furtive march between otherwise boisterous sections; the movement concludes with a long accumulating F of great intensity, a narrow ingot of sound (expanded only by the resonances of the percussion--bell, xylophone, and suspended cymbal) that crescendos to fortissimo and ceases abruptly, leaving a single cornet on a high C to begin the Interlude with an unmeasured solo (Example 13-A). The movement is a brief alternation of solo cornet and trombone with small answering groups of instruments, a free rhapsodic solo yielding to fragments of "Where Is My Wandering Boy Tonight?," whose rhythm pervades the replies of the small groups.

The Parade is a rousing good time, with intima- tions of an actual circus march ("wrong notes" and all) and references also to "The Darktown Strutters' Ball." The brasses and woodwinds are given alterna- tions that are at times interruptive or even argumenta- tive.

Games exploits the contrast between highly kinesthetic and unmeasured phrases in an alternating form (ABABABABABA), with similar but not repeated materials and a more precise reference to the opening in the next-to-last A section. The A sections all use

155

Example 13-A

Summer in Valley City
2, Interlude, first seventeen measures

Example 13-B

Summer in Valley City
4, Games, Measures 36-38

* These notes in any order and as fast as is natural

thirds and are energized either by unanimous accents on off-beats or by regular metric progressions; the B sections alternate between soft, floating, and loud, almost chaotic effects. Thus the whole movement is shaped as an expansive arch; it is more than simple alternation, while at the same time the basic contrast remains central in enlivening the form (Example 13-B).

Fireworks, a brief section, begins softly, projecting individual sounds almost as points of light, rounding a quiet section, then pausing, and suddenly exploding in a tutti fortissimo unmeasured semi-statistical Roman candle of a phrase, immediately subsiding and ending in quietude.

The concluding Night is a short epilogue, a solo cornet playing "When the Curtains of the Night," answered by small groups (as in the Interlude) and coming to rest in a pianissimo brass chord that takes time to produce a final reassuring resonance.

The Works of the 1970s

Finney's works dealing with memory informed his instrumental music in ways both obvious and subtle. Although he returned to nonprogrammatic forms, he carried the newly developed techniques into these works. The Symphony No. 4 (1973) evinces both tighter and freer elements in construction. The three movements are Allegro energico ma cantando, Allegretto capriccioso, and Adagio sostenuto, an over-all scheme unusual for Finney. The pitch matrix is of three trichords expanding from C: C/D-flat/D-natural, C/D-natural/E-flat, and C/D/E. These trichords can be juxtaposed, manipulated, and overlapped in numberless ways; and in spite of the basic simplicity of the matrix, the complexity of its development is virtually limitless. At the opposite pole, that of elaboration, the Symphony is beautifully lyrical; Finney achieved a freedom and flexibility of the melodic line. In the slow movement, the first violins, in Finney's words, "throw their melody over the open spaces of the work."[10]

The Violin Concerto No. 2 (1975) is a two-movement work which begins with a reference to Landscapes Remembered played by harp and vibraphone; it is less a quotation than a memory. The first movement is a lyrical parabola which returns to that same memory in a closure typical of Finney's works a decade earlier.

But the second movement stands as a replying independent force, contrasting the stretching of the first with the confident energy of the second.

The <u>Concerto for Alto Saxophone and Wind Orchestra</u> (1974) is also a two-movement work, juxtaposing a lyrical Moderato and an Allegro energico. A writer compared it with Finney's early work for band:

> In contrast to <u>Summer in Valley City,</u> the two-section piece for saxophone is completely without program, a highly technical work that, nevertheless, makes no effort to disguise the memory of <u>romanticism</u> which is equally a part of Finney's vast musical experience. A particularly intriguing part of the <u>Concerto</u> is the cadenza near the conclusion of the second section in which the winds and the soloist alternate in controlled improvisation in increasing intensity that leads to a brilliantly scored coda in hazardous tempo and technique.[11]

This work has the ornate lyricism and unabashed melodic variation associated with jazz, though the sound is not jazzy. The work is tightly wrought, precisely weighed; it is the consciousness of the melodic elaboration which makes the listener hear the work as romantic.

Variations on a Memory

The search for lyrical structural significance, for greater freedom and yet for valid musical complexity, led Finney to seek a deeper emotional life for his new works, along with structural techniques that would complement that aspect. In 1975 he produced a remarkable distillation of his many interests in a work for chamber orchestra that he called <u>Variations on a Memory</u>. The orchestration calls for ten players, chosen for color and balance: two flutes, clarinet, bass clarinet, two horns, trumpet, trombone, piano, and percussion (vibraphone, four tom-toms, cymbal, and triangle). A program note accompanies the work:

> When I was very young I used to accompany my brother's impassioned performance of his favorite trumpet solo. The bell of his trumpet was always next to my left ear for

he had to read from the music on the piano
and though I was never completely deafened
from the blast, the memory of his enthusiasm
still haunts me. I always longed, but never
dared, to match it at the piano.

As is often the case, the greater precision of
the image freed the composer: not having to attempt a
literal parallel or a musical depiction, Finney could
use the memory as a fulcrum, drawing across it a
musical work for the full savoring of which the
program note is in fact necessary.

The work is evocative, sensual, and masterfully
constructed; it creates its world and fulfills its
span in six and a half minutes, but does not seem
short. It begins and ends with muted trumpet, marked
"ppp--distant," and the trumpet defines the whole,
whether present or absent, playing now metrical and
tonal, now long or unmetrically deployed elements,
coming in and out of the fabric like a golden thread,
and, when present, now clear and now obscured. For
the most part, the other instruments create a ground
upon which the trumpet line comes forth and from which
it takes a good deal of its meaning. The opening solo
is accompanied by a vibraphone F (the opening pitch of
the trumpet solo) marked "pppp," which remains static
while the trumpet moves away from that pitch and then
returns, playing a phrase in B-flat. The pianist
joins this with a strummed sonority (holding notes
down with the left hand and strumming the strings with
the right). As the instruments enter they weave soft
sensuous lines, flutes and clarinets curling like
tendrils around the trumpet line. Finally the lines
descend, leading to a slightly more regular rhythmic
pattern of piano chords and flute repeated notes.
Gradual expansion of energy follows, the trumpet also
becoming more angular, the piano more active; the
texture does not thicken, but it brightens. Finally
all instruments that enter are marked "f," the piano
chords widen, and the trumpet enters forte, with a
motif that will be expanded and developed as a central
span-within-a-span, achieving an orchestral fortissimo
and the final development of the trumpet motif.
This is followed by a short crescendo to the climax:
a sforzando tutti eighth-note chord and ensuing rest,
into which the trumpet plays a sforzando high B-flat
which is held into an unmeasured passage of overlapping
wheels. The vibraphone picks up the trumpet B-flat
(as A-sharp) and that tone finally erupts into its own

wheel. The trumpet leads out of the statistical passage as it had led into it, and initiates the descent from the climax. Materials from the first section return, in new guises but clearly recognizable, and the delicious quiet activity--the curling lines of flutes and clarinets--take on new beauty. The trumpet, now muted again, forsakes the B-flat roots (though it does not enter the serialization), drops two octaves, and finally ends on middle C, made ambiguous by the sonorous ambiance of horns, flutes, and vibraphone, each with its own tonal emphasis.

In general, Finney prefers a larger canvas and a more discursive elaboration of idea; Variations on a Memory is unusually brief and concentrated. It is a study in complementarity: the twofold materials of the trumpet line and the instruments that create its context; the long-limned tonal trumpet phrases and the climactic unmeasured section with wheels beating in rhythmic disorder contained by the hexachordal discipline; the dignity of the trumpet line and the lovely mystery of its setting; the essential simplicity of the concept and the intricacy of the detail. In the end the integrity of the trumpet, which, defining all, nonetheless yields nothing, becomes a poignant integrity, and the score takes on deeper meanings. The program note has prepared the listener, but the music, in a perfect wedding of meaning and technique, transcends its program and speaks to larger concerns.

Choral Music

Finney's music for choir spans virtually his entire creative career, with two periods of more intense work: one before and just after the War, and another in the years 1962 to 1978. The first group came during the years at Smith College and concentrated on works for choir alone or with piano or organ; the second group, a culmination of the years at the University of Michigan, expanded into larger works for choir, soloists, and orchestra.

The choir has never been far from Finney's philosophical life, and it is possible to trace his changing attitudes through his choral works. Like Fischer, he produced compelling philosophical statements, at the peak of his mastery and in retirement, in works for choir and orchestra.

Many of the early works for choir are clearly American in focus: Pilgrim Psalms (completed in 1941), and Oh, Bury Me Not (1940), for example, are straightforwardly American, dealing with historical and folk aspects of the New England and the western (cowboy) traditions in ways that make the music and the national elements accessible to both the choir and the listener. Finney wrote for specific performances and was both energetic and immensely practical in this endeavor. His natural proclivity for oppositions enabled him to draw creative validity from the reality of working at Smith College: he faced the practical necessity for a full choir to result from union of a women's chorus and a men's chorus, when they would have to be rehearsed in large part separately. His early efforts thus deepen his native bent to find structures in which the women's voices are opposed to the men's.

Finney was also well aware that student participation in performances of new music would have to be through choral music, and--as the natural venue for his creative life would lie in chamber music at the University of Michigan--he put vital energy into the venue of the choral concert at Smith College. The Pilgrim Psalms, for example, is an extended work, a string of movements for soloists, choir, and organ, alternating solos (with organ), a capella, and accompanied choruses, and organ interludes, and incorporating items from the Ainsworth Psalter. The tunes are sometimes complete, occasionally harmonized in recognizable fashion, but more often established and then expanded into layers of traditional innovative materials. Old Hundredth (Doxology), for example, enters with the first phrase traditionally harmonized, and is then progressively diffused until it is indistinguishable within the fabric. The fabric itself is similar to that of the early songs: based in diatonic elements with overlapping roots, often with key centers-- magnetic pulls--modally rather than tonally set.

After the War, Finney had turned from obviously national music to an exploration of his own musical centrality. This exploration was not one of musical techniques but of philosophical premises that illuminate personality and, by definition, that musicianship which is indivisible from personality. The interest in physics (Newtonian and quantum theories as complementary) was clarifying the new vision of oppositions that would develop a decade later as the musical

162

concept of complementarity.

More important in Finney's immediate creative life was a musical symbolism that was arithmetical and geometrical, with cosmic (astronomical) implications. This symbolism is ancient, quintessentially expressed in the Quadrivium of the Liberal Arts, and a study of it was being made by Finney's wife. He became interested in the symbolism of the circle, which is particularly strong in practical music, though the more far-reaching aspects of both Gretchen Finney's work and that of the theoretical scientists fascinated the composer in interacting (and complementary) ways.[12]

Spherical Madrigals

Exigency and philosophy combined after the War in the production of a work that stands as a perfect statement: a meeting of personal and musical development in the right medium and at the right time. A decade earlier, Finney's diatonic style would have been less secure and still too new for choir and audience; a decade later, Finney would have turned the corner into serial integration and it would have been too late. The work is the Spherical Madrigals (1947).

The title speaks at once to the symbolism of the circle and to the historical term "madrigal," not musicologically, but within the tradition of the high school and college choirs in which madrigals had been kept within public ken. It is a free concept, yet for Finney it came remarkably close to the essence of the original. First, of course, verbal symbolism lay at the heart of the madgrigal, particularly the English madrigal, which enjoyed popularity during the period of Shakespeare's career. Second, Finney's diatonic, semi-modal, often chromatic fabric, although achieved from an opposite direction, was amazingly similar to the original fabric; the fluidity of modal diatonic materials infused with chromatic and tonal elements is ideal for a fabric put to such use. The implications in relation to text are different, since in the earlier madrigals the chromatic (even enharmonic) elements were yielding to the coming diatonicism and tonality, while in the post-War years it was exactly the opposite.

Finney shaped the concept first by selection of

texts: he turned to seventeenth-century poets (basic to Gretchen Finney's study--for the most part a generation or two later than the period of the English madrigal) and from their works he took short passages that present metaphors of a circle. The symbol of the circle was thus intrinsic to the texts: further, it informed the whole, which is of seven texts numbered as six, with a seventh, a round canon, on the cover (Example 14-A), printed in a circle like Billings' canon in Paul Revere's engraving of 1770. This is perhaps an Americanism, but it is more purely a perfection of Finney's concept of the work as a whole, as is the inclusion of canons (which were not part of the Elizabethan ideal, but which were popular both earlier and later).

The Herrick couplet of the round on the cover deals centrally with love, as does the first of the numbered pieces; the rest unite astronomical metaphors to the personal--words within spinning worlds. As a whole, the texts create a unified metaphor of circles: love, the seasons, the world, the heavens--the heavens become love and close the circle.

The opening cover round is based on $\underline{E}$ as a static

Example 14-A

Spherical Madrigals, cover round

root, over which successive entries accumulate additional color and detail, with a turning figure that "doth restless move" in musical parallel to the text. Finney's tonal technique was ideally suited to such a process, giving as much to the text as he drew from it.

The ensuing pieces exploit the choir in a series of textures that go to the heart of the madrigal. The first numbered piece, "When Again All These Rare Perfections Meet," proceeds chordally, the harmonic life rising from independent lines (Example 14-B) that are basically diatonic, wide-ranging rather than stratified (each part consumes an octave in the initial phrase), and achieving rich cadences through modal means--and also by the full potential of perfect and imperfect intervals characteristic of Renaissance polyphony.

The second piece, "All-Circling Point," is a three-part canon (SAT). the Dux followed by one Comes at the unison and another at the octave below; the combination of the lower pitch of the tenor and its higher tessitura presents additional color that enriches the fabric while making the canon more clearly delineated in performance. The fabric is diatonic but enigmatic in tonal allusion; the first

Example 14-B

Spherical Madrigals
I, "When Again All These Rare Perfections Meet" (text by Lord Herbert of Cherbury), opening phrase

165

section has roots on **E**, **G**, and **B**. Like the round on the cover, the materials tend to create static sounds. But they expand, invert, and return to the opening, in a rounded form.

The next, III, "His Body Was an Orb," presents a series of imitative points. It reaches the most complex phrases in the set, but the central climax and the codetta are in familiar style--chords in unanimous rhythm.

Finney's inclusion of the text by John Donne, which he would set as the first of the Three Love Songs to Words by John Donne in the following year, offers a comparison of two settings of the same text by a single composer (see Example 1). The text is here given the title of its opening phrase, "On a Round Ball;" the opening (Example 14-C) presents a turning figure in octaves, and then expands into thirds in mirror image. The rhythm remains declamatory (except

Example 14-C

Spherical Madrigals
IV, "On a Round Ball" (text by John Donne),
    first seven measures

166

for the word "round"); the choir serves the text by singing unanimously, softly, in rhythmic patterns that give it clarity and thrust. Even the imitative points are managed so that one pair of voices alternates texts with another, or so that rhythmic values are stretched out in individual imitations until the voices conjoin in the text. The opening phrase, pulling between C and D, suggests G, which is indeed its magnetic pull, though the harmonic progressions go further afield than in most of the madrigals. The piece ends with a rising imitative point that swells to fortissimo; the ending is a long phrase that expands but is sung decrescendo and with a retard--a stunning moment of withdrawal.

V, "Nor Doe I Doubt" (text by Crashaw) is longer, but simpler in tonal focus and texture; the interest lies in the imitative points, which follow at nontraditional intervals: G and E; E, A, and G; E, F, D, and G. The second half of the piece proceeds in short alternating passages in pairs (SA and TB), featuring octaves and thirds, which yeld at the climax to chords that alternate A major and minor. Another cycle of alternations leads to a forceful concluding chord, A major and the only fortississimo in the Madrigals.

The final piece, VI, "See How the Earth" (text by Marvel), divides into two choirs, opposing a choir of men's voices with one of women's voices. The dialogue begins with short phrases, which expand and then contract, then expand in quicker rhythms, and conclude the first section with a crescendo and then a soft combined phrase for the words "perfect Hemisphere!" The second section completes the work in minor, with a long imitative running section in four parts (SATB), a continuation in familiar style, a return to alternation, and finally to the eight parts and the dialogue with which it had begun. Overlapping triads finally clarify into an E major quiet ending, returning to the tonal base of the first madrigals.

The Spherical Madrigals as a whole present a group of loosely connected choral pieces for voices alone, forming a series informed first by the delight of a master of choral writing in the textures and interactions of the choral group itself, in its capacity for musical dialogue, harmonic beauty, and textural focus, which no other medium can so prismatically display or so intensely concentrate. The series also represents an expanding of line from the static

167

cover round, of one written part, through diverse deployments both linear and vertical, imitative (worked) and familiar (chordal), to the final expansion to eight parts. In spite of the English texts, the Madrigals find their historical counterpart not in Morley and Gibbons but in Marenzio and Monteverdi, to whose solid vocal productions Finney replies with the same solidity and forthright joy.

Edge of Shadow

A decade later, Finney's musical course had taken him into serialism, and, at the end of the 1950s, to an exploration of "large means." The problems of structure to which Finney was seeking answers centered in instrumental music, and their translation to vocal works presented a number of problems based in the nature and in particular the practical limitations of vocal performance.

In 1959, Finney was offered a commission to compose a choral work for the Grinnell College Choir; he accepted, and selected a text from The Hamlet of MacLeish, using a phrase from the text as the title: Edge of Shadow. The work is substantial, a five-movement structure for choir, two pianos, celesta, vibraphone, xylophone, timpani, cymbals, snare and bass drums, tam-tam, and triangle. Finney elected to limit the pitched instruments to those pre-tuned in equal temperament, creating a neutral base for vocal projection. The opening measure (Example 15-A) presents this neutral ground in steady triplets, pianissimo, one note at a time. The row is twofold, of two like hexachords a tritone apart.

The voices are conceived in four levels of diction: "whispered," "spoken," "spoken at approximate pitch," and "sung on pitch;" and also four means of production: overlapping statements of text, direct unanimous statements of text, "accent words," and "overaccent words."

This new set of variables for the choir is exploited in the extensive (three-section) opening movement which spans imitative and familiar techniques, choral unisons, vocal glissandos--all associated with word painting. A stunning glissando, for example, on the phrase "Their eyes to that vast silence:" all voices together "approximate pitch" and fortissimo,

Example 15-A

Edge of Shadow
I, Moderato, first six measures

* Orchestration: 2 Pianos, Celesta, Xylophone, Vibraphone, Timpani, and Percussion instruments.

Example 15-B

Edge of Shadow
II, Parlando, Measures 27-35

crescendo to a fortississimo at "vast," and then in one quarter-note of time, drop via glissando to the word "silence," piano and in a lower tessitura.

The substantial opening movement is followed by a succession of shorter movements:

        I. Moderato
           Allegro energico
           Tempo primo
       II. Parlando
      III. Andante teneramente
       IV. Andante sostenuto
        V. Tranquillo

The Parlando is a declamatory movement, sung by the altos and spoken by the others. At mid-point, the basses and tenors sing (Example 15-B); after commenting in an interjection (marked to be whispered but fortissimo), the sopranos and altos join; four-part singing, in overlapping diction, continues through the rest of the movement. The movement ends with a structure of perfect intervals in the voices; it is interesting that Finney used the tritone, the relationship between the two hexachords of the row, in setting

Example 15-C

Edge of Shadow
III, Andante teneramente, first nine measures

the text "[whose unseen] shape makes sick men of us."

The Andante teneramente follows. This lovely movement is an a capella love song, which, like the short a capella phrase in the opening movement, moves slowly in sonorities associated more with quartal than with serial techniques (Example 15-C). Soprano and alto together move through one row and the tenor and bass through another, each transposed from the original pitch level--soprano up a major third, tenor and bass down a minor third. The movement ends on an E major triad.

The Andante sostenuto begins with an instrumental section and continues in alternating instrumental and vocal passages; the fabric is variable, the dynamic elements change often and are carefully controlled. It is an emotionally tight movement, holding the lines that sum up the meat of the text and give the title to the work: "Be dumb, be silent only, Seal your mouth, Take place upon this edge of shadow."

The Tranquillo follows with an imitative point in the voices alone. This final movement, though short, covers a wide range of dynamics (pianissimo to fortis-sississimo) but is contained harmonically, with many pulsating repeated notes in the instrumental utter-ances. It ends with low, harmonically spare descending chords in a long instrumental phrase, and a final choral invocation, pianissimo, "Have pity upon us!," in quartal chords, central in range, sustained in a long decrescendo marked niente.

The structure seems to be open to more than one meaning. The long opening movement is followed by two pairs, the Parlando and the Andante teneramente, done without pause, and then the Andante sostenuto and Tranquillo, also done without pause. But the two Andantes are braced by reciprocal ideas and, together with the concluding Tranquillo, balance the three-part opening movement, the Parlando connecting the two groups. It is interesting that two philosophical inflections arise in the two groupings: the first emphasizing the human condition of awed questioning, in the end pitiable (and with the love song a parenthe-tical consolation), and the second emphasizing the affirmation of love in the face of ultimate pitiable-ness. The structure as a whole reflects that twofold possibility, and as is so often true in Finney's work, the hexachord itself seems to incorporate the meaning:

172

the perfect intervals within the hexachord pull
against the tritone by which the hexachords are
related.

Still Are New Worlds

For the University of Michigan's University
Musical Society May Festival of 1962, Finney was asked
to compose a large choral/orchestral work. Still Are
New Worlds was the resulting score. It was as representative of Finney's new thoughts about life and
music as the Spherical Madrigals and Edge of Shadow
had been. Although only three years separated the
production of Edge of Shadow from Still Are New
Worlds, they were crucial years, the years of growing
interest in fantasy and instrumental color (and
study of electronic techniques). At the same time,
Finney's expanding thought led him to combine the
symbolisms of the circle with thoughts of wider
application, particularly of the pulls of the human
and the divine, the world (earth) and the cosmos, the
arts and the sciences. The work represents the ideals
of the university tradition.

As he had turned earlier to his New England
friend Archibald MacLeish for his text, he turned to a
work by a former Smith College colleague, Marjorie
Hope Nicolson, who had brought together a number of
quotations that she termed "voices of the past, as
they echo in science and literature, . . . dealing
with the impact of science upon literary imagination."13
Finney selected quotations from Kepler, Harvey,
Marlowe, Donne, Milton, Fontenelle, (Henry) More,
Galileo, Akenside, and Pindar; to these he added a
long passage from Camus. Further, Finney manipulated
passages from Milton so that "He . . . with ambitious
aim . . . th'Almighty Power Hurled headlong . . ."
referred to nuclear physics; the same poet's description of Hell is made to describe a place rendered
uninhabitable by an atomic blast. Thus the circles
include the atom, and the text speaks to the condition
of humankind in the space age. The final statement is
Milton's conclusion of the General Prologue to Paradise
Lost: "That so I may assert Eternal Providence and
justify the ways of God to men." This too Finney has
turned to his own purpose, inserting a paraphrase,
"May we assert Eternal Providence? Can we justify the
ways of men to God?" before the final couplet.

The work is substantial, in ten movements. The performing contingent is large: choir, solo Speaking Voice, orchestra (with xylophone, vibraphone, and celesta in addition to timpani and percussion), and a tapetrack. Like many of Finney's longer works of that period, it is conceived as two reciprocal parts: in this case the first part is a series of seven short movements that accumulate as a group of variations for chorus and orchestra; and the second part is comprised of two long movements for narrator, choir, tape, and orchestra, and preceded by a short introduction. The texts of Part I, the group of variations, rings changes on wonder at the universe; the short opening of Part II serves as an invocation, and the two long movements define the problem, the dilemma of the space age. The addition of the narrator toward the end of Part II, then the tape track, makes the over-all sense one of accumulation and crescendo.

The row was designed for choral statement, and an important permutation for instrumental passagework. This is manifested at once in the first movement, "The Sun." Both of these forms appear in the opening measures: stinging brass tones establish the opening chord and hand it to the choir, which works the row gradually in a technique familiar from Edge of Shadow (Example 16-A). The orchestra enters in the third measure, playing the permutation, three times forward and then in reverse. The independence of the instrumental and vocal elements is representative of this work, as is the chordal style of the choir.

The second movement, "The Moist Earth," has more rhythmic variety in the choir, deals with more highly worked passages, and contains more highly energized orchestral interludes; a heightened diction is called for by scansion (Example 16-B). Manipulation of the row brings independent tonal cadences in vocal and orchestral components, to end the movement in a lovely and mysterious pianissimo (Example 16-C).

The third movement, "Our Soules," expands the main row into a slow accumulation by imitative entries with the first note of the row stated as a poignant rising octave (Example 16-D). After a soft passage for voices only, the texture thickens and becomes activated (voices and orchestra) in a mirroring of the text's phrase, "always moving." A climax follows (Example 16-E, Measure 37) but it is quickly reduced in dynamics and tessitura (Measure 38); the orchestra

Example 16-A

Still Are New Worlds
I, "The Sun," first ten measures

* Fragment of an early disputation

Edition Peters 6553

Example 16-B

<u>Still</u> <u>Are</u> <u>New</u> <u>Worlds</u>
II, "The Moist Earth," Measures 30-35

176

Example 16-C

Still Are New Worlds
II, "The Moist Earth," last seven measures

enters for a short coda overlapping with final choral
sonority; the spare texture finally concentrates in a
single line (Measures 44-47), rising and disappearing
into the atmosphere like a wisp of smoke.

The fourth movement, "Man Hath Weav'd Out a Net,"
an Allegro marcato, begins with unison choir and
extends into a highly motivated movement in which the
voices span long slow phrases over the more active
orchestra. The fifth movement, "To Ask or Search I
Blame Thee Not," intensifies this in an Allegro con
spirito, with heightened diction, wider orchestral
runs, and wider spread. Then the voices drop to
lower, softer chords, the orchestral runs go downward
and yield to the choir, who complete the movement in a
substantial section (30 measures), ending quietly.

The motion changes with the sixth movement, when
the solo Speaking Voice enters to ask a hushed question: "Is every star a Center of a Vortex?" The
orchestra establishes the mystery (Example 16-F),
punctuated by the choir's whispered interjections:

177

Example 16-D

Still Are New Worlds
III, "Our Soules," first ten measures

* Tamburlaine

Edition Peters 6553

Example 16-E

Still Are New Worlds
III, "Our Soules," last eleven measures

179

Example 16-F

<u>Still Are New Worlds</u>
VI, "Is Every Star," first twenty measures

* Conversations upon a Plurality of Worlds.

** The voice should be electrically amplified. The speaker should seek clear and beautiful diction without a trace of
exaggerated dramatic sentiment Effect must come from the beauty of the words and the sincerity of manner

Edition Peters 6553

as big as ours? Is that vast space— which com-pre-hends our

bov-en, farre a - bov-en

bov-en, farre a - bov-en

Sun and Plan-ets but a part of the U - ni-verse?

a - bov-en, farre a - bov-en

a - bov-en, farre a - bov-en

Edition Peters 6553

Example 16-G

Still Are New Worlds
X, "He . . . with Ambitious Aim," Measures 132-144

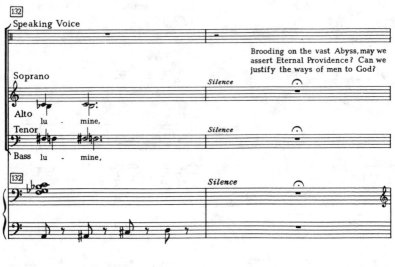

And jus - ti - fy the ways of God to men.

"farre aboven." It is a short movement (only 35
measures), and it leads directly to the seventh and
final movement of Part I, a replying Adagio sereno
that carries out the implications of the Speaking
Voice in a choral answer: "Farre aboven further than
furthest thought of men can traverse, aboven Still are
new worlds, aboven and still aboven . . ."--and again
the narrator continues and the choir interjects the
whispered "aboven." Although orchestral lines are
active, the mood is tranquil and Part I, which had
begun forcefully, ends with a delicate instrumental
question mark.

Part II begins with a spoken quotation from
Galileo and a short movement, VIII, "Give Me to
Learn," loud, jagged, pulsating, but in essence an
invocation. Then the ninth movement, "Here Are
Trees," an extended comment on perception in which
choir, orchestra, and tape recorder present the
surface of the natural--the tape, in Finney's words,
"only for quiet sounds, the chirping of crickets and
of night insects." The choral/orchestral/tape passages
alternate with unaccompanied narration.

The climactic movement is the tenth and last, the
description of atomic energy, "He . . . with Ambitious
Aim." It begins tumultuously, with the tape now
thundering and threatening, the orchestra sparely
harmonized but insistent: the choir enters on a huge
chord (fortississimo, sopranos on high B-flat on the
word "He," forcing a strained sound that adds a new
dimension of commentary, a high tessitura on words
"hurled" and "hideous," in a vocal conflagration, to
speak of holocaust in tones beyond the normal. A new
section, in low tessitura but still forte, describes
the burnt-out city, combining with the fast moving
instrumental lines, over which the longer and longer
choral harmonies sweep like the eye over the burning
ruins. A climax is marked High Point, a long chord
that in six measures takes the voices from fortississimo to pianissimo, a change which inaugurates a new
mood, a recognition of the extent of the dilemma. A
new tempo, Meno mosso, turns to the final section,
asking for illumination. Here the steps in the bass
become detached, and the choir and orchestra suddenly
stop. Into the silence (Example 16-G) the Speaking
Voice projects Finney's paraphrase reversal of Milton:
"Can we justify the ways of men to God?" It is a
stunning moment.

The ensuing Maestoso completes the movement of the work (from Measure 134) with the original Milton quotation, now made equivocal by Finney's paraphrase. Nonetheless, the orchestral conclusion, if brief, is an affirmation and an echo of an echo, awe and wonder reverberating from the opening movement. Finney reverses "What hath God wrought?" to "What has man made?" Ultimately the work speaks to responsiveness and responsibility.

Such a work stands as a statement from an artist of stature and a man of depth and sensitivity. Music was the prism through which the light of many thinkers could be gathered and refracted; the many years of thought, the turning of Finney's art to a point that transcends mastery, the interactions of both Smith College and the University of Michigan—and both Marjorie Hope Hicolson and Gretchen Finney—all enabled the composer to reach an artistic goal that goes far beyond the details of craft. Finney has spoken of the mystery of the relation of thought (in the philosophic sense) to musical production. In the program notes of the premiere performance, he described Still Are New Worlds as "a pattern of feeling rather than an argument," and he delineated elsewhere that Camus had made him feel aware of responsibility, sensing that "thus a dialogue is started." But he continued by questioning, "What does all this have to do with music? I don't know, but it was the motivating force." Thus for Finney, music became "a language of concern."[14]

The concern of the 1960s continued in The Martyr's Elegy (1967), to a text by Percy Bysshe Shelley (based on Adonais); just as Still Are New Worlds dealt outwardly with issues of human arrogance, particularly the salutary counter-recognitions of ourselves (and even the world) as puny, The Martyr's Elegy dealt inwardly with issues of humanity and inhumanity.

A decade later, Finney returned to this material, crowning it with a third spacious choral/orchestral work which both completed and named the trilogy: he called it Earthrise (completed in 1978).

The stance of Earthrise is in a sense both outward and inward. It alternates texts from Lewis Thomas's The Lives of a Cell and Pierre Teilhard de Chardin's Mass on the World, two works which created for Finney the "twofold word" of which Chardin speaks in the

185

Mass. The outward impulse dominates the first half of
the work. "The earth breathes" (Thomas); "I will
climb up in spirit to the high places" (Chardin).
Images of fire and energy culminate in fear and in a
statement of desire for a "reversal," for a renewal of
being in "an overflowing joy" (Chardin). From that
moment the images do reverse, becoming gentler ("The
divine influence secretly defused"--Chardin) and
inward ("Millions of meteorites fall"--Thomas--and
sound like rain). The "inward" image thus transcends
our looking inside ourselves: it culminates in the
perception of an earth-rising seen from the moon, a
compelling reversal of the poetic commonplace of a
moon-rise seen from the earth.

A coda, a tonal affirmation of that which lies
beyond humanity, seems to present a microcosm of the
entire work: "You whose hands imprison the stars,
lock me up within you" (Chardin). It arches from
"you" to "stars" and back, via "imprison" and "lock me
up." Finney beautifully took this line into his own
framework, turning it through the prism of his own
vision, so that the whole trilogy, in the end, speaks
to responsibility. The "outer" voice of the narrator
(called a "Tape Voice") is to be without dramatic
inflection; it is also the "inner" voice, telling us
unremittingly what we must do. The orchestra is also
an "inner" voice which, in a short intermezzo before
the climax (the Earth-Rising), becomes the "outer"
voice, paralleling in advance the final arch-statement.
Like Still Are New Worlds, Earthrise is rich music,
broadly spaced but finely detailed, voices and instruments interacting in elements of line and color that
are incorporated through tremendous rhythmic strength
that becomes for Finney the motion of the universe
itself.

Finney's concern is sensitive, his selection of
texts extraordinarily apposite. Yet it is the excellence of the music which translates the concern into
genuine artistic value and which gives the work that
coherent energy which shapes it as a forceful whole
and makes it so fully representative of its creator.

Notes

1. The significant passages of De Musica are included in Ruth Halle Rowen's collection, Music Through Source Documents (Prentice-Hall, 1979), pages 37-40.

2. Letter of February 27, 1978.

3. Letter of January 1, 1979.

4. From the same letter of January 1, 1979.

5. Still from the letter of January 1, 1979.

6. Paul Cooper, "The Music of Ross Lee Finney," in the Musical Quarterly, LIII (January, 1967), page 4.

7. For an analysis of Three Studies in Fours, see Roger Hines, ed., The Orchestral Composer's Point of View (University of Oklahoma Press, 1970), pages 72-74.

8. "Concerning My Fantasy in Two Movements," in Edith Borroff, ed., Notations and Editions (Wm. C. Brown, 1974, reprint Da Capo Press, 1977), pages 184-190.

9. Ruth S. Edwards, American Music Teacher, Nov-Dec 1978, page 48.

10. Lecture to Phi Beta Kappa, State University of New York at Binghamton, October 4, 1977.

11. John P. Paynter, in notes for a concert on January 16, 1977, of the Northwestern University School of Music Symphonic Wind Ensemble, John P. Paynter, conductor. In his annotation for the recording (NW 211) Paynter discussed the technical means of the work in greater detail.

12. See, among her publications, especially: Gretchen Ludke Finney, Musical Backgrounds for English Literature: 1580-1650 (Rutgers University Press, 1962).

13. In <u>The Breaking of the Circle</u> (Columbia University Press, 1960). The quotations from Nicolson are drawn from the preface to the vocal score (Edition Peters, 1963).

14. Quoted in the program notes for the premiere performance of the <u>Five Pieces For Organ</u> (1967).

Chapter 4
GEORGE CRUMB

The first American concert composers to come into their own in the universities were those born in the second half of the 1920s and trained after World War II. Although they were as a whole educated entirely within the university system, a few were still being trained in apprenticeship--by now very few indeed. And virtually all of the apprenticeship-trained composers would turn to the universities for employment, or change professions, or--in the case of church musicians--continue in the honored tradition of the organist/choir director, writing music on the side and maintaining a venue for performance of church music.

The money that flowed to composers after the War was university controlled, the decisions on recipients made by men in the important Eastern schools, whether the agency be the universities themselves, the government, or private foundations. Those with the money-- the latter-day Prince Esterhazys--no longer had the serene confidence of their predecessors in matters of taste. The twentieth-century patron is the university committee.

The wisdom of the university men to whom the decisions were consigned was the ancient wisdom of the Liberal Arts. They had adapted it to modern concerns, of course, and modern concerns proved quite ready to be taken into the old metaphors: arithmetic and geometric constructs were being energized in scientific work, and could be applied to music in statistical and chance techniques, while electronic music could be taken as a metaphor for outer space. The metaphor was a happy one, catching the popular interest in space exploration and the intellectual examination of alienation as a motivating concept in the arts. The most stylish of these investigations also drew upon the popularity of oriental philosophy; and the deepest of them sought out the creative thought of post-War mathematical theorists.

The young men who saw their way to these conjoining ideas did so under the aegis of John Cage and other like-minded modernists such as Gyorgy Ligeti and Luciano Berio, Witold Lutoslawski and, later, Krzysztof Penderecki. The Americans worked in New York and were

called the "New York School," but they were interna-
tionalists.

Morton Feldman, a New Yorker, was perhaps the
most European of these; although he had studied with
Wallingford Riegger and the eclectic Berlin-born
Stefan Wolpe, his work reflected the European concern
with densities and a new definition of timbre: not as
idiomatic means but as mathematical/acoustical phenomena that can be separated from idiom--another metaphor
of alienation--and synthesized.

Earle Brown was representative of the group who
were active in creating a graphic notation that could
simplify the daunting complexities of notating stochastic or free passages in traditional symbols. From
Massachusetts, Brown studied at Northwestern University
and then with the Russian Joseph Schillinger, who came
to the United States and taught for the last dozen-odd
years of his life, associated with the New York School
for Social Research. Schillinger's system was basically one of composition related to (pre-War) mathematical
theory, but it included graphic notation. After
Schillinger's death in 1943, Brown taught the master's
method; but in the next two decades he expanded the
system. Brown was one of a handful of Americans to be
included in Erhard Karkoschka's important study of
graphic notation in 1966.[1] And he was a frequent
representative of the United States at the Darmstadt
and other international festivals.

Lejaren Hiller was not in the New York group
(though he attended high school in that city); he
studied composition at Princeton with Sessions and
Babbitt while pursuing a chemistry major. He took
music to the computer, in more essentially mathematical
studies. He has been associated with the Polish
radicals.

Pauline Oliveros is a younger member of this
mathematical group, in a day when her being a woman
was still worthy of comment. Also included in the
Karkoschka study, Oliveros worked in virtually every
mathematical type, innovative in all of them. She
worked at the San Francisco Tape Center and lectured at
a number of schools.

With their concern with mathematical structures,
their graphic notation and space metaphors, these were
truly musicians of the Quadrivium. But a number of

composers retained a sense of music in the Trivium.
These composers concerned themselves with sibling
issues, such as alienation, but they used more traditional metaphors to achieve their statements. Ken
Gaburo was born in New Jersey, educated at Eastman
and Princeton. He experimented with layered techniques, combining sound sources. Musique concrète had
entered the ideas of the New Music from the popular
sector, specifically of radio music, where it had
appeared in the early 1930s. (So the full component of
manipulated sound has the strength of two traditions.)
Gaburo's Fat Millie's Lament also included jazz elements. And his choral Three Dedications to Lorca hit
upon the issue of alienation. He taught at the University of Illinois and the University of California.

Paul Cooper, Illinois born but trained (after the
Korean War) at the University of Southern California,
has been concerned with the same issues, but has found
the idiomatic aspect of musical materials of greater
potential than mathematical theory. His university
life has taken him to the University of Michigan, the
University of Cincinnati, and to Rice University in
Houston.

Roger Reynolds and Morton Subotnik are representative of composers who straddle the two camps. Reynolds, from Detroit, studied with Ross Lee Finney and
Roberto Gerhard at the University of Michigan, and was
active in the ONCE Festival; he went to Cologne on a
Fulbright grant (two years later he was awarded a
Guggenheim Fellowship), and taught at the University
of California at San Diego. He took Finney's "complementarity" into expansions that are called "multi-
media" but, with Reynold's sensitivity to text,
approach the theatrical.

Subotnik was trained at Mills College (with
Darius Milhaud and Leon Kirchner), carried forth the
vocal experiments of William Walton and Ernst Toch,
expanding them in such works as Sound Blocks. He
taught at New York University, then at the California
Institute of the Arts and the San Francisco Tape
Center. His Silver Apples on the Moon was the first
electronic work commissioned by a record company.

All of these composers have university affilia-
tions, but within that they make up two categories:
the modernists and the radical avante-garde. It was
George Crumb who most clearly brought the two together,

living with elements of both, sharing their mutual concerns, and, in working out his personal style, incorporating a healthy component of the apprenticeship tradition as well.

Crumb was born on October 24, 1929, in Charleston, West Virginia, where he lived until he was twenty-one. He was one of two sons born to George and Vivian Crumb, musicians of Charleston and significant factors in its unusually strong musical life. A town of about fifty thousand, Charleston maintained a Symphony Orchestra and the Mason College of Music and Fine Arts.

The senior George Crumb was a free-lance musician in the apprenticeship tradition; he was constantly busy in a number of musical activities, into which he drew his family as occasion made possible. First in importance, he was an excellent clarinet player, playing solo, in chamber music, and as first clarinet of the Charleston Symphony Orchestra. He taught clarinet, privately, in connection with a music store, and at Mason College, which was, of course, a conservatory in the apprenticeship tradition. He conducted the Masonic Band, a group which he brought to polished excellence. He conducted a theatre orchestra (and earlier had conducted an orchestra for silent movies). He was the copyist for the entire musical needs of the town, work in which the young George was soon to join his father.

Vivian Crumb was a cellist who played in the Charleston Symphony Orchestra and taught in the home. Like her husband, she was active in solo and chamber music performances. Young George learned the piano as his chief instrument (his brother learned the flute but did not become a musician); and the family trio performed extensively, with particular emphasis on the German Romantic repertoire.

The young boy reared in this household was given un unparalleled apprenticeship, a musical bringing-up beyond value, unpurchasable--a beautiful accident of birth and place. The father, a quiet man and consummate musician, was unusually probing of the science of his art, and had a library of 400-odd scores (based strongly in German Romantic literature) that formed a substantial study for the boy, who learned to read them at the piano. The father, like a good apprentice-master, taught by example as well as precept, drawing the boy into many activities, sharing his art, often

192

wordlessly, and building independence in his son.

The years of World War II did not disunite the family, who straddled the age of service (the father too old, the son too young), and in 1943 Crumb entered high school, graduating in 1947. His high school yearbook, the <u>Charlestonian</u>, lists his activities as music (orchestra--student director; chamber ensemble--student director; and All-State Orchestra, in which he played clarinet) and track.

Crumb seems always to have been composing music: songs, piano pieces, chamber music, and even orchestral music: in 1947 the Charleston Symphony Orchestra performed a work of his called <u>Poem</u>. Another, <u>Gethse-</u> <u>mane</u>, was performed in 1952 by the same orchestra, and, at some time during the early years, his song, "A Lullaby," was done by Fred Waring. His output was constant and profuse, and evidently based upon the models he knew. He never doubted what he would become, and in the fall of 1947 he entered Mason College, where he studied piano and composition, the latter to a large extent on his own, since a separate department of composition was not maintained there. Also studying piano at Mason was Elizabeth Brown, of Chesapeake, who had been listed in the <u>Charlestonian</u> as interested in chorus and Latin Club (although she knew Crumb only casually in high school); they courted, and were married at the end of their second year at Mason. Crumb was not yet twenty.

With his extraordinary background, Crumb was able to complete his baccalaureate degree in three years; he was graduated in June of 1950. The next year was crucial in his development: his father died in the summer, and Crumb found himself at twenty, a baby on the way (a daughter), with need not only to support his family but to make vital decisions concerning his future without the help of the man whose quiet presence had spanned his world. Crumb turned to his father's pattern, free-lancing in a host of musical jobs: he taught, he conducted a church choir, he played piano in a dance combo and served as accompanist in a ballet school, and he took over his father's music copying. This multiplicity schooled him in the life of an apprenticeship musician. It was both educative and daunting: educating him as a would-be composer with a ready and versatile musicianship; daunting him with the dismal financial and cultural prospects of piece-work professionalism in an age when the apprenticeship system was failing and no longer dependable.

In the summer of 1951 the Crumbs moved to Urbana, in time for the summer session at the University of Illinois. He earned the Master of Music in composition in June of 1952, and stayed on an additional year as a teacher. The University of Illinois was a member of a Midwest Consortium of Composition interests, and at the symposia of the group Ross Lee Finney was a significant presence. Crumb decided to continue his work under Finney's guidance, and in the summer of 1953 the Crumb family moved to Ann Arbor, where their life would center for six years--with the year 1955-56 in Berlin on a Fulbright fellowship. In Berlin Crumb composed the Sonata for Solo Violoncello that was his first published work and the earliest still available for performance.

Crumb arrived in Ann Arbor knowing fairly much what he wanted, and it is interesting to speculate on the relationship between the independent young composer's expectation and the kind of discipline that Finney provided. Crumb's work remained largely independent; it was not Finney's goal as a teacher to determine style or to exert force of musical personality; he taught discipline, and he worked above all to develop a capacity for self-criticism in his students. It is the latter which Crumb remembers in connection with his years of study with Finney: "he taught that there is, after all, such a thing as the right note." Finney, in personality so very different from Crumb's father, in a sense gave the young man much the same kind of oblique schooling, though without the sharing of musical activities that with Crumb's father was the fulcrum of the relationship. Crumb was thrown more deeply into himself. His work in Ann Arbor was split by the year 1955-56, with the summer at Tanglewood and the academic year in Berlin, where he worked on his own. Return to Ann Arbor brought him a BMI Student Composer Award and, confirmed by the Fulbright and BMI recognition, he re-entered the discipline of his craft. In 1959 Crumb received the Doctor of Musical Arts in Composition, with the Variazioni, for large orchestra, as thesis--the last of his student works.

The graduation, after the long rigorous University work, was indeed a Commencement for Crumb. His first professorship was waiting for him, at the University of Colorado. The Crumbs moved to Boulder in the fall of 1959 and were to be there for five years; their first son was born there in 1962 (the second after they left, in 1966).

Aside from the sudden (though long-awaited) freedom of the entry into his profession, Crumb enjoyed the encouragement of being among other professionals, particularly the pianist-composer David Burge, for whom Crumb composed the Five Pieces for Piano in 1962. Crumb and Burge had a great deal in common, and the friendship was a fruitful one. Burge's enthusiasm for Crumb's work, along with his abilty to comprehend and interpret it, provided the composer with another confirmation and came at the right time. Crumb, in the Five Pieces for Piano, began his definition of a personal style, based in short subjects characterized by timbre, rhythm, pitch, and technique of performance--a fourfold importance that would expand from the keyboard and gradually form its own discipline through the 1960s in chamber music (with and without voice) and orchestral work. In the inclusion of technique of performance, Crumb retained a vital aspect of his apprenticeship heritage (and one in which he had a strong model in Ross Lee Finney); the presence of music is so vitalizing in his art that he has not sought the avenues of synthesized or manipulated sounds.

But Crumb's strongest influence was internal, and lay in his own musings on the larger matters of life and death ("life, death, love, the earth, water, and rain," he summed them up), and time, philosophical and musical. He found his voice in the dark images of Federico Garcia Lorca (1899-1936), the Spanish poet-dramatist whose works had been translated after the War and were popular among young intellectuals. Crumb wrote a half-dozen works using Lorca texts: Night Music I (1963), four books of Madrigals (1965-1969), Songs, Drones, and Refrains of Death (1968), and Night of the Four Moons (1969).

In 1964 Crumb took a one-year professorship at the State University of Mew York at Buffalo, and at the end of that year he was appointed Professor of Music and Composer in Residence at the University of Pennsylvania (in Philadelphia). The appointment brought him to the attention of Foundation governors, and commissions began to come his way. His schedule of two semesters of teaching and the third off (not counting summers) enabled him to work somewhat faster, though Crumb is neither quick nor prolific.

195

In 1967 he completed a commission from the University of Chicago for a work for the Chicago Symphony Orchestra, producing Echoes of Time and the River. When the work won the Pulitzer Prize in 1968, Crumb's acceptance as a leading composer began. But he was still either a mountain or a Midwestern man, and the New York critics were not ready to accept him. Irvin Kolodin, for example, wrote that he found it "difficult to believe" that Echoes of Time and the River could be the best choice; "if it, or any other work of his, has been performed in New York by a major orchestra, it escapes recollection."[2]

In 1970 Crumb reached the peak of his mature style, with two works that created his fame among audiences. Black Angels: Thirteen Images from the Dark Land, for electric string quartet, was commissioned by the University of Michigan and was premiered by the Stanley Quartet in Ann Arbor at the Contemporary Music Festival, conducted by the composer. It was praised as a work of "authentic beauty and power" by the reviewer.[3] Ancient Voices of Children was commissioned by the Elizabeth Sprague Coolidge Foundation and was completed at Tanglewood (where Crumb returned, fifteen years after his study there, as a faculty member) during the summer. It too was praised in its initial reviews as "powerful and moving."[4] It is undoubtedly one of the most successful of Crumb's works; a setting of fragments of Lorca texts, put into a new order by the composer, it crowned the series of works on texts by that author, transcending them in an integration of Crumb's ideas, fulfilling them with remarkable power in the music. This work, premiered at the Library of Congress, was performed in Paris under the auspices of UNESCO soon afterwards. In 1971 it won the UNESCO International Rostrum of Composers award, and its issuance on disc in that same year brought it the Koussevitzky International Recording Award.

Just as important as the academic honor was the welcome granted this work by the public. The Lorca texts (indeed, the entire dark poetry, with its suggestions equally of earth essences and other-worldly auras) were close to the cultural pulse, particularly of the young; and the quality of the fabric, which contained much that was new, yet was grounded in traditions of East and West. And in creating a rapprochement between hemispheres, it was close to the musical pulse of the nation. These factors were fortuitous and show Crumb as having worked at the cusp of his culture. But most important of all, Ancient Voices of Children was the culmination of an ideal preparation, and in relation to Crumb's career, it comprised a stunning internal climax. It is a pithy, beautifully organized work, whose form is audible and penetrates beyond the surface of text or fabric, and it is a work of deep colors--dark, to be sure, but at the end turning in a new way toward the light.

Ancient Voices of Children formed a turning point in Crumb's style; the earlier style was grounded essentially in Baroque concertato technique, in which the music accrues by contrasts of successive elements of the performing forces, through subjects informed by the nature of the instrument (or voice) producing them; spatial contrasts were vitalizing as well. In Ancient Voices of Children the contrasts were broader, the colors more pungent, and the percussion used with greater regularity of beat (as well as for sonority). This, along with the consciously Moorish effects of the low, throaty oboe, plus the melodic subjects and vocal techniques associated with Medieval music, brought Crumb to more universal concerns.

Subsequent works dealt with Medieval texts and cosmic concepts: the Voice of the Whale (Vox Balaenae) used concepts of prehistory, the beginning of time and the end of time, and the formation of the world. Lux Aeterna used part of the traditional text of the Dies Irae, a Medieval hymn describing the Day of Judgment. Music for a Summer Evening (Makrokosmos III) contemplates the sky as a mystical phenomenon, with "Nocturnal Sounds (The Awakening)," "Hymn for the Nativity of the Star-Child," and a finale called Music of the Starry Night" that includes "Fivefold Galactic Bells."

The music at the end of the 1970s turned in two directions in its poetic reference and equally to two directions in musical content: toward the spare and the lavish. The Dream Sequence, of 1976, and Makrokosmos IV, of 1979, required small ensembles and sharply reduced extraneous reference; in Makrokosmos IV the contingent is only two players at one piano (with a few brief contributions from the page turner), a jovial reduction to a companionable minimum. At the opposite end of the scale, Star-Child, of 1977, called for a soprano soloist, large orchestra, large child-

197

ren's choir, and men's speaking choir with handbells. It required four conductors.

Interestingly, <u>Star-Child</u> is musically spare, an economical work that spins its message from minimal basic musical content. It is also, with the exception of the central "Musica Apocalyptica," very quiet and sustained.

Thus at the end of the 1970s Crumb found himself, having fulfilled his early style, in a period of honing down, refining, of arriving at a consummation. He is acknowledged as a composer of significance, is "all but swamped with commissions,"[5] assured of a ready audience for new work, and secure in his basic employment at the University of Pennsylvania. He has won virtually every major award, including Guggenheim, Fromm, Rockefeller, and Ford Foundation grants and commissions, plus one from the National Institute of Arts and Letters, in addition to the Pulitzer Prize. His accomplishments are beyond question, and his contribution to American music secure. He thinks of himself as a West Virginian and as a "composer" rather than as an "American composer." He is, of course, a "teaching composer" within the uniquely American university system. As one would expect, Crumb's teaching techniques reflect above all that quality shared by the two men--so different in personality--who most deeply influenced him: his father and Ross Lee Finney. Both taught indirectly, both let the young scholar see a deeply intelligent musicianship at work, and both left him with the lesson not of style but of discipline and commitment, a method that Crumb has often called "low-key." He strives for the same indirection in his own teaching: "by the end of the term, Crumb's students (he ordinarily has in his charge from five to seven would-be composers) wind up knowing `an incredible amount about music without realizing how it happened.'"[6]

The vital question for Crumb is the new direction into which his music is now expanding, in the 1980s. Both Fischer and Finney arrived at the same node of creative vibration, at about the same age; both expanded into a new fulfillment and wrote remarkable works in their sixties and seventies. It is predictable that Crumb's new path will be informed by craft and imagination; but the shape of his work and its unfolding style--the galaxies to come--lie in the mystical progression of the Children of Light.

Plate VIII
Crumb at ten

Plate IX
Crumb at fifty-one

(Photo by Harry Zeitlin,
         Los Angeles)

The Music

Like Fischer and Finney before him, Crumb began his systematic advanced study of composition with a twofold background of musical experience: of the general musical lore of his culture and the specific tradition of the concert hall. For Fischer, who had no music at home and a strong, positive influence within the concert tradition, the studies developed upon that tradition, and Fischer's personal style developed within it. For Finney, who had a strong musical life at home as a child, the concert tradition was not yet central; moreover, he was caught in an ill-defined university musical system which could not provide him with authoritative training (indeed, used him as a faculty member before he had a university degree). From necessity (as well as, one suspects, by proclivity), Finney unfolded his personal style in a continuing interaction between his own turning mind and the many venues and systems which impinged upon it. For Crumb the strong background in home music, akin to Finney's in its power but much more professional, was set aside, and the training began anew as a discipline within the newly-defined university system, specifically within the discipline developed by Finney.

Crumb's early works reflected that discipline, particularly in its coverage of atonal (Schoenberg) style, as shown in his String Quartet of 1954, and in looser techniques, more or less integrated and more or less tonal.

The Sonata for Solo Violoncello

The Sonata for Solo Violoncello, composed in Berlin in 1955, reflects Finney's musical personality in more than one way—the cello was Finney's instrument, of course—but without imitating Finney's sound or fabric. The sonata is tonally free, projecting a series of pitch centers—not centripetal centers as in tonal process, but centers of activity, less vital to memory and the perception of structure than the type of activity or subject. The subject material is rhythmically characterized and clearly shaped, so that elements can be recognized in repetition, development, and restatement, even in altered forms.

199

The <u>Sonata</u> is shaped as three movements, all of them using forms associated with Baroque traditions; the work pulls against these traditions, taking meaning from them and also revitalizing them. Two "free" forms, a Fantasia and a Toccata, frame a central Theme and Variations which is a tightly wrought five-part form in itself.

The Fantasia begins with a slowly arpeggiated chord, rolling upwards as <u>D</u>-sharp, <u>B</u>, <u>D</u>-natural, and <u>A</u> (Example 1-A). A series of chords follows, sibling to the first, but now arpeggiated rapidly downwards and creating a tension between the ostinato fifth (<u>D-A</u>) and the shifting sixths beneath. The opening chord is repeated, completing the opening element. A contrasting monophonic subject follows (arco, Measures 3-4): a falling minor third from <u>F</u> above middle <u>C</u> in a Lombardy rhythm, a rising <u>C</u>-sharp minor triad, and repetition of the falling minor third from <u>F</u>. The pizzicato chords return, now expanded so that the sixths rise within the ostinato fifth. The monophonic

Example 1-A

Sonata for Solo Violoncello
I, Fantasia, first fifteen measures

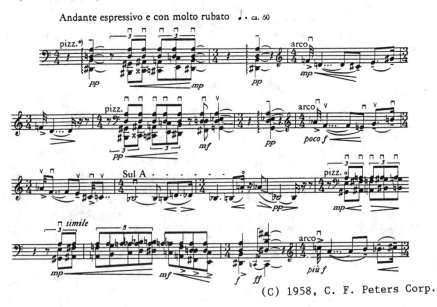

Andante espressivo e con molto rubato ♩ = ca. 60

Example 1-B

Sonata for Solo Violoncello
I, Fantasia, Measures 32-48

Example 1-C

Sonata for Solo Violoncello
II, Tema pastorale

Example 1-D

Sonata for Solo Violoncello
II, opening measures of each variation

Var. I - Un poco più animato ♩. = ca. 60

Var. II - Allegro possibile e sempre pizzicato

Var. III - Poco adagio e molto espressivo

Example 1-E

Sonata for Solo Violoncello
II, Tema pastorale con variazioni, Coda

Coda: Tempo primo (♩. = ca. 56)

202

subject follows again, now from A-flat, expanded to more than twice the original length (Measures 7-11). Thus the structural principles are quickly established: short subjects in alternation; delineation of character by texture and rhythm, pitch areas of focus rather than key centers, and performance style (pizzicato, arco; loud, soft). The two elements are systematically expanded, developed, and brought to a conclusion (Example 1-B) in which the twofold nature of the cello is never clouded and the two subjects remain distinct. The final morendo, leading to pizzicato chords derived from the opening sonority, gives an over-all arch to the perception of the movement.

The second movement, Theme and Variations, marked "pastorale," exploits the dotted rhythm of the previous movement, sharpening it with a double dot but at the same time softening it by making it Grazioso e delicato and in 6/8 measure. The theme is a modified Baroque format of two short units (seven plus eight measures), with only the first unit repeated (Example 1-C); the first ends on E, the second on A, producing a cadence pattern of E, E, A. But although the pattern is a traditional one associated with tonal function, the approach to the cadence tones is not functional, but is anti-tonal: the E preceded by the fifth B-flat/F, and the A by the fifth E-flat/B-flat.

There are three variations: Un poco piu animato, Allegro possibile e sempre pizzicato, and Poco adagio e molto espressivo (Example 1-D). The first two variations proceed in steady motion but in variable groupings, the first within a constant meter, the second in changing meters; both retain the clear two-plus-one (E, E, A) formula. The Poco adagio breaks the formula: the two units are eight plus six measures without repeat, and although the first ends on E, the second is open, descending into a slower and softer turning figure and ending in a rest. A Coda follows (Example 1-E); it is a truncated version of the Tema, skipping from the brink of the first cadence, after a long pause, to the cadence on A.

The finale, a Toccata, begins with an introductory Largo e drammatico (Example 1-F) which sets forth an octave C and a striding upward; a precipitando descent leads to the Allegro vivace (Example 1-G), an extended, discursive movement characterized by rising lines: the opening line is accented, but the exposition continues softly. The lines arpeggiate triads, first C minor and A-flat major, and then B minor and E-flat major, and so forth, juxtaposed in running relationships of variable consanguinity. A middle section, in 9/4, relates these materials to the subjects of the Fantasia; return to the opening materials of the Allegro vivace is subtle, slipping into the B minor/E-flat major pairing as an outgrowth of the extended middle section. The climax returns to the first movement, now alternating a B-flat/G-flat sixth with the fifth C-G, then in a quick pattern

Example 1-F

Sonata for Solo Violoncello
III, Toccata, Introduction: Largo e drammatico

Example 1-G

Sonata for Solo Violoncello
III, Toccata, Allegro vivace, first eleven measures

turning, descending, pausing, and reversing the Largo in a striding fortississimo descent to the same octave C with which the movement had begun.

The relative tonal ambiguity of the Fantasia and Toccata, along with their common subjects, creates a focus of stability in the middle movement. The cumulative succession of small sections that become members of similar forms in a larger pattern, is perceivable and successful. It is an interesting technique for the 1950s; integrated but not serial, vitalized by pulls to contrasting tones but not tonal, dependent upon process but not on progression. The effect is of crystalization: the organic combining of smaller into larger segments, while maintaining clarity at the several levels.

This effect is underscored both by the use of closed forms and by differentiation of fabric. The closed form, particularly an ABA structure with its presentation, departure, and return, lends itself to clarity of section with particular thrust. The opening subject of the Sonata, for example, is a miniature ABA (chord, series of chords, chord), which itself becomes an A in a dialogue with the monophonic subject, B, which is also a miniature ABA form; the dialogue enlarges as ABAB, and itself becomes an A in a three-movement whole. Nothing could better exemplify the young composer's independence from his mentor, for whom the idea that the "small means" should become the "large means" was simply a contradiction.

Differentiation of fabric vitalizes the structure at all levels: two types of pizzicato clarify the ABA of the short opening subject: the change of direction draws the attention of the listener to the opening elements in the chords (the static upper fifth, the shifting lower sixths) as well as to the internal structure of the subject. (This opposition of pizzicato directions is resolved at the final chords, which the cellist is asked to play as single, simultaneous sonorities.) These subtle differentiations then yield to the larger one of the dialogue, in which pizzicato and arco subjects are contrasted, as well as chordal and melodic textures. The importance of color to clarity is evidenced in the composer's care with dynamic markings, mute (for the Coda of the Variations), bowings, the color of the A string, and the use of the octave to clarify the opening and closing gestures of the Toccata.

Thus at twenty-five Crumb was using finely calibrated elements to produce a work of considerable artistry, within the traditions of the concert hall, keenly alive to the actualities of performance, and serene within its own projections of fabric and form.

Music for Solo Piano

It was as an expansion of such means as displayed in the Sonata for Solo Violoncello that Crumb's personal style began to unfold. It was natural that a disciplined and more-or-less systematic exploration of medium begin with the piano, and it was fortunate that the composer found himself at Boulder, where he could feel very much on his own and establish a working basis operandi in his post-student life. He was fortunate also to find in Boulder a sensitive and encouraging colleague, David Burge, with whom he could exchange ideas, and who was eager to perform his music.

Five Pieces for Piano

The first work of this new discipline was called Five Pieces for Piano (1962). It is actually a single work in an arch form (ABCBA):

   I. Quasi improvvisando
  II. Ruvido, molto energico--Prestissimo--
        Tempo primo
 III. Notturno--sempre pizzicato
  IV. Ruvido, molto energico--Prestissimo--
        Tempo primo
   V. Senza misura, liberamente--Solenne--
        Tempo di primo pezzo

As in the cello sonata, the instability of the outer movements throws focus to the center three, all of which are ABA forms.

The opening Quasi improvvisando is carefully designed of four elements or subjects: discrete three-note chords, set off by rests; a group of repeated notes, shaped by accelerando and ritard; a cadenza-like flourish, of varying components but including quick breaks between registers; and a rapid tremolo on the strings described in the score as "a smooth band of sound."

The movement exploits the effects of these elements: playing in the middle register, pianissimo, on the strings with finger-tips (a warm sound); in the very high or very low register, pianississimo, on the keys; repeated-note groups; seemingly random flourishes; notes played both pianissimo with the key and pizzicato on the string, with fingernail (a sharp, almost nasal sound), and so forth. A coda presents the material of the flourishes, and adds a final chord. This is deployed as a single F-sharp approached by a double grace-note, and enriched as it resonates by the touch of a metal loop (to be made from a partially unbent paper clip according to a precise design given in a footnote).

The structure of the movement accrues from small elements in a design whose over-all plan is traditional: ABAc (c being a coda), but whose detailed plan is a unique deployment of three elements. The additive structure can be shown schematically by referring to the first three subjects as a, b, and c, a continuing tremolo as d, and the enrichment of a by use of the paper clip as A (all groups end with a rest, so they are set off clearly):

A	B		A	c
aaaba	c	baccc	aaaba	cA
			d	

The second piece (movement) contrasts chiefly in its greater sense of energy. Ruvido (rough, coarse), Molto energico uses forceful gestures, then allows them to resonate (with the help of the sostenuto pedal),--three such gestures in the opening section. Then a soft, fleet Prestissimo, still of separate gestures. A violent ("feroce!") fortississimo measure serves as punctuation, and an extended related section follows and crescendos to repeated-note figures. A series of four discrete chord figures of decreasing force ends the section with delicacy. A final section, Tempo primo, is shorter than the first but uses the same gestures.

The third, central movement is a calm night music, Notturno--sempre pizzicato, a leisurely movement of two spacious short sections framing a longer middle section of greater activity as well as faster tempo (Poco piu mosso). The two outer sections each use two long bass tones, over which shorter gestures appear. The two tones rise in the first section and fall in the second; all four of the bass tones are enriched by the application of the paper clip.

The fourth movement, again Ruvido, is essentially an inversion of the second, reversed in order and in many details with the gestures turned upside down. The framing sections are reversed, the opening of the fourth movement derived from the short last section of the second, and the longer opening of the second serving as the final section of the fourth--with a climactic enlargement of the penultimate gesture. The long central section is an almost constant inversion of the model, its sweeping gestures and repeated notes recognizable.

The last movement begins with a free section (Senza misura, liberamente) that contains the largest, most beautifully shaped subjects in the Five Pieces. The substantial Solenne presents the most complex and intense fabric of the work; a counterpoint of elements played with the keys and the strings, along with the strong metric force of the section, give it dignity and a certain serenity. At the end of the section, elements of the opening section appear: discrete chords, tremolo, and a final bass G enriched with the paper clip. The last section, calling for "The tempo of the first piece," reverses elements of the A section of the opening movement. The reversal is not exact, but the opening discrete chord of the first movement slowly accumulates as the final sound of the last.

Thus the Five Pieces for Piano present an intricate set of relationships; as in the earlier Sonata for Solo Violoncello, small forms are used as microcosms of larger structures. And, as in the earlier work, the elements are clarified by differentiation of fabric. The many types of pizzicato, specified quite exactly in the score, are used not only to set off gesture from gesture, but also to characterize the gestures and to ensure clarity of reference. The use of the paper clip, increasing reverberation of bass notes in the first, third, and fifth pieces, serves a function in delineation of the form as a whole.

Pitch materials support the ideas of over-all form. The work is integrated and in part serial, but its structural basis is the piano keyboard and the octave as composed of four quadrants or vectors, used systematically but not slavishly. For example, the four chords of the opening systematically span the octave: B-flat, A, G-sharp in the first; G, F-sharp, F in the second; E, D-sharp, D in the third; and C-sharp, C, B in the fourth.

The notation of the Five Pieces is precise, highly controlled, and helpful to the performer in setting forth the fine distinctions desired and specifying the means of attaining them. Both pizzicato (including types of tremolo) and pedal techniques are formulated in detail, with footnotes where necessary, in addition to the set of principles presented in the introduction. Notation of rhythm is for the performer: everything but the opening of the last piece is notated in meter, but the music itself is anti-metrical (that is, with the exception of certain parts of the Solenne the meter cannot be perceived by the listener). Gestures are regular or irregular within themselves, but they cannot be placed within a measure (seldom within a beat) or related temporally to each other in metrical terms. The effect is of succession in the theatrical sense, of prose or choreography, of progression from idea to idea, without pressures of meter but with a logic of order and repetition.

In retrospect, Crumb looked back upon the Five Pieces for Piano as opening "a whole new world" of piano idiom to himself and others. He was, he wrote a decade later, "much excited about the expanding possibilities of piano idiom."[7] He acknowledged his debt to Debussy and Bartok, both of whom expanded the rainbow of color (though one suspects that Bartok's string writing was more influential than his piano writing in this regard), but omitted reference to such predecessors as Cowell and Cage. The omission is instructuve, for as an avant-garde score, the Five Pieces are conservative, and in this Crumb was setting forth a position that would remain vital for him and would be basic to his mature style: he had dealt with musical idea and he had made use of whatever would clarify it, deepen it, fulfill it, and convey it. It is clear that Crumb did not search for new sounds, but rather for the right sounds. In his latter-day statement about the Five Pieces, Crumb hazarded that his musical ideas owe more to the Romantic than to early twentieth-century composers, more to structural thought than to fabric or piano idiom. "I suspect," he wrote, "that the `spiritual impulse' of my music is more akin to the darker side of Chopin, and even to the child-like fantasy of early Schumann."[8] Both composers had dealt in depth with succession and prose elaboration of musical idea, Chopin particularly in his dramatic forms rather than in the popular dances, and Schumann in the early piano works.

Makrokosmos

It would be interesting to date Crumb's view of Chopin's elaborated form as a "dark side," to know when this idea occurred to him. The statement came ten years after his completion of the work which prompted it, and the years between had centered in his long dealings with texts by Lorca (certainly a "dark" poet), the development of an extra-musical symbolic thought, virtually all of it in "dark" metaphors, and the confirmation of direction by professional and public recognition extraordinary for a composer of Crumb's age. One suspects that in 1962 the thoughts expressed later had been inchoate, felt rather than defined, sensed as beckoning direction rather than as ideas already secured. In any event, the sequel to the Five Pieces had to be hard won in a struggle over a period of years in which Crumb admitted to "germinal ideas" and "abortive attempts."[9] It is probable that Crumb's style could mature only in vocal works, and that he had to achieve a maturity in other spheres and then turn, within that maturity, back to the piano.

The sequel to the Five Pieces was in fact a double set, two dozen "fantasy-pieces," two volumes, each with one piece associated with each sign of the Zodiac. Crumb called these pieces Makrokosmos; Volume I was completed in 1972, Volume II in 1973. The zodiac, like the metaphor implied in the idea of a macrocosmos, is a spatial concept, with a special implication of the night--the only time when the cosmos as astronomical/astrological phenomenon can be observed. The complex associations of the zodiac provided the composer with an ideal motivation: verbal, suggestive, expandable, but not so specific as to delimit form or to require a voice or a text. Further, the idea had the advantage of placing the pieces as a substantial work in a continuum of musical idea, through tacit allusion to works by Crumb's much-admired predecessors: the Mikrokosmos of Bartok, the 24 Preludes of Debussy, the two volumes of the Wohltemperiertes Clavier, and the type of form such as the string of pieces in Schumann's Carnaval. The advantages, along with the processes of expansion, are

suggested at once in the titles of the pieces of the
first volume:

Part I
  Primeval Sounds (Genesis I), Cancer
  Proteus, Pisces
  Pastorale (from the Kingdom of Atlantis,
    ca. 10,000 B. C., Taurus
  Crucifixus, Capricorn

Part II
  The Phantom Gondolier, Scorpio
  Night-Spell I, Sagittarius
  Music of Shadows (for Aeolian harp), Libra
  The Magic Circle of Infinity (Moto Perpetuo),
    Leo

Part III
  The Abyss of Time, Virgo
  Spring-Fire, Aries
  Dream Images (Love-Death Music), Gemini
  Spiral Galaxy, Aquarius

The twelve pieces form three parts; the last
piece of each part is notated in the shape suggested
by the title (though the Magic Circle at the end of
Part II contains a cross-bar like the Greek theta);
these are labeled SYMBOL. Each of the pieces, dupli-
cated from the composer's beautiful inscribing,
concludes with bracketed initials and zodiacal symbol,
which Crumb admitted as whimsical attempts at enigmatic
reference to people born under the sign: one immediately "recognizes" Ross Lee Finney (#4), David Burge
(to whom the work is dedicated, #10), and the composer
himself (#5). These arcane, extra-musical addenda,
like Schumann's SPHYNXES, cast a penumbra of mood
suggestive to the performer (the listener, of course,
cannot hear them) and supportive of the emotional
intention in abstracto--and of course the page of
music has an aesthetic value in itself.

The designation of the twelve pieces further
clarifies the three-movement structure; the three
parts have three movements each, connected without
pause (all but #4 and #8 end "attacca"). The shape of
each group is roughly the same: a slow, "dark"
opening; a more energized continuation; a quiet,
interior piece; and a slow closing. The ABCA shape of
the sections is intensified by the use of common
materials in #1, #4, #9, and #12, as well as by

211

closing each group with a SYMBOL.

The scheme is:

    I. 1. Darkly mysterious
       2. Very fast; whimsical, volatile
       3. Moderately, with incisive rhythm
       4. Darkly mysterious

    II. 5. Eerily, with a sense of malignant evil
       6. Poised, expectantly
       7. Gracefully, with elastic rhythm
       8. A. Luminous
          B. Joyously, like a cosmic clock-work;
            with mechanically precise rhythm

    III. 9. Dark, with a sense of profound mystery
       10. Prestissimo; breathlessly, with elan
       11. Musingly, like the gentle caress of
           faintly remembered music (flexible
           and expressive)
       12. Vast, lonely, timeless

The structural techniques of the Five Pieces for Piano have both relaxed and intensified: the tight structures of the earlier style have loosened and become more elaborate, and the delineation of idea through color and idiomatic effects has been marvelously enriched, refined, and sharpened; this integrity of subject, color, and technique—a total Anklang or integrity of sound—has become one with the subjects and indispensable to the form. Although the repeated elements still serve, and precise dynamic control adds to organic shaping of the pieces, they essentially are rhetorical forms in which one "sentence" follows another to build a "paragraph." At the same time, the work is a succession of sounds, some of them remarkably beautiful, all of them carefully controlled, in a coherent progression whose logic is perhaps closest to the concertato principle of Baroque style, in which the physical and sonorous potentials of the performing forces suggest interactions that create organic forms through repetition and contrast, dialogue and accommodation.

The work opens with seven stately chords, rising slowly and deliberately (Example 2-A) in the low register; seven seconds of slow glissandos follow; the seven chords reappear a tritone higher; then, a stunning thunderation occurs: a light metal chain is

Example 2-A

Makrokosmos, Volume I
Primeval Sounds (Genesis I), Cancer

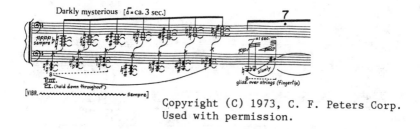

dropped onto the bass strings, precisely synchronized
with a heavy quick glissando on the same strings,
sforzando and with a quick crescendo, and the instrument seems to roar. Other effects include harmonics
(second and fifth partials), scraping over the metal
windings of the strings, strumming with a thimble,
striking the soundboard and the metal crossbeam,
humming, calling out, whistling, and moaning. But not
many effects appear in a single section, so that
individuality and integrity are maintained.

Structural procedures include wheels, layered
fabrics, and memories not only of subjects within the
work, but of materials outside. A revival hymn, "Will
There Be Any Stars in My Crown?," is invoked in Night-
Spell I. But a dialogue that interpolates Chopin's
Fantaisie-Impromptu in the next-to-last piece, is a
serious and lovely contemplation. It is a three-layer
fabric, with bass triads (B and F-sharp major alternating) and an iterative melody establishing two layers
of dialogue at the start (Example 2-B). Then the
Chopin excerpt is superimposed upon this, entering "as
if emerging from silence" (Example 2-C); after three
measures, blurred, the melody stops and a B major
triad reinstitutes the first two layers. Three
fragments of the Chopin are used, laid into the matrix
of bass triads and treble melody; superimposed upon
this structure of seven sections (alternating two- and
three-layered fabric) is a development and climax in
the extended fifth section, following the second
Chopin quotation. A major, F major, and E-flat minor
triads in the bass occur in a slow progression in a
single layer (for the only time), followed by an

213

Example 2-B

Makrokosmos, Volume I
Dream Images (Love-Death Music), Gemini, opening

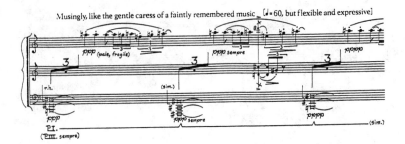

Example 2-C

Makrokosmos, Volume I
Dream Images, (Love-Death Music), Gemini,

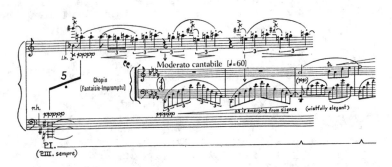

introduction of the first Chopin excerpt "cadenza" in middle and upper registers that seem to grow from the treble layer. The final (and shortest) quotation enters, and is followed by a final B major triad, fortississimo, and two short phrases of the iterative melody, first very loud, and finally very very soft, "as from afar," dying away. The silence prepares for the "Vast, lonely, timeless" finale.

Pitch materials are integrated only in the sense that, over the length of the work, one can expect any and all pitches of the piano keyboard--and, through use of the harmonics and amplified reverberations, some pitches unavailable in the tempered scale. But subjects--indeed, whole pieces--are also frequently restricted: the cosmic clockwork (the Magic Circle of Infinity) uses wheels that limit the scope to a group of notes that, like a gamelan sound, pulsate with a constant reinforcement of a single "ground of being," equally melodic and harmonic; such a delimitation, however "centered" in a dominating pitch, is not tonal. It can, however, be used as a point of reference, a unit in a cross-work relationship.

The materials of the three-layered eleventh piece are: the triads of the bass, beginning and ending with B major; the iterative melody, which, except for one three-note extension of the figure, dwells within the fifth D/A (of D minor); the Chopin is of course in D-flat major. But there is no tonality in the basic two layers. The root B, supported in the initial alternations with its upper fifth, F-sharp, yields to the impressionist non-progression of the climax: the last four triads are A major, F major, E-flat minor, and B major, interlocking tritones, and anything but a tonal progression. The iterative melody is based in two recurring elements: F-G-A (heard four times) and E-G-A (heard nine times); as discrete entities, the first has the "root" of F and the second of A. It would be a mistake to impute a "key" to either of the two layers, which rather use separate selected materials, clusters of notes to be perceived as groups--vertical or horizontal--and not ironed out in a "scale." The whole is not conceived as twelve-tone: the B-flat of the E-flat minor triad, for example, is not simply another spelling of the A-sharp of the F-sharp major triad, but arises from a separate impulse and is heard as a different tone. A twelve-note "scale" of the bass layer could be extracted: C/C-sharp/E-flat/D-sharp/E/F/F-sharp/G/A/B-flat/A-

215

sharp/<u>B</u>. This could also be reduced to a ten-note scale by elimination of the enharmonics. Either would be misleading, for the reality of the layer lies in the triads and their deployments in the bass, in open position, with roots spanning the augmented fifth <u>E</u>-flat to <u>B</u>.

The rhythmic life of the work is rich: theatrical time, measured succession, and metrical sections are free to interact as a significant element in contrast and coherence. The notation has been substantially clarified, reflecting the intention of the pieces (and anti-metrical notation obviated, which is a great help to the performer). The eleventh piece incorporates all three types: the approximate connections of the subjects are theatrical (that is, as dependent upon acoustical and psychological elements of a particular performance, but structured as three-second units); the treble layer is measured but not metered, so that the two rising figures are heard as two forms of the same idea; the Chopin quotations are in 4/4 meter. Two of the pieces have meter signatures, and all of them contain measured elements.

As a whole, <u>Makrokosmos</u>, <u>Volume I</u> is a succession of opulent images, each one complete, and strung into a coherent whole through contrast, inter-sectional reference, the grouping into three shaped parts (again a crystal growth from smaller to larger vectors), and a judicious over-all balance. Except for the inventiveness in the devising of the particular techniques of performance, the work is not innovative: much wilder pianistic free-for-alls preceded Crumb's work by nearly half a century. What characterizes the work is the relation of these effects to the musical ideas they support and embody. In preferring the appropriate to the surprising, musical effectiveness to unconnected flamboyance, Crumb became part of a continuum of composers who, like Mozart, declined merely to astonish his listeners (for which crime he labeled Clementi a "charlatan"), seeking instead to enlarge them.

Chamber Music with Solo Voice

Crumb's expanding world of piano idiom and its concomitant role in the delineation of form, as evidenced in the <u>Five Pieces for Piano</u> in 1962, led inevitably to the extension of the piano with percussion instruments, as well as to an increase in the

216

number of techniques in the use of the piano itself (most of these on the strings and hence basically percussion in type). Chamber music of percussion instruments came into considerable focus in the 1960s, and Crumb's interest in percussion instruments was very much of its time. But this "new world" came at a time when the composer was deeply interested in the poetry of Lorca, and the expansion into percussion choirs coincided with Crumb's personal exploration of the human voice, not choral (as with the Polish avant-garde), but solo. Lorca's work, full of darkling imagery--the night, time lost, water, and death--found fertile ground in Crumb's creative thought, and in the next decade Crumb would explore three worlds at once: the imagery of Lorca, the human voice, and the potential of percussion instruments.

Night Music I

The first of the Lorca works was Night Music I (1963), for soprano, keyboard, and percussion. "Keyboard" means a pianist who also plays celesta; "percussion" means two players: one with xylophone, glockenspiel, antique cymbals (three mounted, three detached), tenor drum, suspended cymbal, and timpano; the second with vibraphone, marimba, bongos, triangle, bell, and three tam-tams (one of which is to be used as a "water gong" by immersing it half-way in a tub of water).

Night Music I is a set of seven nocturnes, conceived, like several of Crumb's works, as a mirror form with a central focus. Five of the Nocturnes are instrumental pieces; two (*) are settings of Lorca texts.

```
      I. Giocoso, estatico
     II. "Piccolo Serenata"--grazioso
   *III. Lirico;  fantastico
     IV. Vivace;  molto ritmico
    *V. Oscuro;  esitante, quasi senza movimento
     VI. "Barcarola"--delicato e tenero
    VII. Giocoso, estatico
```

As usual, Crumb set up the work with clarity of title: the first and last nocturnes are based on the same materials: alternating sections of measured (M) and unmeasured (n) structures, eleven measures in all:

```
3   1   2   1   3   1
M   n   M   n   M   n
```

In the opening movement, luminous splashes of
sound (of piano, celesta, glockenspiel, vibraphone,
and triangle) seem regular but not metered;   the
unmeasured sections are labeled "senza misura;
improvvisato," and deal with repeated-note patterns
(Example 3-A).   In the final nocturne the measured
sections are identical with those in the first;   but
the unmeasured sections are labeled "senza misura;
oscuro e minaccioso" and deal with tremolos.

The second and sixth nocturnes are set pieces,
the second a "little serenade," the sixth a barcarole.
They are short and piano-centered (the serenade is for
piano and celesta only).

The third and fifth are settings of Lorca poems;
the third, "La Luna Asoma" (The Moon Rises), a surreal-
istic series of four short stanzas of ominous night
visions;   the fifth, "Gacela de la terrible Presencia"
(Gacela--an Arabic verse form--of the terrible Presence), eight couplets presenting parallel fragments of
thought in the ancient tradition, and based in juxtapositions of physical and metaphysical concepts, such as

Example 3-A

Night Music I
Notturno I, Measures 7 and 8

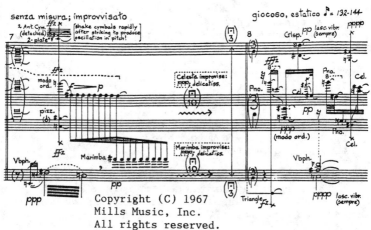

218

Example 3-B

Night Music I
Vocal techniques

1.

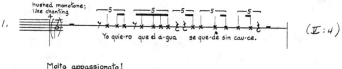

2.

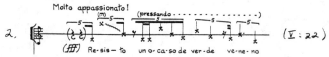

3.

4.

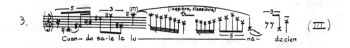

5.

Example 3-C

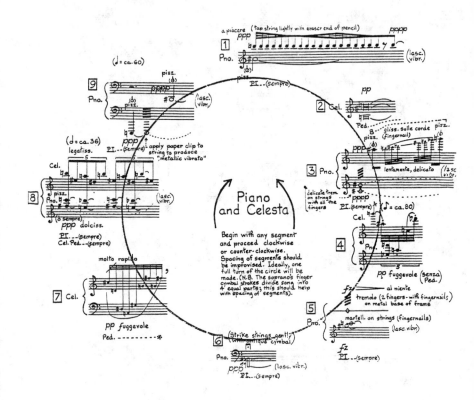

"the broken arches where time suffers." The two songs provide the opportunity to set forth a continuum of controlled vocal techniques between speech and song. Sprechstimme (Example 3-B) includes plain speech (with no musical notation at all), a flat-line notation (1), a semi-specified intonation against a single line (2), and an almost-specified pitch notation, with and without staves (3). Song includes humming, sotto voce, and normal singing (4), but also, to complete the circle, a flat-line "uncolored" voice becoming speech (5). Like most polarities, speech and song here are no longer two choices, but are two defining ends of a continuum, the whole central area of which was to be explored, in this and ensuing works.

Crumb experimented with chance effects in the nocturnes: the pianist, for example, is asked to improvise for ten seconds in the serenade. The moon of the first song is represented on the page as a circle of elements (one circle for piano and celesta, another for the percussions). Players may start anywhere on the circle and proceed in either direction (Example 3-C).

The presence of the voice, and the size of the songs--the second is an extended form--gives them a strong focus. The danger of a weak center-piece was, of course, keen. Crumb avoided it by having the fourth nocturne emerge as the most forceful of the group: it is loud, accented, thickly scored, and closely concatenated (A), and it contains a long crescendo for the bongos (B) that whips up a considerable broth, and which is repeated (after a variation of A) on the mounted antique cymbals. The form of the piece is ABABc, two pairs plus a coda, a form of coherent and contrasting energy spheres.

The form, like a mirror, reflects from a central position outward; but the mirror metaphor does not convey the vitality of the central section(s), and a more accurate one is of a semi-circle, a form rising to a rhythmically vital central movement, then falling away from it.

The techniques evidenced in Night Music I were refined and deepened in a number of volumes: four volumes called Madrigals (two in 1965, two in 1969, all for soprano and various instruments), Songs, Drones, and Refrains of Death (1968), for baritone, and Night of the Four Moons (1969), for contralto. In these the vocal and instrumental techniques tighten; longer lists of instructions, including precise stage set-ups, are given in the prefaces; and the writing-- particularly for the voice--is surer. The definition of the structural unit is vital to delineation of structure, and the unit--a phrase or event--is set off by rests like a Medieval punctus, with little overlapping and either more repetition (obsessive patterns) or very little (rhetorical form). An increased battery is apparent: <u>Songs, Drones, and Refrains of Death</u>, for example, divides thirty-five instruments (counting sets, such as "four antique cymbals," as one) between two percussion players. The (electric) piano is included, the pianist also playing (electric) harpsichord, but no longer central, vying for preeminence not only with the singer (who plays seven percussion instruments and must also sing into a speaking tube), but with (electric) guitar and (electric) contrabass. Altogether, six people manage fifty instruments.

The Performance Notes outline the spectrum of vocal techniques, from "half-whispered" and "whispered" to "half-sung," "normal `bel canto' singing," "falsetto" (indicated as a harmonic), and "unvoiced singing." Refinements are noted in the score.

Example 4-A

<u>Songs, Drones, and Refrains of Death</u>
Refrain One: Primitively, with quasi-mechanical rhythm
Opening

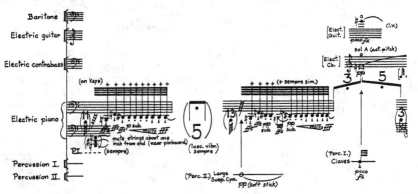

Example 4-B

Songs, Drones, and Refrains of Death
Refrain One: Primitively, with quasi-mechanical rhythm,
    Second section

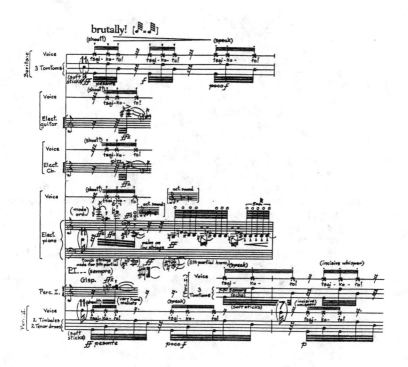

Time has become theatrical, with the lengths of
delineated rests stated in seconds (Example 4-A);
many sections are notated in "meters" that help the
performer group an event but are not perceivable to
the listener (Example 4-B). Techniques of singing on
syllables added to the texts ("Isai-ko-to" in Example
4-B), with instrumentalists joining to create choral
accents, recall Lutoslawski's Trois poèmes d'Henri
Michaux (1963), but Crumb's reference is broader and
includes, of course, the solo voice. Toward the end
of the decade, Crumb tended to use oriental idioms
(Far Eastern and "Moorish" techniques, the latter
perhaps a natural result of submersion in Spanish

223

thought); to seek significant continuation of impulse (as in the alto flute solo that begins the Night of the Four Moons); and to symbolize structure both to the ear and to the eye.

Ancient Voices of Children

By 1970, Crumb's tools were remarkably well honed, and in that year he completed two works that together defined his mature style. One of these was Ancient Voices of Children, a musical evocation of a central mood derived by Crumb from fragments of Lorca poems. The five fragments deal with lost childhood, memory, and a climactic and definitive invocation to Christ to return to the child's soul.

The work is scored for soprano, boy soprano, oboe, mandolin, harp, electric piano, and three percussion stands (with twenty-eight instruments). The mandolin players also play musical saw and mounted antique cymbals, the oboe player plays a small chromatic harmonica, the soprano two mounted glockenspiel plates. The battery calls for vibraphone, marimba, tubular bells, tam-tams, finger cymbals, Japanese temple bells, Tibetan prayer stones, tuned tom-toms, maracas, and sleighbells, as well as the more "usual" tambourine, triangle, claves, and timpano.

The design format is an arch form:

    1. Song I
    2. Dances of the Ancient Earth
    3. Song II
    4. Song III & Dance of the Sacred Life-Cycle
    5. Song IV
    6. Ghost Dance
    7. Song V

The central fourth movement is both a song and a dance; it begins with the voice, singing alone, and then incorporates the song into the instrumental dance. The dance (in reflection of the title) is notated as a circle of elements for oboe, piano, mandolin, harp, and soprano, to be performed in specified order two and a half times (with an alternative vocal element--for boy soprano--the second time). But there are no "chance" elements in the circle (both the events and the order of events are specified); notation in linear order would have been possible.

"Chance" exists only in the superimposition of the circle elements as an independent over an ostinato, a bolero rhythm, in the drums, with a relentless beat and a long crescendo (then decrescendo), and this is a variable of rhythmic detail, not of effect. But the central movement is not the only forceful one; the outer movements are substantial, and although the central Dance/Song is climactic, the other movements are potent enough to deny it unchallenged supremacy.

The emotional life of the work is independent of the arch format. It is suggested by the designations of the movements:

1. Very free and fantastic in character
2. Very rhythmic
3. Musingly
4. Freely; with dark, primitive energy
5. Hushed, intimate; with a sense of suspended time
6. Eerie, spectral
7. Luminous

The form is strong, with a forceful opening pair of movements, a dark central four, and a spacious final movement whose strength (like the strength of the work as a whole) lies in progression and arrival rather than in complexity or simple rhythmic and dynamic vigor. The indication "Luminous" suggests a mood rather than a tempo or dynamic level; the finale does not balance the opening, but transcends it, as the emotional form transcends the arch structure. The emotional life of the work is thus superimposed on the format in a strong progression which is fulfilled in the long final movement.

Ancient Voices of Children is built of three basic elements: the solo voice as song; the solo voice as instrument (singing syllables); and the instruments, variously solo (particularly oboe) and employed as ensemble.

The vocal and oboe lines are melismatic and vivid, with Moorish qualities of both basic intervals and decorative shakes, slides, and grace notes. The Moorish character is strong also in the use of the oboe itself, particularly in the low register (and with the instruction "raw, primitive, shawm-like"), and in the use of gongs and delicate high (pitched and unpitched) percussion instruments. The over-all

Example 5-A

Ancient Voices of Children
1, Very free and fantastic in character, Introduction

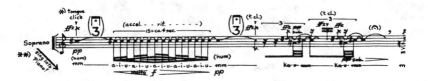

Example 5-B

Ancient Voices of Children
1, Very free and fantastic in character, cadenza

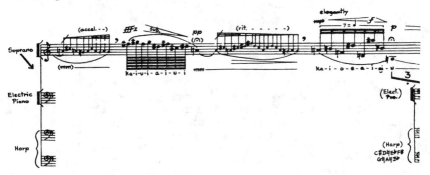

Example 5-C

Ancient Voices of Children
1, Very free and fantastic in character, text entry

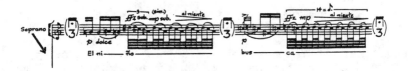

fabric is thus, for Crumb, relatively restricted in types of sound, though unusually robust in effect; the work unfolds within a demarcation that tightens it and gives it greater thrust.

The work begins with a substantial introduction for the solo voice as instrument; Crumb has chosen percussive consonants and hard vowels for incisive elements and softer sounds for supple ones. The slight interjections of electric piano and harp serve to divide the introduction into three sections, which do not duplicate materials, but expand upon a pitch and rhythmic core. An opening C-sharp (Example 5-A) expands to a figure that will prove vital: an augmented fourth with a major third within. This figure in turn expands in cadenza (Example 5-B). The increasing tension and drive of the solo culminate in a loud rapid rising figure (of unspecified pitches) and lead to the song proper, after a three-second pause. The song begins with solo voice softly spinning out the main element as a melisma on the word "niño," child (Example 5-C); that word, which begins and ends the text, is the heart of the work. The song concludes with a line of text divided among the instrumentalists, followed by a coda sung by the boy soprano off-stage-- the alter-ego of the soprano (Example 5-D).

Example 5-D

Ancient Voices of Children
1, Very free and fantastic in character, Coda

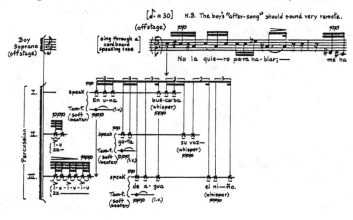

The Dances of the Ancient Earth begins with the "raw" oboe in a solo cognate with the introduction, but with an expanded accompanying contingent. The opening centers on F (Example 5-E), expanding first upwards to configurations including F/G/B, and then to concatenations of the figure in various forms and at various levels that produce undulating, ululating, dithyrambic gestures. These appear in the paperstrung

Example 5-E

Ancient Voices of Children
2, Dances of the Ancient Earth, opening phrase

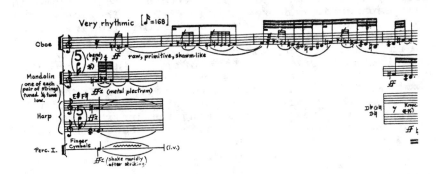

Example 5-F

Ancient Voices of Children
2, Dances of the Ancient Earth, middle section

harp and the mandolin, and finally in the beautiful, desiccated yet bright Tibetan prayer stones (Example 5-F). The Dances end in a concluding section with the scale passages at two speeds, the players reinforcing the three-note element with shouts.

The ensuing song presents a diametric contrast: a soft floating movement that is basically a dialogue between musical saw (which has the haunting, other-worldly quality of a theremin), the figure narrowed (to various enharmonic formulations of a major third with a minor third inside—such as the initial E-sharp/G-sharp/A in the electric piano), the time span widened, and the events rhythmically free (there is no meter signature). The soprano whispers through a speaking tube; the dialogue between the whispered song and the piano involves the pianist altering pitches with a chisel, a poignant effect of great delicacy. A pianissimo breathy rising glissando (on "Ah") in the voice is pitched; it is followed by a gentle melisma. A vocalise hum (on "mm") incorporating the narrowed figure concludes the movement. This, the most restrained of the songs, serves both as an afterpiece to the rough Dances and as a connection to the large central movement.

The double movement combining the central song (of five) and the central dance (of three) is a complex, layered piece. It opens with the greatest expansion of the three-note element, in a vocal introduction, sung in syllables (Example 5-G). This yields to a dialogue between soprano and boy soprano

Example 5-G

Ancient Voices of Children
4, Song III, opening

Freely; with dark, primitive energy ♩ = ca. 84

Soprano

ka-i- o, — Ka-i- o, — ha! ta-i-o-Ka, ta-i-o-Ka, ta-i-o-Ka!

(off-stage), metered and insistent, notated in semi-specific registers against a single staff line, and performed forte. The Dance of the Sacred Life-Cycle and the ostinato are superimposed on the dialogue, creating an opulent brocade and a rhythmic thrust that combine, in spite of the "dark" quality essential to the concept, in a coherent and forceful statement.

The afterpiece of the vigorous dance is also a quiet, contemplative song; the text is brief, and is stated at once by the soprano after an introduction of a low, throbbing, pianississississimo triad. The voice reduces the three-note figure to two before releasing the three briefly in a final melisma. This is answered as a second part, by the playing of "Bist du bei mir" (from the Anna Magdalena Bach Notenbuch) on a toy piano, gradually running down and not finishing--still over the throbbing pianississississimo triad, which is left as a cantilever of sound reaching to the Ghost Dance, which follows.

The Ghost Dance is a mandolin solo (played in "bottle-neck" style), four long phrases, two of them in dialogue with maracas (and with syllabic interjections by the maracas players), the third together with the maracas, and the last alone. The mandolin, in the high register and with that earthy technique, has a piquant sound, and the bending pitches are capable of stringent, penetrating effects; the third phrase is loud and pungent, and the fourth (a repetition of the third) is done solo, slowly and softly, the "slow motion" turning the sound into a supple, lambent afterimage of the preceding phrase. This too reaches toward the movement to follow, the final song.

The last movement begins with a substantial introduction (balancing rather than mirroring the vocal introduction of the first movement). Memories abound: elements of earlier movements, the oboe of the first Dance, an octave higher, becoming a reference to a Mahler phrase, and the voice, when it enters, expanding into a new expansion of the three-note figure (Example 5-H). The oboe player has left the stage just before the singer begins, and the main body of the last song is a dialogue between soprano and oboe, now off-stage, and increasingly more distant (and with a decreasing importance of the other instruments); the last long (six-phrase) oboe solo is a slow fade over a pianississississimo roll of sleighbells and a single pizzicato chord. A five-second fermata

Example 5-H

Ancient Voices of Children
7, Song V, entry of the voice

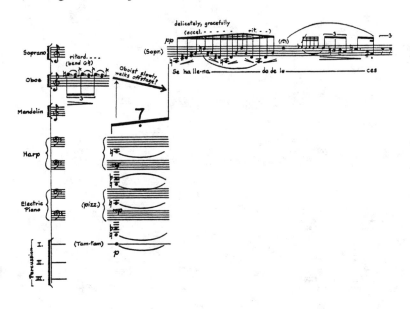

Example 5-I

Ancient Voices of Children
7, Song V, start of vocal climax

Example 5-J

Ancient Voices of Children
7, Song V, vocal climax

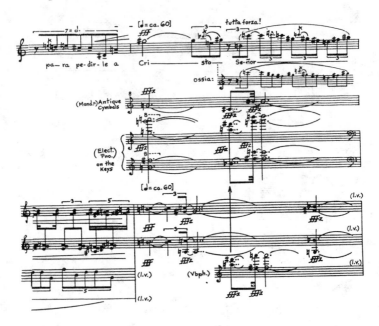

Example 5-K

Ancient Voices of Children
7, Song V, conclusion

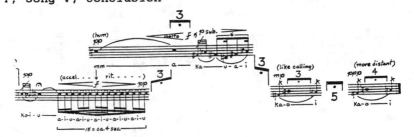

forms a caesura in preparation for the concluding sections.

First, the soprano sings the climactic invocations, starting slowly (Example 5-I), a clear line etched against a shining background of bells and tamtam, and rising to the most intense phrase of the work. This is a thickly-set phrase of unanimous impulse (Example 5-J) and sonorous splendor, allowing an operatic high G-sharp on the Name "Cristo" and a melisma ("tutta forza!") on the title "Señor", and ending with the figure D/F-sharp/G-sharp.

Second, the soprano sings the final phrase of text, alone, expressing the desire to be granted the return of "my ancient soul of a child;" the phrase goes from fortissimo to pianissimo, while slowing from sixteenth- to quarter-note motion, and falls to the lower register. During the phrase, the boy enters and moves to the piano.

The coda is a duet dialogue sung in syllables by the two singers into the piano (with no instruments except the sympathetic sounds of the piano, whose damper pedal remains depressed). The coda-dialogue is well and clearly shaped: an initial crescendo tremolo by the boy leads to a fortississimo, high-tessitura phrase by the woman; the boy answers, overlapping, then continues alone. Both decrescendo, so the transition to the quiet sound of the soprano's lower tremolo, though with crescendo, does not seem as forceful as the previous phrase. The boy answers with repeated notes, pianissimo (Example 5-K), the soprano picks up the pitch in a hum which is left as a bridge to her final statement of the original figure (now D/F-sharp/A-flat), and answered by the boy's final form of it: F/B/A, an inversion of D-sharp/A/C-sharp, with which the work had begun. The boy echoes it himself, and the music evaporates with this fragile evocation of the introduction.

In the end, it is not the generous and splendid color of the work which defines it but its tension between the pungent and the delicate: extrovert splashes of sound and introvert, haunting echoes; exotic brocade with comfortable, homely universals beneath. And it is not the lavish array, but the discipline and containment that brings so much power to the work as a formal structure. It reflects the textual premise in its ambiguity of number; although

233

sustained in a continuing series of solos and dialogues, the music yet creates the reality that all the
voices are one, that the experiences (the verbal and
the ineffable) are everyone's. It is one of the
mysteries of art that so vivid a specificity can speak
so powerfully to universality.

There is much of the universal in <u>Ancient</u> <u>Voices</u>
<u>of</u> <u>Children</u>: the mandolin, with each double course
tuned with one string a quarter-step flat and with
after-pitches, becomes oriental; the oboe sound and
its arabesques, the temple bells and prayer stones,
and the expanded fourth and its concatenating figures,
are oriental as well. References to Bach and Mahler
speak to Western traditional concert music. But some
pithy home-grown elements speak of the root and soil
of American heritage that never knew a concert hall:
the harmonica, the sleighbells and musical saw,--and
the bottleneck technique, though put by Crumb to very
different service, is well known to mountain banjo
pickers. The toy piano is perhaps the most specific
sound of all, conjuring up visions of piano lessons in
childhood, an image with which the musical clockwork
is not inconsistent.

The strong central thrust of the work justifies
its divergent elements: it is a good honest eclecti-
cism that forges a meaning from components previously
held to be disparate. That thrust may in part come
from two important features of the work which derive
from universal musical practices that transcend style.

The singing to syllables, which provides the
opportunity equally for idiomatic virtuosity and a
compelling unity, is a potent symbol. For Crumb's
purposes it can stand for those elements of experience
that rise in the heart beyond the limits of words,
ultra-violet to the spectrum of conventional feelings.
But singing to syllables is known from earliest times
and is found on all continents, north and south.

The vital three-note figure spanning the augmented
fourth has roots in universal practice as well. The
cognate figure, spanning the perfect fourth (as <u>D</u>/<u>F</u>/<u>G</u>)
seems to have been basic even in ancient days, and it
has taken on a variety of intonations and expansions
in modern times. It is common in Crumb's work. But
the expansion to the augmented fourth is specifically
eastern and supports the "Moorish" effect of the
whole. But even so, the figure has the strength of

the elemental and adds earthiness and musical energy
to the work.

For the public, Ancient Voices of Children was,
in the early 1970s, a surprising, even confusing
display of virtuoso sound effects. But within Crumb's
creative life it was a reining-in; it is a disciplined
work, a stunning coming together of idea and technique
at the right time in the composer's development. Thus
it does not have the selfconscious congratulatory aura
of a work at the outer edge of a composer's technique.
It is, if not Crumb's text, Crumb's gathering of
fragments of Lorca texts into a new meaning, a meaning
that the texts themselves leave incomplete and which
is fulfilled in the musical entirety.

The Instrumental Chamber Music

Between 1962 and 1978 Crumb composed seven
chamber works for more than one instrumentalist. Two
of them are for piano only (four hands: Makrokosmos
IV) or for two pianos and percussion (Makrokosmos
III); five of them are for combinations traditionally
classed as chamber music. Those before 1970 lay
within an expansion of instrumental techniques parallel
to the vocal works of the same period and centered in
the piano as pivotal to the texture and hence, in
Crumb's terms, to the design.

Eleven Echoes of Autumn, 1965, for violin, also
flute, clarinet, and piano, completed in 1966, is an
excellent example of Crumb's reaching toward expanded
materials in fabric and form. The movements are:

1. Fantastico	Piano only
2. Languidamente, quasi lontano (hauntingly)	Piano and violin
3. Prestissimo (Allegro possibile)	All players
4. Con bravura	All players
5. Three cadenzas, all "Dark,	Flute cadenza
6. intense," all with	Violin cadenza
7. broken piano circles	Clarinet cadenza
8. Feroce, violento	All players
9. Serenamente, quasi lontano (hauntingly)	All players
10. Senza misura (gently undulating)	All players
11. Adagio; like a prayer	Piano and violin

A modified semicircular form, the eleven sections begin with a short piece for piano alone. The second expands to two players, and the third to the full component. The eleven pieces clarify themselves into an introduction and three larger sections, by the use of fermatas at the end of the first and fourth pieces, and by the setting off as a significantly different central section a series of three cadenzas. This long triple section is symbolic in itself as an incorporation of the Lorca quotation " . . . and the broken arches where time suffers," a text part or all of which is whispered before each cadenza begins. The piano layer that lies under each cadenza is a broken circle (Example 6-A). An "attacca subito" signals immediate progession into the eighth piece. The last two movements are very short and serve as a single decrescendo, the violin and piano alone again in the last piece, then the violin dropping out to leave the piano to complete the last movement with the short figure with which the work had begun. Thus the work is both

Example 6-A

Eleven Echoes of Autumn, 1965
Eco 6, Dark, intense; the broken circle

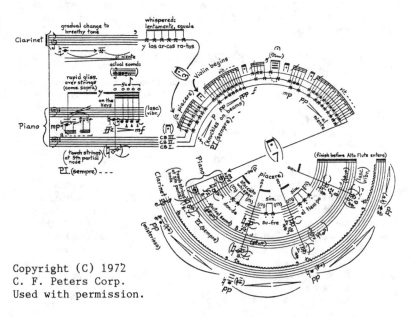

an arch, broken in the center by the threefold cadenza, and a clear multi-section form.

Crumb is a careful notator, calling for precise effects and making sure that the performer can grasp both the technique and the result. For the pianist, for example, the dialogue of the opening solo, which could have been notated on a single staff, is opened up into its dynamic/speed levels on five staves; and the added help of giving the "actual sounds," which is not mandatory (one might assume a violinist to know that high G-sharp is the fifth partial of E), gives a ready reference. Similarly, the pianist is told on which crossbeam to strike with knuckles (Example 6-A). The instrumental techniques are expanded in ways that would become more important, chiefly through the extensive use of grace-note figures that expand range (Example 6-B), speaking over the flute mouth-hole, and

Example 6-B

Eleven Echoes of Autumn, 1965
Eco 5, Dark, intense; start of the flute cadenza

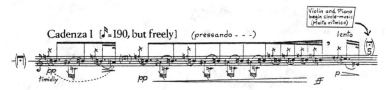

playing into the piano strings (while the pianist holds the damper pedal down). The violinist is asked to bow above the left hand, to play with the bow-hairs "completely" slack, and with other non-traditional techniques. The instructions, typical of Crumb, are careful as to both what to do and what to expect:

> Hold the violin like a mandolin. Make a very rapid tremolo on the G string with the fingernail (forefinger) or the fingernail and thumbnail (held closely together). A very rapid lateral motion of the nail should produce an effect resembling a plectrum tremolo on a mandolin.

Crumb's interest in harmonics extended to whistling, which is normally a fourth partial, combining a whistle with standard violin harmonics, in which he presumably desired the flat tone of an untrained whistler.

Black Angels

In fact, the violin techniques are of special interest, for they came to a fruition in 1970 with the completion of Black Angels: Thirteen Images from the Dark Land, the second of the works of that year to define Crumb's mature style. It is a compendium of new string techniques and a textbook on number structure as an extra-musical element ordering the shape of musical components. The "dark" images, now without text, became a congeries of spooky titles and directives that suggest a spectral battle between Thirteen and Seven, the midpoint in an arch form of thirteen movements.

Crumb detailed the structure in the score:

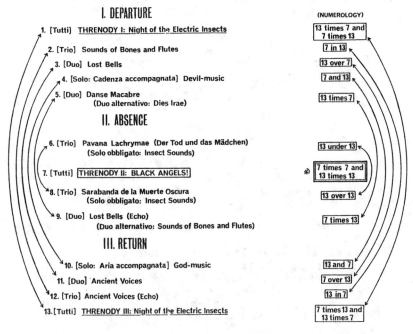

I. DEPARTURE

(NUMEROLOGY)

1. [Tutti] THRENODY I: Night of the Electric Insects — 13 times 7 and 7 times 13

2. [Trio] Sounds of Bones and Flutes — 7 in 13

3. [Duo] Lost Bells — 13 over 7

4. [Solo: Cadenza accompagnata] Devil-music — 7 and 13

5. [Duo] Danse Macabre
   (Duo alternativo: Dies Irae) — 13 times 7

II. ABSENCE

6. [Trio] Pavana Lachrymae (Der Tod und das Mädchen)
   (Solo obbligato: Insect Sounds) — 13 under 13

7. [Tutti] THRENODY II: BLACK ANGELS! — 7 times 7 and 13 times 13 ✳

8. [Trio] Sarabanda de la Muerte Oscura
   (Solo obbligato: Insect Sounds) — 13 over 13

9. [Duo] Lost Bells (Echo)
   (Duo alternativo: Sounds of Bones and Flutes) — 7 times 13

III. RETURN

10. [Solo: Aria accompagnata] God-music — 13 and 7

11. [Duo] Ancient Voices — 7 over 13

12. [Trio] Ancient Voices (Echo) — 13 in 7

13. [Tutti] THRENODY III: Night of the Electric Insects — 7 times 13 and 13 times 7

✳ This central motto is also the numerological basis of the entire work

238

There is no symbolic moral structure, however.
The larger three parts are built of 5, 4, and 4
movements, a separate rhythm superimposed upon the
arch, so that the powerful central movement (7) comes
between two short, staid trios playing archaic strains
(the second followed by an "echo"). The scheme of
movements, in musical terms, reveals the balanced
imbalance of the total structure; perhaps a more
important balance inheres in deployment of forces
within the quartet (given here as numbers indicating
the members of the quartet from first violin--1--to
cello--4):

```
 1. Vibrant, intense!                    1 2 3 4
 2. Delicate and somewhat mechanical      1 2   4
 3. Remote, transfigured                      2   4
 4. In romantic-phantastic style          1 │2 3 4│
 5. Grotesque, satirical                      2 3

 6. Grave, solemn;   like a consort          2 3 4
       of viols
 7. Furiously, with great energy!         1 2 3 4
 8. Grave, solemn;   like a consort       1   3 4
       of viols
 9. (continues from #8)                       2   4

10. Adagio (with profound calm)           │1 2 3│ 4
11. (continues from #10)                  1 2
12. Grazioso, flessibile                  1 2 3
13. Disembodied, incorporeal              1 2 3 4
```

In the tenth piece, called "God-music," the cello
solo, balancing the first violin solo of the fourth
movement, is accompanied by the three other instruments
bowing across "crystal glasses" to create a "glass
harmonica." The cello plays normally (on the cello),
"molto cantabile," a long turning melody, in the high
register and designated as "Vox Dei." The players are
also asked to play maracas and tam-tams, to bow above
the left hand, and to play "pedal tones," as well as
to call out numbers (from one to thirteen) in seven
languages.

The three tutti movements (#1, 7, and 13) are the
most remarkable, however, because of the raw sound of
the electrified instruments, particularly in the
stunning sudden fortississimo bursts, made all the
more raucous by tremolo figures (Example 7-A). The
jeux d'esprit of the whole concept of the work is
mirrored in an exuberant notation, at which Crumb is

Example 7-A

Black Angels
1, Threnody I. Vibrant, intense!;   third system

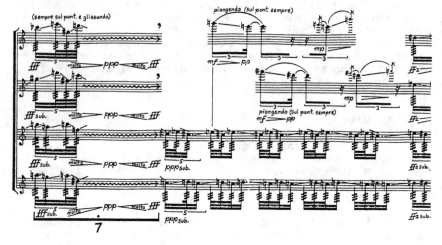

Example 7-B

Black Angels
7, Threnody II. Furiously, with great energy.
The note *** at the beginning of the system says
that the players are calling out the number 13
in Swahili and gives the correct pronunciation.

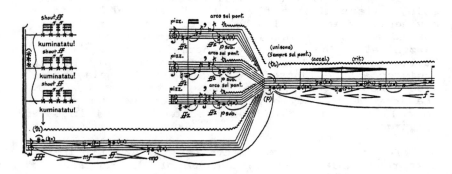

a master (Example 7-B). Enjoyment of the score is
keen, and the realization that the notation is clear,
and in most respects simple, comes only after appreciation of its aesthetic visual quality. In putting
extra-musical symbolism into the notation, Crumb
touched the Medieval mind once more.

Voice of the Whale

Originally conceived (and published) with the
Latin name, Vox Balaenae, with the English subtitle
For Three Masked Players, Voice of the Whale, composed
in 1971, superimposes the image of the whale sounds
(which had been recorded two years earlier and which
Crumb captures with eerie accuracy) upon a movement
structure symbolizing the creation of the world.

The three instruments, all electrified, are
flute, cello, and piano. The flute sings and plays (at
once) a complex fioratura; the cello (tuned to B/F-
sharp/D-sharp/A) introduces a variety of harmonic
techniques, including glissandos and a "Seagull
effect." The pianist draws basically from the techniques developed in the Five Pieces and other earlier
works.

A jewel of a piece, it unfolds as a set of
Variations on Sea-Time (A Sea-Theme and five variations
named for great ages in the formation of the earth:
Archeozoic, Proterozoic, etc.), framed by an introductory Vocalise (" . . . for the beginning of time") and
the concluding Sea-Nocturne (" . . . for the end of
time"). Crumb wrote of it:

> The concluding Sea-Nocturne ("serene,
> pure, transfigured") is an elaboration of
> the Sea-Theme. The piece is couched in the
> "luminous" tonality of B major and there are
> shimmering sounds of antique cymbals (played
> alternately by the cellist and flutist). In
> composing the Sea-Nocturne I wanted to
> suggest "a larger rhythm of nature" and a
> sense of suspension in time. The concluding
> gesture of the work is a gradually dying
> series of repetitions of a 10-note figure.
> In concert performance, the last figure is
> to be played "in pantomime" (to suggest a
> diminuendo beyond the threshold of hearing!)[10]

The final movement does indeed have a five-sharp key signature and features guises of the "universal" figure C-sharp/D-sharp/F-sharp.

Crumb also envisioned theatrical components, and wrote of them:

> Each of the three performers is required to wear a black half-mask or (visor-mask). The masks, by effacing the sense of human projection, are intended to represent, symbolically, the powerful impersonal forces of nature (i.e., nature dehumanized). I have also suggested that the work be performed under a deep-blue stage lighting.[11]

In other works Crumb's staging directives have been given as suggestions, and although these specifications were obeyed in the premiere, other performances have not bowed to the theatrical fiat. This is a testimony to the strength of the work; the symbolic underpinning of the masks may or may not ring true (the "ages" of the variations are all pre-human, so who is to say?), but the work of music stands secure and without the need of extra-musical addenda.

The Orchestra

The expansion of forces that began with the Five Pieces for Piano in 1962, and which revealed Crumb's essence in works of small size, also included an orchestral work, perhaps of more importance to the composer's career than to his musical development, since it gained the Pulitzer Prize for him. Yet Crumb's treatment of the orchestra was interesting and important, and the single work for orchestra alone, Echoes of Time and the River, has proved to be of influence. Like Ancient Voices of Children and Voice of the Whale, Echoes of Time and the River was produced for television, an important venue for Crumb, since the visual aspects of the work were fundamental to its concept.

Echoes of Time and the River

Echoes of Time and the River (1967) has two subtitles, and each reveals aspects of the work that are close to its heart. First, it is subtitled Echoes

242

II, indicating that it had its genesis as a continuation of certain impulses in Eleven Echoes of Autumn, 1965, which preceded the orchestral work by a year. He dealt particularly with aspects of time bound up with the idea of echoes and of cosmic time (that is, of the music of the spheres and the creation of the universe) and pre-human worlds, along with Medieval ideas that were just beginning to be of influence in Crumb's musical thought. Ancient and Medieval thinkers equated time with gesture and motion, and Medieval musicians used both space and gesture in musical constructs and in performance.

The second subtitle of Echoes of Time and the River is Four Processionals for Orchestra. The four movements deal with intersections of time and space by including measured parades by certain members of the orchestra--on stage (a pale echo of Medieval church festivals in which performers drew their melodies across both exterior and interior spaces). The four movements carry "time" titles:

I. Frozen Time
II. Remembrance of Time
III. Collapse of Time
IV. Last Echoes of Time

The third and fourth movements are played as one, but the effect of random ordering throughout makes the entire work a single long movement, the last section a substantial coda with memories of earlier materials.

Crumb included a great many references to himself, most of them arcane (such as having his name incorporated into the rhythm of the xylophone part in Morse code), some of them exuberant (such as having the percussionists in the first procession recite "Montani semper liberi" ("Mountain men are always free," the state motto of West Virginia)--but he added a roguish question mark at the end. But the musically relevant comprise memories of his previous works (including the Lorca quote " . . . the broken arches where time suffers," which had appeared in both Night Music I and, with the broken circles, in the cadenzas of Eleven Echoes of Autumn), along with music of his earliest memories (mandolin idioms, the spiritual "Were You There When They Crucified My Lord?" disguised in string harmonics).

But it is the accessible which matters. And the

work replies to the questions concerning the use of the orchestra in new idioms, as an expanded chamber group. The music is amazingly Medieval in fabric, even in its love of the bell-like sounds, which serve to announce its beginning and then to close the work. The orchestral choirs are used separately, and they process separately: percussion in the first movement, brass in the second, then woodwinds (alone, then with brass), and finally strings, with bells. The processioners call out sometimes in syllables, using the syllables that Aristophanes had given his frogs, in a more conscious unity with the past. The diversity is clear enough.

Rhythmic motion, though carefully controlled in the score, is impossible to perceive as regular, though within events a clear impetus can often be felt. The long sustained sounds, like the single-tone events separated by seemingly random lengths of time, make the music hover, suspended, in the first movement. The second movement is the vivid center of the work, with a mountain of a crescendo and a concurrence of loosely related energetic figures (on stage and off). The third movement contains circles--as in earlier works--of elements to be layered freely into the fabric; it then gradually subsides into the coda. The figure of a descending second expands in space and time, to fourths majestically stretched and doubled upon themselves, rising, then falling from a central tone, whistled in a final fade that seems to condense all, to leave the adventure of physical and metaphysical time with the single irreducible element of the human presence.

Star-Child

If Echoes of Time and the River contracts into the finitude of human presence, Crumb's later work with orchestra, Star-Child (1977) begins with human consciousness and expands from it to a suggested transcendence of human limitation. Like Echoes of Time and the River, Star-Child is a twofold expansion. First, it is a development of ideas used earlier. And second, it is an enlargement of the chamber group with voice. The basis of the work is the soprano solo, set now into a stretching orchestral matrix, scored (as stated in a long subtitle) for Soprano, Antiphonal Children's Voices, Male Speaking Choir with Handbells (in the 1979 revision--originally, orchestra

244

members spoke and the children played the handbells), and Large Orchestra. Four conductors are required. It carries a subtitle, A Parable, and it uses metaphors developed from Music for a Summer Night; these newly-developed materials are based in but transcend medieval Latin texts, which (Crumb stated in his notes to the premiere program) "convey universal meaning." The Star-Child, from the earlier work, is associated with the "Children of Light" of John 12:36, which is the final text. Crumb returns to portions of the Dies Irae and adds lines from the Massacre of the Innocents (both thirteen-century texts). These verbal elements are superimposed upon orchestral layers deriving from the independent instrumental movements; of particular inmportance are the opening sections, Musica Mundana and Music of the Spheres, over which he projected a "progression from darkness (or despair) to light (or joy and spiritual realization)," symbolized by the playing of the handbells. With its four conductors, its geometric staging, and its references to tradition-al facets of the study of music in the Quadrivium, conjoined with clear concerns for a musical Rhetoric, Star-Child reveals Crumb as a peace-maker between Trivium and Quadrivium, spanning both views of his art in a single work.

It is a departure from Crumb's structural norm; it is not an arch form, even modified, but a progres-sion from those forces symbolized by the instruments to those symbolized by the voices, use of which is indicated with asterisk in the list of movements:

   I. Musica Mundana
  *II. Vox Clamans in Deserto
  III. Ascensus Potestatum Tenebrarum
  IV. Musica Apocalyptica
  *V. Adventus Puerorum Luminis
 *VI. Hymnus pro Novo Tempore

The opening Music of the Spheres establishes a ground of being, and the events transpire in layers over it (it is notated, of course, as a circle); the texts are Medieval--this is the movement that includes parts of the Dies Irae and the Massacre of the Inno-cents--with a final verse from the New Testament (John 12:36). The first text, in the second movement, is the Libera me, also from the Dies Irae, sung by the soprano; the Voice Crying in the Wilderness (II) of the title is never sung, but is represented by a solo trombone, who stands alone between singers (front of

245

the stage) and orchestra (in the rear, save those spaced around the hall). The crucial line of the Voice is that which follows in the scripture (but only suggested in the work): "Prepare Ye the Way of the Lord." It is this preparation which is the business of the third and fourth movements, within the metaphor of a progression from darkness to light, despair to joy. The Apocalyptic music, in the center, maintains Crumb's proclivity for putting the most active music at the midpoint of a work: it invokes the seven trumpets (five spaced throughout the hall, two on the stage) and the four horsemen (for percussionists each with four tom-toms), "a considerable racket, and a most exciting one,"[12] that "shakes the rafters."[13]

The fifth movement introduces the Star-Child, the idea expanded to Star-Children and then to the scriptural Children of Light--as well as boys on the stage. "Star-Child" had been used in Makrokosmos II as the subject of a hymn (Hymn for the Advent of the Star Child), and this had been developed in Makrokosmos III, in the third movement, The Advent, which had culminated in a Hymn for the Nativity of the Star-Child. Here, in the new work, the text is shared in dialogue between the soprano and the children, climaxing in the text from John (12:36): "While ye have light, believe in the light, that ye may be the children of light," sung by the soprano. The children respond, but symbolically: their voices are transmogrified into handbells--they have become the light.

The work is powerful; Crumb's imaginative canvas of "ingenious sonorities" and "moments of breathtaking beauty"[14] is vital to the progression, leading from the dark to the luminous over the leisurely course of the work; the vital musical element in the structure is the use of subjects of a variety of length. In his earlier works, Crumb's creative process was essentially Baroque and rhetorical, whether for voices or instruments; he presented a series of gestures, phrases, or events which established an organic logic by dialogue, alternation of performers, intensification, or accumulation, all techniques characteristic of monophonic structures. Here the layers move independently, overlapping in varying degrees, with repetition of certain subjects and with interpenetration of elements, techniques characteristic of polyphonic structures. Some of the intense delicacy is lost in so vast a deployment of forces--critics found the work too finely calibrated for "so populous an ensemble" in

which "the intentness is lost."[15] But to this the
enriched structural texture replies with meanings
unavailable to the more finely-etched chamber works.
It may be that in requiring huge assemblies for such
introvert and subtle personal statements, Crumb lost
the dimension of suitable freight, an old musical law
which would claim that a large orchestra should present
large and socially robust ideas.

In his notes for <u>Makrokosmos, Volume I</u> (in 1972)
Crumb wrote of the pervasive issue of the "`larger
world' of concepts and ideas which influence the
evolution of a composer's language." Among these he
mentioned "the `magical properties' of music," an
article of faith, most probably, of every composer who
lives his or her art. Certainly one of the "magical
properties" of all the arts is the ability of a work
to speak simultaneously on many levels, and one
level of magical vitality is the capacity of a work to
reflect the personality and the inner luminosity of its
creator. <u>Star-Child</u>, in its progression out of
darkness, repeats, symbolizes, and ramifies the
composer's own progression from the darkling images
that dominated his earlier works to the numinous
vision of the Children of Light.

Notes

1. Erhard Karkoschka, Das Schriftbild der Neuen Musik (Moeck Verlag, 1966).

2. Saturday Review, May 25, 1968.

3. Edith Borroff, in the Ann Arbor Daily News, October 29, 1970.

4. Alan Rich in New York magazine. Quoted by Donal Henahan in "Crumb, the Tone Poet," in the New York Times Magazine, May 11, 1975, page 16.

5. "Composers in Focus," BMI, Winter 1976, page 19.

6. In Donal Henahan, Op. cit., page 56. The quotation is from Richard Wernick, Chairman of the Music Department of the University of Pennsylvania.

7. Notes to the recording of Makrokosmos I, Nonesuch H-71293, and reprinted by C. F. Peters in the score of that work.

8. Ibid.

9. Ibid.

10. Notes by the composer, in Modern American Music Series, First Recordings, M 32739.

11. Ibid.

12. Harold C. Schonberg in the New York Times, May 7, 1977.

13. William Bender, in Time, May 24, 1979.

14. Donal Henahan, in the New York Times, May 24, 1979.

15. Andrew Porter, in the New Yorker, May 27, 1977.

Chapter 5
STYLE AND HISTORY

The three composers of this study--Irwin Fischer,
Ross Lee Finney, and George Crumb--display the combination and interaction of personal and cultural factors
that make the consideration of musical style so
fascinating. Each style resulted from a strong
personality shaped by the path of education, at home
and in formal training, and by the venue of music in
which each immersed himself. To the extent that the
paths differ, the styles differ. Yet the deepest
fascination lies not in the cultural differences, the
heating of their craft at different forges and the
emerging of three incorporations of musical individuality, but in the central commitment which the three men
shared: in the end, the wonder lies not so much in
what separated them as in what their work has in
common.

First, all three have given voice to a conviction
that the profession of composing begins in craftsman-
ship, and have spoken with forceful respect for the
thorough grounding and mature skill which is sought
through continuing study and which transcends period or
type. Second, all three have acknowledged (as theory)
and exemplified (in practice) the commitment of craft
to the service of musical idea. And third, in their
careers they have succeeded in their several paths to
the extent that together they incorporate the shifts of
a half-century in works of depth and significance,
while retaining that individuality which both embodies
and transcends school and type.

Fischer

Irwin Fischer was without doubt the most important
of the conservatory composers at the end of that
tradition, and his career was a classic of that venue.
He sought to steep himself in the European tradition
that he honored, and to cherish it through entering it
and leading it forward, as a modernist, from within.
This he accomplished to the extent of out-distancing
the tradition as maintained in the conservatory which
was the center of his career, and, in the last seven
years of his life as a composer, working alone, without
connections to any school or camp, producing works of

249

unique character. While neither the administration nor the faculty of the American Conservatory of Music had any idea of his creative work, he was equally an outsider to the university critics and theorists. Essentially, Fischer as a composer was without a musical home after the second World War.

His teaching life lay within the conservatory only in part; he taught piano, organ, composition, theory, and conducting in other schools, at church, and at home (as well as at Camp Wonderland in the summer). He also directed an orchestra, maintained a church console, and gave recitals, all with undiminished vigor to the day of his death. He was, like his eighteenth-century counterparts, the master of a unique balance of skills and was involved with many kinds of work; he believed that his profession encompassed them all. Like the Kapellmeister or Surintendant at the roots of his tradition, he professed music and was a musician whole.

Fischer's mainsprings of influence were the great conservatory figures of the past, particularly those whose careers were most intimately connected with performance. Adolf Weidig, his composition teacher, was a living link to the German nineteenth-century tradition: he was born in Hamburg in 1867 and was a product of the Hamburg Conservatory as a violinist and of further study in Munich (under Riemann and Rheinberger); his father worked as a secretary/copyist to Brahms, who was his model. In Chicago from 1892, Weidig joined the faculty of the American Conservatory but also played (violin) in the Chicago Symphony Orchestra, was an assistant conductor to that group, was active in chamber music performances, composed and was widely known as a conductor, a theorist, and a critic.

Fischer found in him a potent model. But equally potent were Fischer's instrumental studies, which led him to the French school and to the organ works of J. S. Bach. Fischer met Bach as an organist, not as a theorist. His work as a conductor broadened and intensified his concern with instruments, and he became aware of the nature of the orchestral instruments in the fullest sense--of color, technique, and presence, at one with the creative impulse and as close to it as the muscle of an athlete to his will. As a student he was drawn to Nadia Boulanger, both for her sense of craft and for her respect for individuality of talent; but, after five years of work in his profession, he was drawn to Kodaly for his supreme sense of musical reality. He drew from Kodaly the respect for folk music that would become so important in his mature style. Fischer drew folk elements into the tradition, enlarging its content and meaning, expanding rather than deflecting it. For Fischer, the tradition was all-inclusive, strong and capable of change in the best sense. This confidence enabled him to plumb the depth of his style, while his naturally thoughtful nature led him to compose fewer works that span an amazing variety of style; to hear one of his works is to accomplish nothing in the possible recognition of another. And his confidence in his tradition enabled him to include humor--sometimes a positively delicious wit--in his work as well.

What was exceptional in Fischer was not his command of the tradition he espoused nor even his rejection of the idea that it was static or retroactive; it was, he thought, the normal thing to enter a tradition, conceiving it as fluid, with the purpose of changing it, moving it forward. What was exceptional was the degree to which he sought to integrate the forces of contemporary life and aesthetic communication, to consider the composition of music as the production of works that reach outward, speaking of music and through music, to issues of the nature of humankind and the world. For that was not at all within the goals of the conservatories, but was within the nature of the universities, where it was natural for department to reflect upon department. For a man of the conservatory tradition, this had to be accomplished as transcendence of that tradition's inward view, and for Fischer it was a slow and lonely growth; his last works, particularly the String Quartet (1972) and Statement: 1976, live in the granite integrity of that hard-won victory.

Finney

Ross Lee Finney was, within the concerns of this study, the most remarkable man of the transition. Like that of most composers of his generation, his training was a somewhat random convergence of forces and influences, random in the sense that the childhood experiences of music, so vital to the formation of both personality and musical style, are beyond the reach of choice. As Fischer's path was determined by the nature of his earliest musical experience (his move to the

251

city of Chicago and his work there with his first teacher), Finney's was decided by the splendid strength and diversity of his family's musical life, together with the isolation of the Valley City years and the happenstance that the university community was the natural habitat of his father. The coming together of these two factors was unlikely: the natural development of a midwestern musician was to have professional parents or to take lessons with a local conservatory-trained teacher and to follow in the path of that teacher.

Finney's university experience was exceptional; there was no program for training in composition at the University of Minnesota, and the young man had to make his own channels as a composer, while putting the broadening studies of the history and theory of music, along with more peripheral subjects, to his own use. Finney had no models, save of individuality.

Typically for the university composers of his generation--and in this, Sessions was a model--Finney elected to consider himself a composer, in the sense that he specialized within the profession of music. The university system, in cooperation with foundations in providing composers with whole years away from the campus, specifically for composition,[1] discouraged musical versatility, while also making composers responsible, not to the public or indeed any audience, but to the group of university faculty who determined the recipients of foundation funds. But from the beginning, Finney was exceptional: he continued to perform (though not his own music--he toured as an American folk singer), and he made himself available to performers wherever he taught. He composed choral works at Smith College and made the amicable interrela- tions with resident performers at the University of Michigan a consistent and fruitful concern. In spite of his consistent affiliation with university rather than with conservatory institutions, Finney displayed throughout his teaching years a consistent awareness of the total musical community. He wrote for performers, in the sense both of viewing himself as a craftsman who accepted commissions from performers and performing groups of whatever provenance, and also of providing to the performers the kind of music that is rewarding to play.

In his creation of a doctoral curriculum for the training of composers, Finney made use of the potential of the university structure, while sidestepping its faults: he encouraged his charges to seek interactions both in and out of the university, both in and out of music, he increased composer-performer interaction through student performances of student works--and discussion of the works; through the Composers Forum,[2] he avoided the commitment--or even the appearance of a commitment--with any theoretical camp. His students were not indoctrinated; he received them already at the graduate level (for the most part), and he strove chiefly to provide the frame in which they could develop self-criticism and musical independence, both of which he personally had good reason to value.

At a time when many university composers were defining themselves in theoretical camps and moving inward to an aesthetic stance which excluded responsibility toward either the performer or the audience, Finney maintained open channels of mutual responsibility in these directions. He strove to provide clear and helpful titles;[3] he strove to make process audible, and hence retained the traditional view that an informed audience finds the perception of unfolding structure to be a keen pleasure; he grew more and more sensitive to the musical reality of performance, and in such works as Two Acts for Three Players and Variations on a Memory made the physical presence of the performers a vital element of the concept and a pleasure for performers and listeners alike. It is not surprising that by far the most substantial backing of Finney's music has come from performers and performance organizations, many of them outside of the university community.

A transitional phase by definition attains no norms, and it is difficult to speak of Finney as typical or exceptional. But if his election of a university career can be considered typical of his generation, his refusal to allow the university to form his musical thought must be considered exceptional. In his early acceptance of serial theory, in his production of a great amount of chamber music, and in his placement of students in university positions throughout the country, Finney is representative though unusually prolific. But in his ready acknowledgment of the total musical interactions (as evidenced, for one, in the broad range of styles represented in the guest composers he brought to the University of Michigan), in his bending of serial technique to his own goals (choosing techniques which, like Fischer's, made the

253

music more vital to the listener), and in his disinclination to stamp students with his own theories and techniques, Finney remains strongly himself.

If Fischer displayed characteristics of the university composer unusual in a conservatory musician, Finney bent toward the conservatory tradition in his outward concerns. They shared both the commitment to craft and the awareness of tradition. Their generation was divided between those who acknowledged Western music and the Romantic--particularly the German--and post-Romantic styles, and those who were bent upon repudiating or even destroying them. The conservatory composers were "acknowledgers" fairly much as a bloc; the iconoclasts and destroyers were given harbor in the universities, fairly much as a bloc: Fischer as an acknowledger was representative, but Finney was not. The two men, working in opposing traditions, were similar in their refusal to be limited, similar in their growth in defining issues of larger and larger contexts. Fischer's <u>Statement</u>: <u>1976</u> is philosophically not far from Finney's <u>Earthrise</u> trilogy, and the layered sounds of Fischer's <u>String</u> <u>Quartet</u>, invoking cultural memory, are very like Finney's more personal <u>Variations</u> <u>on</u> <u>a</u> <u>Memory</u>, meeting at an Omega Point of shared concerns.

Crumb

George Crumb, like Fischer, embraced a tradition to lead it forward. From his entry to the University of Illinois in 1951, he was part of the new university structure. He was one of many doctoral graduates (from Michigan and other universities) who fanned out through the United States to build and to strengthen the university system as the producer of composers.

He benefited directly from Finney's pedagogy; Finney's gifts as a sower of seeds is nowhere clearer than in Crumb's success in guiding and disciplining himself once he was off on his own.

Like his teacher, Crumb acknowledges the Western tradition. He has consistently made referenece to his predecessors, acknowledging them by direct quotation in his music as well as in his titles: Bach, Beethoven, Schubert, Chopin, Strauss, Mahler (certainly a German apotheosis) and Bartok.[4]

Crumb also carries tradition forward. The arch form, important to his predecessors, he rethought. For earlier composers, from Brahms through the Fischer-Finney generation, this was a mirror form, usually with stable beginning and the center a kind of development, less stable. For Crumb the arch form is not a mirror image; the center is sought, from less stable to more stable elements, and the most compelling central section seems to define what preceded it. Seen as a whole, such a form is like water when a pebble hits it: the periphery expands, wavering, enhancing but not disturbing the defining center.

Crumb turned also to the new techniques, built up by the radicals of the preceding generation, and attempted new means of wielding them into significant forms; this meant pulling them into the craft (where their originators in many cases had no intention of placing them).

Crumb's craft, to which he brought new sounds of his own as well as those inherited from others, necessitated the consideration of musical "events" as single elements, each unified subject made like a fabric of interwoven colors; Crumb's structures required the techniques of monophony, the techniques of succession developed in Medieval Europe (and with ties to music the world over).[5] Crumb's natural proclivity is toward additive structures: the crystalization of small elements in the Sonata for Solo Violoncello, as early as 1955, was similar to techniques of West African structure.[6] He developed these techniques in the chamber works, with and without voice, of the 1960s, and they culminated in Ancient Voices of Children (1970), in which the Medieval structures are incorporated in sibling "Moorish" sounds. This work also yields readily to analysis in monophonic terms, which enlighten it. In turning to a strongly exotic fabric, Crumb was speaking to issues of philosophic and musicological concern that were common in universities after the second World War. He was, it seemed, the fair-haired boy of the university community, with awards from virtually every important Foundation and in a position of growing if tacit leadership in American music.

Yet it is here, strangely enough, where he would seem to be so representative of university interests, that Crumb is in fact independent (and has never sought leadership--and may in fact decline to take it on as a conscious mantle). For his work is not with ethnomusicological phenomena but with exotica; his development of the sonorous body had been carried out in his own studio, a well-equipped, spacious room at the back of his house, where he precedes every effect called for so carefully in his scores with hands-on experiments. He is one of the composers that Ross Lee Finney has designated as "American tinkerers," men in the tradition not of erudition but of practical know-how. Nothing in Crumb's music, no seemingly far-out effect, is theoretical; everything has been tried and found practicable and dependable. In these experiments Crumb has used whatever has come to his attention, from the mountain music of his boyhood, from his tool case, or even from the kitchen, from whatever he has heard or read--in short, within the homely tradition of the inventor rather than the erudite speculation of the university scientist.

It is precisely this which is Crumb's essence, and in it lies his independence of the university tradition. For the apprenticeship tradition had cradled him as an infant and sustained his early musical yearnings, in the person of his father, and had given him his first college-level training (at the Mason College of Music and Fine Arts). He grew up with a native curiosity, which his father fostered gently by quietly providing avenues for musical growth; and he found in Finney a mentor who similarly accepted his musical personality--Charleston in the 1930s had something in common with the Valley City of Finney's boyhood--and gave him much of the same indirect support. Finney nourished the capacity for discipline but made no attempt to deflect the essence. And like both Fischer and Finney, Crumb has that ability to protect that interior creative essence. He is, like the two older men, entirely genuine.

It is in part Crumb's genuineness which has brought him so much public acclaim. It was also in part the luck that his extra-musical concerns (particularly his fascination with "dark" images and the writings of Lorca), as well as the Medieval and exotic fabrics that he enjoyed, happened to be high in the public mind, especially of the younger generation; in this he had the force of a musical bellwether. In 1973 at a performance of <u>Ancient</u> <u>Voices</u> <u>of</u> <u>Children</u>, Crumb was besieged by clamoring highschoolers asking for his autograph. Even Crumb's "almost desperate reticence"[7] has contributed to an image of leadership: in a time when the young are bombarded with saturating communication, silence may have taken on the glamor of a frontier.

Conservative vs. Avant-Garde

In Crumb, the ascendance of the university system is made plain. His is the first generation to have been given advance training in the university programs leading to the doctoral degree in the post-War "complete" university departments (or accredited schools) after the subsumption of the conservatory elements.

The advantages of the younger man are perhaps most clearly seen in the matter of publishing. Publication was part of the university hegemony early on, but more specifically of the northeastern schools, since New York was the heart of that industry and publishers called on university advice near at hand. It is an extremely powerful influence. The shift to university control can be seen in Fischer's career: he had no trouble getting early works published--his early songs and organ pieces--but was unpublishable by the time he was thirty-five. Finney, as a midwestern composer had difficulties being taken seriously in the east (as Crumb would have, but only briefly), and had to develop publishing connections slowly over the years; But Crumb, with clear support from the university system from the days of his doctoral work, found his publisher very early.

The ascendancy of the university system was accomplished in counterpoint with (and in certain senses as a counterpart of) the transfer of critical and pedagogical power from the traditionalists to the iconoclasts. And this transfer too is to be understood through historical parallels, particularly through an understanding of the transfers to the proponents of the Ars nova in the fourteenth century and the Nuove musiche in the seventeenth. History becomes practical when it enables us to comprehend forces at work in our own day.

The bitter denunciations of "modern music" by critics at the start of a period of new definitions in music are natural enough. The critic who studies long to learn what music is cannot welcome a work so radically different that his vocabulary cannot cope with it. The entrenched Romantic tradition defined music as based in melody, harmony, and rhythm (by which was meant the rhythm of regular meters--it is hard to remember now that Tchaikovsky was castigated for producing a symphonic movement in 5/4); for a critic schooled in that definition to deal with Crumb's <u>Five Pieces for Piano</u> (for example) would be extremely frustrating, and the story of Crumb's success has been in large measure the story of the development of critical skills during the period of his youth and the new ability of critics to speak to a work composed in the new style without having to write about the style as an anomaly.

It is speaking to the style--particularly the theoretical basis of the style--that characterizes criticism in the initial turmoil of a major change, but only in such a time. It is important to realize that this concentration is not typical and, in historical terms, represents a special (and short-lived) emphasis brought about in periods of serious musical redefinition.

For the most part, a work of music is examined to reveal its materials and its techniques (its means), then studied to explore the relations of these materials and techniques to the essential musical ideas of the work (its ends), and finally evaluated on the basis of the ideas and of the integrity of the whole. Excellence in a play is not held to be a matter of grammatical competence (which is assumed) but of a high quality of its Idea in relation to the means of embodiment, support, and heightening of that Idea. And a work of music is held to be a fine one not because it is theoretically competent (which is also assumed) but because of compelling musical Ideas and the relationship of materials and techniques to their fulfillment.

In periods of musical change, a temporary switch occurs in which critics line up, not in relation to musical ideas, but to basic grammatical content, the new against the old style. Such critical battlelines are doubtless a necessary aspect of establishing a new style, and the resulting paper wars help to make possible a general acceptance of new sounds and techniques. But only later, when criticism reverts to its normal role of evaluation of specific works of music on the basis of their inherent quality (and on their own terms), can a sifting process be begun and a genuine heritage be established.

Specifically, in periods of change, the line-up deflects from a critical sorting-out of, say, superficiality vs. integrity, to an overriding concern for the single issue of Old vs. New Style--with assumption that one is bad and the other is good, without regard for the suitability of the musical idea, or even disregarding musical idea altogether.

Battle lines are drawn between proponents of the Ars nova and the Ars antiqua, or the Nuove musiche against the Stilo Antico, and, in our times, the Modernist vs. the Traditionalist, Avant-Garde against Conservative. To a certain kind of conservative, avant-gardism is the senseless and censorless going after the new, even at the cost of rationality; to his opposite number among the avant-garde, conservatism is an equally mindless following in well-worn musical footprints, at the sacrifice of originality. Neither is true; no composer sets out to write music that is either mindlessly New or repetitiously Old. Every composer strives to be original--that is, to originate musical statements not previously made, to convey new musical ideas. Theory and methodology have reality only as matrices for musical ideas, and in ordinary times are evaluated only within the microcosm of the individual work and not in relation to arbitrary concepts. No method can be considered independently from the idea it serves, any more than the dramatic line can be evaluated by some grammatical standard without reference to the character and dramatic situation from which it rises.

The critical upheaval of a period of New Music is painful but vital. Historically, the composers that we label as top rank (including all of those whose music has been quoted by all three of the composers of this study) have been conservative rather than avant-garde, conspicuously so if the organization of pitch materials is the primary concern of the critic. But these composers worked at times when the critical upheaval was over and originality of idea was the issue and not method. "Originality," Eugene Ormandy said, "lies not in devising new musical elements but in using acknowledged elements in new and individual ways."[8] He was speaking of Schubert. He spoke, of course, for the public and for the performing organizations of the public arena. But it is in the public arena that a new style finally emerges, as a folding in of styles, the vitalization of the traditional with new energy of the

259

new, and disciplining of the new within the wisdom of the old, until they have interpenetrated to the extent that the distinction, first blurred, is no longer useful.

Critical writings concerning Fischer and Finney were exactly what these considerations would lead one to expect. Those critics who were concerned with Idea gave warm praise to their works; but those critics were rare. The avant-garde critical establishment after the War labeled Fischer a Conservative and simply dismissed him without a hearing, whereas both the critics and the public had admired his work before the War. Finney has been something opposite, and more complicated: he was too conservative for the avant-garde but too modern at the start of his career for much of the public. As both men matured and their work took on aspects of the new techniques, the critics declined to follow their developing styles, ignoring them in favor of the younger, more extreme composers, in large part European, who were "proclaimers of the word" of the New Music.

There is probably nothing that Fischer and Finney could have done to achieve the critical recognition that their work merited. They were simply born at the wrong time, too late to be included as "modern traditionalists" and too soon to be standardbearers for the "radical modernists." They were in a sense the fulcrum of that span, and lost between.

An American Focus

It was while Crumb's mature style was becoming established that a critical acknowledgment of musical leadership by American composers in the international arena became common. Theodor Adorno, the German sociologist, wrote in 1962 of "a certain shift of the musical center of gravity from Europe to America," but he was concerned only with the radical avant-garde (a limitation typical of critics in a period of transition), and the radical avant-garde still depended upon "the premise of an absence of tradition."[9] But this is only the first half of the process, the erasing of the blackboard so that it may be written on anew. The coming of a new style is the distancing from tradition and then the returning to it, absorbing it rather than re-entering it, a counteraction already described.

Crumb was born at the right time, as his two predecessors in this study were born at the wrong time. He was old enough to have experienced something of the old tradition himself, and to have lived through the distancing and the returning in his own career, an abbreviated course through which he had the fortune to pass simply by dint of his age and by the luck of his early circumstances.

In matters of musical subject, for example, his mature style represented a reining in of extravagance to a goal of commandably economical idea. The use of both fewer and more clearly delineated subjects involved for Crumb the association of instrumentation (or instrumental technique) with the subject, as well as an increased scope of rhythmical devices. Whereas the radicals tended to give up metrical notation altogether, Crumb returned to the use of metrical subjects, pitting them against contrasting clock-time subjects. The pervasive short gesture, on the other hand, expanded, so that long continuous and coherent passages, often developmental in monophonic terms, could pull across musical time in organic growth. In their intense condensations, composers had been asking even greater intensity from their listeners, who were asked to take the music in on one hearing, with ears only (while the composers reveled in the niceties of notation)--rather like being served coffee powder without the boiling water. Crumb's extensions of subject types (the long spinning-out of the solo vocal sections in _Ancient_ _Voices_ _of_ _Children_, for example), while seemingly discursive, actually gave coherence and comprehensibility to the music, making it accessible and satisfying to the listener who stretches out to meet it.

The instrumental relationship is in itself an incorporation of distance and return. In his expanding sonorous world, Crumb became estranged from performers, demanding of them more and more willingness to try new effects. But he was thoughtful in matters of notation, which he had learned in both its practical and aesthetic aspects from his father (and indeed the appeal of his notation is strong--and his production of master pages easy to duplicate makes publication cheaper and hence easier to obtain).[10] In his expansion of techniques he was considerate of the performer, specifying both method and expectation of effect as a twofold guide.

But estrangement resulted from the demands that transcended the normal sphere of activity: flute players perhaps cannot sing, "perfectly balanced," while playing a complicated fioratura; a violinist may not want to play the tam-tam or the musical glasses, possibly ruining an expensive bow on the water they hold. More important, performers may, even with good will, be unable to improvise effectively.[11] Clearly the interaction between composer and performer is a dialogue, with technique stretched by the demands of new works, and virtuoso capacity demanding music to fulfill and expand itself. But in an era when performer and composer are no longer the product of the same training (or even are embodied in a single person), the performer must in the end declare the limit of the stretching and determine when the techniques are no longer germane. It is not so simple a matter as the relegation of performers to servant status.

Crumb has been fortunate in the granting of foundation funds to performers to give thThe success was perhaps too great. University professors had become over-cosseted, endowed by a deferential public (and, alas, even at times by themselves) with hierophantic status and unquestioned authority.

The crucial step that Crumb has taken is to broaden the university frame of reference. Established in his profession within the insulated university system and in his youthful maturity enjoying the independence that permitted his development without interaction with either the performers or the audiences of the commonwealth, he has turned from that closure and opened his art to dialogue from other spheres of influence.

In this too Crumb has the force of a bellwether. For the splendid isolation of the university is over, as its financial power is over. The task of the next generation will be to re-establish communication among the several channels of activity in the nation; the scientist is no longer an unquestioned figure, the universitiy expert is no longer an unassailable sage, and the public stance is no longer respectful and obedient. As American scholars learned to value their own native abilities vis-à-vis their European counterparts, so now are the members of the body politic learning to value their own capacity to seek the answers to cultural dilemmas vis-à-vis the awesome university panjandrums.

In music this will mean the reopening of non-university channels; the re-establishment of the performance quadrant (perhaps alongside a quadrant of mechanically reproduced electronic music); and the revitalization of the dialogue with public audiences. Over the long haul of Western musical history, the public has by far a better batting average in the evaluation of new works of music than either critics or musicologists, and the loss of the public voice (however inevitable during a period of aesthetic turmoil and redefinition) has been a grievous one. As Henahan indicated, it is the province of the arts to communicate in the broad scope of an outward stance. Every profession must balance the exterior with the interior dialogue: doctors cannot treat only doctors; lawyers cannot limit their services to other lawyers; house builders cannot build homes exclusively for those in the building trades; truckers cannot deliver goods only to members of the brotherhood of teamsters; playwrights cannot produce plays exclusively for other playwrights; and composers cannot create works of music solely for the pleasure of other composers. If the signs can be read, it is time for composers to see themselves again as part of the larger profession of music and to reaffirm that profession as part of the larger cultural firmament, to "get back in touch," as Henahan put it, "with their own artistic instincts."[12]

Three for America

It is possible that the issue of Americanism in concert music, to which so many composers and writers have devoted so much time, will fade into the new aesthetic values of the near future. The Italianate beginning of the Baroque faded into an eighteenth-century internationalism, and the Austro-German nationalism of Romanticism came to serve as a European lingua franca (and the immediate background of Western musical tradition). If the issue of Americanism fades, it will do so like the Cheshire cat. leaving its smile like a blessing upon a new internationalism. Adorno found nationalism a dead issue as early as 1962. "Since 1945 the modern movement has liquidated national differences," he wrote.[13]

Yet in the years after 1970, Fischer, Finney, and Crumb all explored American issues in new ways,--less self-consciously perhaps and certainly without apology. Fischer raised a Negro spiritual to the status of a chorale in his String Quartet in 1972; Crumb turned from Lorca to Walt Whitman in Apparitions in 1980; and Finney directed his energy to the creation of an opera (to his own libretto) about the historical figures of the American West, William Bent and his sons.

Yet there is no consensus on the meaning of American subject matter; perhaps if there were, more could remain than the smile. But there is unanimity only in the issue, basically a reiteration of the proposition that there ought somehow to be an American national style in concert music. The answers have been as various as the men and women who have proposed them, from Dvorak to MacDowell, Gershwin, Copland, Schuman, and the proposals have worked for individual pieces (or not), but have not proved productive beyond themselves. It is unlikely that a nation of so multifarious a mosaic of backgrounds could develop an artistic unity through retrospection. And in fact the post-War American universities themselves provided the single country-wide general cultural unifying force that the nation had known since it had spanned the continent.

If a new international style is emerging, with the United States in the vanguard, the next generation will be working out its definition. Now that the circle is complete, the business can get underway; it is already underway among several of the younger generation.

The reconciliation of extremes is a vital process, the energizing of the traditional and the taming of the radical elements already seen as informing the styles of the three composers of this study in the fifteen years from 1960 to 1975. Critics, having spent a generation probing the new and justifying the avant-garde, are now well started in the counter-action of re-examining the conservatives of the past three generations, and are returning, after a concentration on techniques, to the business of probing musical Idea and enlarging the public understanding of works of music in an ever-widening spectrum of styles.

A style can be understood most clearly in scanning its scope, in clarifying its boundaries, walking its fences. To accept the entire scope is to see the style whole; to reject either end is to diminish it. The hypothetical center can be determined only through bisection of the extremes, which are thus as indispensable as the two prongs of a sling-shot.

It is important in the creation of a musical basis operandi to explore the two prongs of the conservative and the radical, and to be assured that we have indeed a marvelous heritage on both sides and that the consummation (devoutly to be wished) is a valid coming together of two substantial traditions, both of which had American proponents and practitioners of undoubted luminosity.

Irwin Fischer, Ross Lee Finney, and George Crumb represent a span of American music, one span among many that could have been selected for this study. They incorporate the recent past, which, with its span of conservative and innovative elements, its probing of tonality and personalized serialism, and its variable views of Americanism, displays a splendid scope. Above all, their careers, taken in total, illustrate that transfer of power from the conservatories to the universities, from the traditionalist to the avant-garde side of the musical spectrum, which it is one aim of this study to examine.

Certain characteristics of their styles are inevitably tied to their separate paths and commit-ments: the types of music that they chose to write (Fischer's concentration on songs, orchestral works, and concertos; the central position of chamber music in the work of the two university men); their relation to tonality and serialism (Fischer and Finney adding serial techniques to a personal style of tonal writing; Crumb viewing tonality and serialism as two among many factors, neither terribly important); their relation-ships with performers (Fischer's indispensable and intimate; Finney's cordial and institutionally convenient; Crumb's somewhat demanding, sometimes strained); and their use of instruments (Fischer's intensely idiomatic, expanding the tradition; Finney's forceful, dramatic, deflecting the tradition; Crumb's highly colored, sporadic, confounding the tradition and setting on the path for a new view of instruments).

But also they are strong musical personalities bringing equally their own character to their work, to raise their music beyond school or generality of style: the specific uses of tonality (Fischer as fulcrum; Finney as complementarity; Crumb as transient focus); the typical sounds (Fischer's layered chords and augmented intervals; Finney's diatonic clashes and hexachord units; Crumb's sumptuous colors and fastidious pianissimos); the rhythmic character

(Fischer's long line and rhythmic variety; Finney's unison rhythmic driving force; Crumb's suspensions of time and occasional short metric thrusts); the use of repeated notes (Fischer's as melodic intensification; Finney's as rhythmic compulsion; Crumb's as pointillistic subject matter); their use of musical quotation (Fischer's integral, in worked structures; Finney's motivational, in and out of focus in layered structures; Crumb's mystical, as dimensions of thought--sometimes extra-musical--in fragmented structures). Their choices of text are all of interest at the end of the 1980s: Fischer's use of religious texts and the writings of Patience Worth, who purportedly dictated her work from beyond the grave, has its mirror in the interests of young people sixty years later, and his absorption in thoughts of death is close to Crumb's long immersion in the dark depths of the Lorca poems. Finney alone has chosen American writers more than others, but Finney also has chosen the texts--Thomas and Chardin, for example--that express the full commitment and moral hope of the American university community.

These three composers stand as symbols of a vibrant American art, of a creative elan behind the mid-twentieth-century musical turmoil, of a splended gamut of style and accomplishment. As a new international style unfolds, the work of these men and the other composers of their times and traditions will be seen anew, freshly appreciated as displaying the richness and defining the scope of the new music and America's secure place within it.

Notes

1. Sessions held a succession of fellowships that enabled him to live abroad, concentrating on the composition of music, for six consecutive years: 1926–1928, two Guggenheim Fellowhips; 1928–1931, three years at the American Academy of Rome; 1931–1932, a Carnegie Fellowship.

2. The early university music programs did not include performance, so it was normal and unquestioned practice for a composer to be graduated, having written a number of works but without having heard any of them. Students at conservatories after World War II found themselves in a similar predicament because the connections to local performing groups, previously one of the conservatory strengths, were no longer viable. It is notable that Fischer, as a teacher of composition, arranged for his students to hear their works at readings by groups unaffiliated with the conservatory.

3. In the Piano Concerto movements, for example: Entrance and Crescendo, Ornaments and Dialogue, Cadenza and Climax.

4. Crumb's works also contain subtle allusions, such as the sectional titles of Departure, Absence, and Return (in Black Angels), otherwise extraneous to the eerie metaphors of the work, but clearly a reference to Beethoven's Les Adieux.

5. It is interesting that the three composers turned to three different historical periods: Crumb to Medieval and Baroque techniques, Finney to sixteenth- and seventeenth-century techniques, and Fischer to eighteenth-century techniques.

6. Edith Borroff, Music in Europe and the United States (Prentice-Hall, 1971), contains an analysis of two West African songs (page 439) that clearly reveals the consanguinity.

7. Henahan, Op. cit., page 56.

8. On the PBS radio presentation of First Hearing, broadcast of April 14, 1979.

9. Theodor W. Adorno, Introduction to the Sociology of Music, trans. E. B. Ashton (New York: The Seabury Press, 1976), page 153.

10. It is interesting that Crumb's notation, which looks at first meeting to be in the technique of the New Music as documented by Erhard Karkoschka in Das Schriftbild der neuen Musik (Celle: Moeck, 1966), is independent of it. The new notation is basically piecemeal, Crumb's is organic. On June 18, 1979, in an interview at his home, Crumb told me he had never seen the Karkoschka. He is not, of course, included in it.

11. In my review of the premiere of Black Angels (in the Ann Arbor News, October 29, 1970, page 38), I spoke of "the arrival of the New Music [in works of this caliber] at a position of authority equal to that of the old. . . . The [Stanley] quartet searched out its meanings in the kind of genuine musical excitement that only new music can offer. It is time for the new music to enter the repertoire and not be segregated in special programs; this remarkable quartet could serve well to break the trail." But the Stanley Quartet, who had played the premiere performance, told me that they had refused to electrify their valuable instruments and had used cheap substitutes, believing that the process of electrification was harmful. They were uncomfortable with these strange instruments. They would not use their good bows with the musical glasses, and got cheap substitutes for them as well. Further, they were uncomfortable with the vocal demands, for which they had not been trained, and found the "extraneous effects" undignified. They did not play the work again.

12. Henahan, Op. cit., page 67.

13. Ibid., page 174.

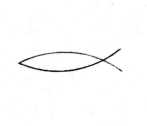

Appendices

Note on the Catalogues

Each work is listed by title, followed by the author of its text, if any; its instrumentation (if known and necessary), its date of completion, its date of first performance (fp), its date of publication (pub), its publisher, and its discography (rec), if any.

Failure to give a date of first performance means that I have been unable to establish such a date; it does not mean that the work has not been performed.

Appendix A:

CATALOGUE OF WORKS BY IRWIN FISCHER

Fischer's published works are noted.
The others are available through:
   American Composers Alliance
   170 West 74th Street
   New York, NY 10023

Orchestral works

Hungarian Set (The Pearly Bouquet) for string
   orchestra and celesta, 1943, fp 1948,
   rec CRI-122.
Lament for cello and orchestra, 1938, fp 1939.
Marco Polo (Fantasy Overture), ?1937, fp 1937,
   withdrawn.
Mountain Tune Trilogy, 1957, fp 1960.
N. Y. A. Film Music, filmed in 1941, concert
   version 1942, fp 1942.
Overture on an Exuberant Tone Row, 1964, fp 1965,
   rec Louisville LOU 676.
Passacaglia and Fugue, 1961.
Rhapsody on French Folk Tunes, ?1933, fp 1934,
   withdrawn.
Short Symphony for Full Orchestra, 1960, fp 1972.
Symphonic Adventures of a Little Tune, for
   narrator and orchestra (with tape). 1974,
   fp 1974.
Symphony No. 1, 1943, fp 1960.
Variations on an Original Theme, 1942.

Concertos

Chorale Fantasy, for organ and orchestra, 1938,
   fp 1954. Rescored in 1974 for strings,
   double reeds, brass, and percussion (organ
   solo unchanged), fp 1974.
Concerto Giocoso for clarinet and orchestra,
   1972, fp 1972.
Concerto in E minor for piano and orchestra,
   1935, fp 1936.
Idyll for violin and orchestra, 1949.
Poem for violin and orchestra, 1959.

Chamber Music

Divertimento for eight solo instruments: flute, clarinet, bass clarinet, horn, trumpet, violin, cello, and string bass, 1963.

Fantasy with Fugue Plain and Accompanied, for solo violin, flute, oboe, clarinet, harp, and strings, 1958.

String Quartet, 1972, fp 1973.

Trio in D minor for violin, cello, and piano, 1928, fp 1929.

Works for piano solo

Ariadne Abandoned, 1938, fp 1938.

Burlesque, ?1927, fp ?1927.

The Cliff Dwellers: A Musical Portrait (four hands), ?1965, fp 1965.

Etude in A minor, 1952, fp ?1953.

From Far, From Eve and Morning, 1924, fp 1924, pub 1924 The Circle (University of Chicago student magazine), withdrawn.

Intermezzo, ?1925, fp ?1925, withdrawn.

Introduction and Triple Fugue, 1929, fp ?1929.

The Moonlit Road. ?1925, fp ?1925, withdrawn.

Rhapsody, 1937, fp 1937.

Sketches from Childhood, 1937, fp 1937.

Sonata for Piano, 1960, fp 1961.

Works for organ

Chorale preludes:
Als Jesus Christus in der Nacht, ?1955, fp ?1955

Das walt Gott, 1957, fp 1957.

Jesu, meine Freude, ?1950, fp ?1950, pub 1953 Highgate

Jesu, meine Freude, No. 2, 1955, fp 1955.

Liebster Jesu, wir sind hier, 1948, fp 1948, pub 1949 Summy

Nun ruhen alle Wälder (Innsbruck), 1951.

Legend, 1955, fp 1955.

Prelude on "Franconia," 1946, fp 1946.

Recitative and Aria, 1930, fp 1930, pub 1946 Witmark.

Toccata, ?1950, fp 1950.

Transcriptions for organ

Bach, _Adagio for Sonata VI in G Minor for Flute and Clavier_, pub 1948 Summy.
Bach, _Andante from Sonata in A Minor for Violin Alone, and Sonata in D Minor for Clavier_, pub 1950 Summy.
Bach, _Sheep May Safely Graze (from Cantata #208)_, pub 1948 Summy.
Handel, _Arioso: Dank sei dir, Herr_, pub 1940, Summy.

Works for concert band

Meditation, 1970.
Wonderland March, 1958, fp 1959, rec 1959 Central Music Institute (private recording).
Fanfare for brass and percussion, 1976.

Choral works

Blessed Be Thou (I Chronicles), for 1970.
The Call (Anonymous), 1968.
He Is the Gentleness (Patience Worth) for chorus and piano, 1929.
An Indian Serenade (Shelley) for male chorus and piano, 1930, withdrawn.
In the Lord Put I My Trust (Psalms).
I Will Lift Up Mine Eyes (Psalms).
Lord, Our Dwelling Place (Psalms), pub 1959 De Luxe.
Manger Song (Silence Buck Bellows), 1960.
Statement: 1976 (Franck, Bates, Johnson, Matthew, and the composer), for soprano solo, chorus, and orchestra, 1975, fp 1976.
Sussex Carol (Anonymous), ?1946, pub 1947 FitzSimons.
Symphonic Psalms (Psalms), for soprano solo, chorus, and orchestra, 1969, fp 1980.
The World of Dream (de la Mare), SSA and piano, 1934.

Non-scriptural songs

"Ay, Gitanos!" (Velma Hitchcock Seeley), 1936.
"Can I Then Hope" (Patience Worth), ?1927.
"Christmas Message" (Hazel Harper Brandner), 1974.
"Friendship" (Patience Worth), 1928.
"Go From Me" (Elizabeth Barret Browning), 1957.
"The Horseman" (Walter de la Mare), 1932.
"The Hour Is Come" (E. Lyndon Fairweather),
     1959.
"Increase" (Edith Coonely Howes), 1959,
        pub 1976, Coburn.
"I Saw the Moon" (Gertrude Steel), 1950.
"Lullaby" (Patience Worth), 1927,
        pub 1927 Phillips (now at ACA).
"Newcomer" (Anita Fitch), 1927.
"Nocturne" (Marion Fischer), ?1930.
"Now Sweeping Down the Years" (Laura C. Nourse),
     1976.
"Requiescat" (Oscar Wilde), 1927.
"A Sea-Bird" (William Alexander Percy), 1933,
        pub 1971, in Edith Borroff, ed., Notations
        and Editions (Wm. C. Brown), reprinted by Da
        Capo Press 1978.
"Season of Star-Song" (Bonnie May Malody), 1974.
"Song of Shadows" (Walter de la Mare), 1931.
"Song of the Willow Branches" (Marion Fischer),
     1931.
"Stampede" (Velma Hitchcock Seeley), 1937.
"Still There Is Bethlehem" (Nancy Byrd Turner),
     1958.
"That Which Is" (Doris Kerns Quinn), 1977.
"There Is No Time" (Verne Taylor Benedict), 1959.
"Vista" (Sidney King Russell), 1947.
"The Walk in the Wilderness" (Doris Peel), 1961.
"When From the Lips of Truth" (Thomas Moore),
     1960, pub 1976 Coburn.
"Where Hath My Ship Agone?" (Patience Worth),
     1927.
"Winter Winds" (Anna Benfer), 1950.
"You Were Glad Tonight" (Siegfried Sassoon),
        ?1926.

Songs on poems by Mary Baker Eddy

"Christ My Refuge" ("O'er Waiting Harpstrings"),
1958, fp 1958.
"Christmas Morn," 1958, fp 1958.
"Communion Hymn" ("Saw Ye My Saviour?"),
pub 1952 Carver.
"Feed My Sheep," 1965, fp 1965, pub 1976 Coburn.
"Love" ("Brood o'er Us"), 1953, fp 1953.
"Mother's Evening Prayer" ("O Gentle Presence"),
1954, fp 1954.
"Satisfied," 1951, fp 1951.

Scriptural songs

"Come, Take the Water of Life" (Revelation), 1958,
fp 1958.
"Come Unto Me" (Matthew), 1956, fp 1956,
pub 1976, Coburn.
"Delight Thyself in the Lord" (Psalms), 1959,
fp 1959.
"Fear Thou Not, For I Am With Thee" (Isaiah),
1963, fp 1963.
"God Is Our Refuge" (Psalms), 1959, fp 1959.
"God Shall Wipe Away All Tears" (Revelation),
1954, fp 1954.
"God So Loved the World" (John I), ?1935,
fp ?1935.
"How Beautiful upon the Mountains" (Isaiah), 1951,
fp 1951.
"If I Take the Wings of the Morning" (Psalms),
1969, fp 1969.
"If Ye Love Me, Keep My Commandments" (John),
1962, fp 1962, pub 1975 Coburn.
"Let the Beauty of the Lord Be Upon Us" (Psalms),
1969, fp 1969, pub 1975 Coburn.
"The Lord by Wisdom Hath Founded the Earth"
(Proverbs), 1967, fp 1967.
"The Lord Is My Shepherd" (Psalms), 1975, fp 1975.
"Lord, Teach Me Thy Statutes" (Psalms), 1957,
fp 1957.
"Love One Another" (I John), 1937, fp 1937.
"Make a Joyful Noise Unto the Lord" (Psalms),
1972, fp 1972.
"O Lord, How Manifold Are Thy Works" (Psalms),
1957, fp 1957.
"Praise Ye the Lord" (Psalms), 1966, fp 1966.
"Psalm of Praise" (Isaiah, James, Psalms), 1951,
fp 1951.

"Quicken Me, O Lord" (Psalms), 1968, fp 1968.
"Suffer the Little Children To Come Unto Me"
    (Mark, I John), 1957, fp 1957.
"Taste and See that the Lord Is Good" (Psalms),
    1937, fp 1937.
"Ye Shall Know the Truth" (I John), 1973, fp 1973,
    pub 1975 Coburn.

Miscellaneous

    Piano teaching pieces (pseudonym)
    Organ transcriptions
    Orchestral transcriptions
        Ariadne Abandoned (Fischer)
        Cantabile (Franck), for organ and orchestra
        Legend (Fischer)
        Pièce Héroique (Franck), for orchestra
        Pièce Héroique (Franck), for organ and
            orchestra
        Sketches from Childhood (Fischer)
    Transcriptions of songs for soprano and string
        quartet
    Transcription of songs for soprano and orchestra
    Two-piano versions of works originally for one
        piano
            Ariadne Abandoned
            Burlesque

Books and articles

    Canon and Fugue, 1942, rectographed and used in
        teaching.
    "The Challenge of the Gifted Student," The Piano
        Teacher, July-August 1965.
    "A Delicate Balance," Clavier, Vol. XIV, No. 3,
        (March 1975).
    First Year Composition, 1940, rectographed and
        used in teaching.
    Free Counterpoint, 1940, rectographed and used
        in teaching.
    "From the Organ Bench at the Symphony," Clavier,
        Vol. VII, No. 8 (November 1968).
    A Handbook of Modal Counterpoint, with Stella
        Roberts, pub 1967 Collier-Macmillan,
        The Free Press.
    Harmony, 1950, rectographed and used in teaching.
    Harmony Supplement, 1940, rectographed and used
        in teaching.

"Modern Music: Problem Child," _Music Journal_,
     March 1966.
"Music and the Community," lecture, read in 1951,
     Milwaukee-Downer College, Milwaukee.
"Musical Unity in the Church Service," _Clavier_,
     Vol. VII, No. 2 (Feb 1968).
"A Note in Opus 27, No. 2, of Beethoven,"
     Music and Letters, Vol. XXXII, No. 1,
     (January 1951)
"Phrasing," _Clavier_, Vol X, No. 2 (March 1971).
"Steeltown Symphony," _American Composers Alliance
     Bulletin_, Spring 1953.
"Twenty-Two Years on the Organ Bench," _Clavier_,
     Vol. VII, No. 7 (October 1968).

Appendix B:

CATALOGUE OF WORKS BY ROSS LEE FINNEY

Finney's works are published by:

AME   American Music Edition, now Theodore Presser
AMP   Arrow Music Press, Inc., now Boosey & Hawkes
BC   Bowdoin College Music Press
BH   Boosey & Hawkes
CF   Carl Fischer, Inc.
CFP   C. F. Peters Corp (Henmar Press)
G   Galaxy (Columbia University Press,
          Music Division)
GS   G. Schirmer, Inc.
MM   Mercury Music, now Theodore Presser
NM   New Music, now Theodore Presser
P   Theodore Presser
SP   Summy Publishing Company
SPAM Society for the Publication of American
      Music,, now G. Schirmer, Inc.
V   Volkwein Brothers, Inc.
VM   Valley Music Press (Smith College)

Orchestral works

    Concerto for Strings, 1977, fp 1977,
        pub 1977 CFP.
    Hymn, Fuging, and Holiday, 1943, fp 1947,
        pub 1965 CF.
    Landscapes Remembered, 1971, fp 1972,
        pub 1979 CFP.
    Slow Piece, for string orchestra, 1940, fp 1941,
        pub 1943 VM.
    Spaces, 1972, fp 1972, CFP rental. (Transcribed
        for concert band 1986, fp 1986,
        pub 1986 CFP.)
    Symphony No. 1 (Communiqué 1943), 1942, fp 1962,
        pub 1962 CFP, rec Louisville LOU 652.
    Symphony No. 2, 1958, fp 1959, pub 1959 CFP,
        rec Louisville LOU 625.
    Symphony No. 3, 1960, fp 1964, pub 1964 CFP,
        rec Louisville LOU 672.
    Symphony No. 4, for large orchestra, 1972,
        fp 1963, pub CFP 1985.
    Symphony Concertante, 1967, fp 1968, pub 1968 CFP.

Three Pieces for chamber orchestra & tape
    recorder, 1962, fp 1963, pub 1975 CFP.
Variations for Orchestra, 1957, fp 1965,
    pub 1962 CFP.
Variations on a Memory, for ten players, 1975,
    fp 1975, CFP rental.

Concertos

Concerto for Alto Saxophone, with wind orchestra,
    1974, fp 1975, pub 1976 CFP. rec NW 211.
Concerto for Percussion and Orchestra, 1965,
    fp 1966, pub CFP 1966.
Concerto in E for Piano and Orchestra, 1948,
    fp 1951, pub 1977 CFP, parts rental.
Concerto No. 2 for Piano and Orchestra, 1968,
    pub 1977 CFP, parts rental.
Concerto for Violin and Orchestra, 1935, fp 1951,
    revised 1952, pub 1977 CFP, parts rental.
Concerto No. 2 for Violin and Orchestra, 1973,
    fp 1976, pub 1976 CFP, parts rental,
    revised 1977.
Narrative for cello and fourteen instruments,
    1976, fp 1977, pub 1977 CFP, parts rental.

Chamber music

Chamber Concerto (Heyoka), for violin, flute
    (and piccolo), clarinet (and bass clarinet),
    trumpet, bass trombone, percussion, and
    string bass; 1981; fp 1982, Erick Hawkins
    (dance); CFP rental.
Chromatic Fantasy in E, for solo violoncello,
    1957, fp 1957, pub 1971 CFP,
    rec CRI SD 311.
Divertissement, for piano, clarinet, violin,
    and cello, 1964, fp 1965, pub BC 1965.
Fantasy in Two Movements for solo violin, 1958,
    fp 1958, pub CFP 1958.
Fiddle-Doodle-Ad, for violin and piano, 1945,
    fp 1946, pub 1949, GS.
Piano Quartet, 1948, fp 1949, pub CFP.
Piano Quintet, 1953, fp 1953, pub CFP 1957,
    rec COL ML 5477.
Piano Quintet No. 2, 1961, fp 1961, pub 1974 G.
Piano Trio No. 1, 1938, fp 1939.
Piano Trio No. 2, 1954, fp 1955, pub CFP 1958,
    rec CRI 447.

Quartet for oboe, cello, percussion, and piano,
    1979, fp 1980, pub CFP 1980.
Seven Easy Percussion Pieces, 1973, fp 1976,
    pub 1981 CFP (see Books).
Sonata for Saxophone and Piano (Sonata in A Major
    for viola and piano transcribed by Laura
    Hunter), 1981, fp 1981, pub CFP 1984.
Sonata No. 2 in C for cello and piano, 1950,
    fp 1952, pub VM 1953, rec CRI SD 311.
Sonata in A minor for viola and piano, 1937,
    fp 1939, pub CFP 1971 (see Sonata for
    Saxophone and Piano).
Sonata No. 2 for viola and piano, 1953, fp 1955,
    pub 1971 CFP.
Sonata No. 2 for violin and piano, 1951, fp 1952,
    pub 1954 AME (P).
Sonata No. 3 for violin and piano, 1955, fp 1956,
    pub 1957 VM.
String Quartet in F minor, No. 1, 1935, fp 1935,
    pub 1939 AMP (BH).
String Quartet No. 2 in D minor, 1937, fp 1940.
String Quartet No. 3 in G, 1940, fp 1940.
String Quartet No. 4 in A minor, 1947, fp 1947,
    pub 1949 SPAM (GS).
String Quartet No. 5, 1949, fp 1950.
String Quartet No. 6 in E, 1950, fp 1951,
    pub CFP 1961, rec CRI 116.
String Quartet No. 7, 1955, fp 1956, pub 1961 VM.
String Quartet No. 8, 1960, fp 1960, pub 1961 VM.
String Quintet (with two cellos), 1958, fp 1959,
    pub 1966 CFP.
Three Studies in Fours, for solo percussionist,
    1965, fp 1965, pub 1974 CFP.
Tubes I, for one to five trombones, 1974,
    fp 1975, pub 1974 CFP.
Two Acts for Three Players, for clarinet,
    percussion, and piano, 1970, fp 1971,
    pub 1975 CFP.
Two Ballades for flutes and piano, 1973, fp 1974,
    pub 1974 CFP.
Two Studies for Saxophones and Piano, 1981,
    fp 1981, pub 1984 CFP.

Works for piano solo

Piano Sonata in D Minor, 1933, fp 1933,
   pub NM 1937.
Fantasy, 1939, fp 1942, pub 1942 AMP (BH).

(24 Piano) Inventions (children's pieces), 1956,
   pub 1957 SP, second edition pub 1971 CFP.
Lost Whale Calf, 1980, pub in Whales, a Celebration, Little, Brown, 1982; now available
   through CFP.
Narrative in Retrospect, 1984, fp 1985,
   pub 1985 CFP.
Nostalgic Waltzes, 1947, fp 1948, pub 1953 NM (P).
32 Piano Games, 1968, pub 1969 CFP.
Piano Sonata No. 3 in E, 1942, fp 1944,
   pub 1945 VM.
Piano Sonata No. 4 (Christmastime, 1945), 1945,
   fp 1946, pub 1947 MM (P).
Sonata quasi una Fantasia, 1961, fp 1962,
   pub 1966 CFP.
Variations on a Theme by Alban Berg, 1952,
   fp 1954, pub 1977 CFP.
Waltz, 1977, fp 1978, pub 1979 CFP.
Youth's Companion: Five Short Pieces for Piano,
   1980, fp 1980, pub 1981 CFP.

Work for harpsichord

Hexachord for Harpsichord, 1983, fp 1983,
   pub 1984 CFP.

Work for organ

Five Fantasies for Organ, 1967, fp 1968,
   pub 1970 CFP.

Works for concert band

Skating on the Sheyenne, 1977, fp 1978,
   pub 1977 CFP, rec Crest T824.
Summer in Valley City, 1969, fp 1971,
   pub 1971 CFP, rec Ed Rec Ref Lib 35-154.
Spaces, orchestral work transcribed 1986,
   fp 1986, pub 1986 CFP.

Choral works

Earthrise (Chardin, Lewis Thomas), for soloists,
    choir, and orchestra, 1978, fp 1979,
    pub 1978 CFP. (Earthrise is the final
    member of trilogy, with Still Are New Worlds
    and The Martyr's Elegy.)
Edge of Shadow (MacLeish), for chorus and instru-
    ments, 1959, fp 1959, pub 1960 CFP.
Immortal Autumn (Whitefield), for tenor solo and
    choir, 1952, fp 1952.
The Martyr's Elegy (Shelley), for high voice,
    chorus, and orchestra, 1967, fp 1967,
    pub 1967 CFP.
Oh, Bury Me Not (Folksong), 1940, fp 1941,
    pub 1940 V.
Pilgrim Psalms (Ainsworth Psalter), 1945, fp 1946,
    pub 1951 CFP.
Pole Star for This Year (MacLeish), for tenor,
    contralto, choir, and orchestra, 1939,
    fp 1943.
The Remorseless Rush of Time (composer), for
    choir and orchestra, 1969, fp 1970,
    pub 1970 CFP.
Spherical Madrigals (Herrick, Herbert, Crashaw,
    Dryden, Donne, Marvell), SATB, 1947, fp 1948,
    pub 1965 CFP. CRI recording in process.
Still Are New Worlds (Kepler, Harvey, Marlowe,
    Donne, Milton, Fontenelle, More, Galileo,
    Akenside, Pindar [all used by Marjorie Hope
    Nicolson in The Breaking of the Circle],
    Camus, and the composer), for narrator,
    tape, choir, and orchestra, 1962, fp 1963,
    pub 1963 CFP.
A Stranger to Myself (Camus), for men's voices and
    brass, ?1935.
Trail to Mexico (Folksong), for male chorus,
    1941, fp 1942, pub 1941 V.
When the Curtains of the Night (Ogle), TTBB or
    SSAA, 1940, fp 1941, pub 1940 V.
Words To Be Spoken: Modern Canons (MacLeish),
    1946, fp 1946, pub 1946 NM (P).

Theater works

Ahab, for violin, flute (and piccolo), clarinet
  (and bass clarinet), trumpet, bass trombone,
  percussion, and string bass; dance, 1985;
  fp Erick Hawkins 1986.
Chamber Concerto (Heyoka), for violin, flute (and
  piccolo), clarinet (and bass clarinet),
  trumpet, bass trombone, percussion, and
  string bass; dance, 1981; fp Erick Hawkins
  1982; CFP rental.
The Joshua Tree, for violin, flute (and piccolo),
  clarinet (and bass clarinet), trumpet, bass
  trombone, percussion, and string bass;
  dance, 1982; fp Erick Hawkins 1984.
Nun's Priest's Tale (Chaucer), for soloists,
  small chorus, and chamber orchestra,
  1965, fp 1965, pub 1977 CFP.
Weep Torn Land: Opera in 2 Acts (7 Scenes)
  (the composer), 1984, pub 1985 CFP,
  parts rental. Premiere scheduled for
  the fall of 1987, University of Michigan
  Opera Theater.

Songs

Bleheris (MacLeish), for tenor, contralto, and
  orchestra, 1937, fp 1940, pub 1969 CFP,
  parts rental.
Chamber Music, 36 songs (Joyce), 1951,
  pub 1985 CFP.
The Express (Spender), 1955, fp 1958.
Poems by Archibald MacLeish, 1935, fp 1936,
  pub 1955 AME (P).
Poor Richard (Franklin), 1946, pub 1950, GS.
Three Love Songs to Words by John Donne, 1948,
  fp 1959, pub 1958 VM.
Three 17th Century Lyrics (Vaughan, Shakespeare,
  Milton), 1938, pub 1948 VM.

Books

The Game of Harmony, 1947, pub 1947 Harcourt,
   Brace.
Landscapes Remembered and other essays, Frederick
   Goossen, ed., publication in process,
   University of Alabama Press.
Making Music: A Trilogy
   1. Time Line (contains Seven Easy Percussion
      Pieces), 1974, pub 1981 CFP.
   2. Pitch Curves (unfinished)
   3. (Projected)

Appendix C:

CATALOGUE OF WORKS BY GEORGE CRUMB

Unless otherwise noted, Crumb's works
are published by:
    C. F. Peters Corporation
    373 Park Avenue South
    New York, NY 10016

Orchestral works

    Echoes of Time and the River: Four Processionals
        for Orchestra, 1967, fp 1967,
        pub 1967 Belwin-Mills, rec Louisville
        First Edition Records LS-711.
    A Haunted Landscape, 1984, rec New World Records
        NW326.
    Variazoni, for large orchestra, 1959, fp 1965,
        pub 1973, rec 1981 Louisville LS-774.

Chamber music

    Black Angels: Thirteen Images from the Dark Land
        (Images I), for electric string quartet,
        1970, fp 1970, pub 1971, rec CRI-283,
        Vox SVBX 5306, Philips 6500881.
    Dream Sequence (Images II), for violin, cello,
        piano, percussion, and off-stage glass
        harmonica (2 players), 1976, fp 1977,
        pub 1976, rec Col Odyssey Y 35201.
    Eleven Echoes of Autumn, 1965, for violin, alto
        flute, clarinet, and piano, 1966, fp 1966,
        pub 1972, rec CRI-233.
    Four Nocturnes (Night Music II), for violin and
        piano, 1964, fp 1965, pub 1971,
        rec Mainstream MS/5016, Desto DC 6435/37,
        Col Odyssey Y 35201.
    An Idyll for the Misbegotten, for flute and
        three drummers, 1985, fp 1986.
    Sonata for Solo Violoncello, 1955, fp 1956,
        pub 1958, rec Desto DC-7169, Gasparo GS 101,
        B1565.
    String Quartet, 1954, fp 1955.

Voice of the Whale (Vox Balaenae) for Three
    Masked Players, for electric flute,
    electric cello, and electric piano,
    1971, fp 1972, pub 1972, rec Modern
    American Music Series (Columbia) M32739,
    Cameo Classics (England) GOCLP 9018 (D).

Piano works

Celestial Mechanics (Makrokosmos IV), for piano
    four hands, 1979, fp 1979, pub 1979,
    rec Smithsonian Institution NO67.
Five Pieces for Piano (electric amplification
    suggested in large halls), 1962, fp 1962,
    pub 1963, rec Advance FGR-3.
Gnomic Variations, 1981, fp 1982, pub 1982.
A Little Suite for Christmas, A.D.1979, 1980,
    fp 1980, pub 1980.
Makrokosmos, Volume I: Twelve Fantasy Pieces
    after the Zodiac, for amplified piano,
    1973, fp 1974, pub 1973, rec Nonesuch
    H-71293.
Makrokosmos, Volume II: Twelve Fantasy Pieces
    after the Zodiac, for amplified piano, 1973,
    fp 1974, pub 1974, rec Columbia Odyssey
    Y 34135.
Music for a Summer Evening (Makrokosmos III),
    for two amplified pianos and percussion
    (two players), 1974, fp 1974, pub 1974,
    rec Nonesuch H-71311 (1975).
Processional, 1983.

Work for organ

Pastoral Drone, 1982, fp 1984, pub 1984.

Chamber music with solo voice

Ancient Voices of Children (Lorca), for soprano,
    boy soprano, mandolin, oboe, harp, electric
    piano (and toy piano), and three percussion-
    ists, 1970, fp 1970, pub 1970, rec Nonesuch
    H-71255 (1971).
Apparition (Walt Whitman), for soprano and piano,
    1979, fp 1981, pub 1980, rec Bridge 2002.

<u>Lux Aeterna for Five Masked Musicians</u> (from the
<u>Requiem Mass</u>, thirteenth century), for
soprano, bass flute (and soprano recorder),
sitar, and two percussionists, 1971, fp 1972,
pub 1972, rec Col Odyssey Y 35201.
<u>Madrigals, Book I</u> (Lorca), for soprano, vibra-
phone, and contrabass, 1965, fp 1965,
pub 1971, rec Turnabout TV 34523, AR-Deutsche
Grammophon 0654 085 (1973).
<u>Madrigals, Book II</u> (Lorca), for soprano, flute
(and alto flute and piccolo), and percussion,
1965, fp 1965, pub 1971, rec Turnabout
TV-S 34523, AR-Deutsche Grammophon 0654 085
(1973).
<u>Madrigals, Book III</u> (Lorca), for soprano, harp,
and percussion, 1969, fp 1970, pub 1971,
rec Turnabout TV-S 34523. AR-Deutsche
Grammophon 0654 085 (1973).
<u>Madrigals, Book IV</u> (Lorca), for soprano, flute
(and alto flute and piccolo), contrabass,
and percussion, 1969, fp 1969, pub 1971,
rec Turnabout TV-S 34523, AR-Deutsche
Grammophon 0654 085 (1973).
<u>Night Music I</u> (Lorca), for soprano, keyboard, and
percussion, 1963, fp 1964, pub 1967 Mills
Music, Inc., rec CRI-218, Candide CE 3113.
Revised edition pub 1979, Mills Music, Inc.
<u>Night of the Four Moons</u> (Lorca), for alto, alto
flute (and piccolo), banjo, electric cello,
and percussion, 1969, fp 1970, pub 1971,
rec Columbia M 32739.
<u>Songs, Drones, and Refrains of Death</u> (Lorca),
for baritone, electric guitar, electric
contrabass, electric piano (and electric
harpsichord), and two percussionists,
1968, fp 1969, pub 1971, rec Desto DC 7155.

Choral work

<u>Star-Child: A Parable for Soprano, Antiphonal
Children's Voices, Male Speaking Choir with
Handbells, and Large Orchestra</u> (Texts freely
adapted from Medieval sources of the thir-
teenth century: <u>Dies Irae</u> and <u>Massacre of
the Innocents</u>, and <u>John XII:36</u>), 1977,
fp 1977, pub 1977. Scoring revised 1979.